L. K. Wood

L. K. WOOD

AS EVERYONE SHOULD

His branches sheltered many.

L.K. WOOD

WITH ROBERT J. SCUDIERI

Published by The Spirit Of Naples and Southwest Florida, Inc.
http://SONStudios.org

Library of Congress Cataloging-in-Publication Data
(Applied for)

Cover design and interior layout: http://PearCreative.ca

Hardcover: ISBN: 978-0-9970642-0-9
Ebook: ISBN: 978-0-9970642-1-6

Table of Contents

Foreword

Words cannot truly express my heart or feelings for the great man named L.K. Wood. He was my everything and I was blessed to also be his. Our life was not perfect, but at the end of the day we were for each other, loving each other without condition, and living in full devotion to each other. The only real difficulty we ever encountered was the world always trying to dictate what we were supposed to be, what a married couple should look like, or what behavior was acceptable. The world didn't win with us, though. We believed we were supposed to be together and lived in that joy to the end.

L.K. taught me something new every single day. Whether it was one of his famous diddys, a real life story from his past, or an important life lesson, the offerings he showered onto my life were plenty and they helped me to know that our marriage was a true gift from God. But while both the world and I received his generosity, I was most grateful for one gift in particular: his transparency. My love allowed me to know the wounds of anger and hurt left in the wake of his mother's abandonment. They were still festering when we set out on our life together. When, in our latter years of marriage, he allowed me to introduce him to the powerful release of forgiveness for that long-ago hurt, I knew I'd experienced my greatest joy as a wife and given him a gift that mattered.

Often, after we'd enjoyed a dinner with friends and L.K. had told a story about teaching Clark Gable how to knife fight in basic training or about going on a blind date with Shirley Temple before shipping off to the war, people would ask L.K. questions. What else did he see over there? How did he go from penniless to real estate mogul? What relationships and learning moments took him from an abandoned child to a man who helped put governors in office and bring The Arch to St. Louis? Often, my love would smile and say, "Those stories can be told once I'm dead."

I thought about that in the days after he passed. And, as my heart began to heal, I knew there was one more worthy gift I could give to this man who gave me so much. I could honor his wish to tell his story once he left this earth for Heaven.

My best friend, companion, husband, and love lived an extraordinary life by the raw way he overcame numerous challenges, how he brought the spice of life to others through his humor, and by sharing his knowledge and opportunities with others. He will forever live through those who had the gift of knowing him as Father, Brother, Husband, Grandpa, Great Grandpa, Uncle, Cousin, Business Associate, and, of course, Friend.

It is my great honor now to introduce you to my champion, a man unlike any other, L.K. Wood.

His Loving Wife,
Patty Wood

Chapter One
A PROMISE TO DAD

Mom was dead. Dad told us so. And then, before too long, he died, too. Yet there I sat, years after we put Dad into the ground, aboard a bus headed to Chicago to meet a very alive woman.

My mother.

Alive.

In 1939.

I shook my head and thought back to the phone call that sent our late summer afternoon spiraling into a sea of questions. Had it only been a few days since then?

I was sixteen, my brother, Dick, three years younger. Despite the difficulties and losses, we'd made a form of family—two boys grafted into the home of our older sister.

We were all together when the phone jangled, and as my sister answered it, the noise woke my newborn nephew. My sister spoke a few words; then her face turned white. She handed the receiver to me. I didn't recognize the voice on the other end of the line, an aunt gone silent more than a decade ago. My mother's sister.

"Lowell, we're pretty sure that your mother is alive."

My mind instantly flashed further back to life a decade earlier. Dad broke the news then: your mother is gone. We presumed by "gone," he meant she had gone to God in heaven above. I was six, Dick three. A year later, Dad was gone too and Dick and I found ourselves in a home for orphans.

I stayed until I'd had enough. One night, I ran off to live with hobos and search for any relatives who might still be alive. Eventually I found my way to my sister's house and summoned my brother to join us.

"She's living in Chicago." The voice on the phone drew me away from my orphanage memory. "I know how you can find her."

My tongue went dry. I couldn't speak, unusual for my talkative mouth.

This had to be a big mistake. Maybe a con job—some trick to wheedle us out of what little money we had. Could it be real? My sister was too stunned to respond, my brother too young to grasp the gravity of the call. But I had to know. I had to make the two-hundred-mile journey from our small Michigan town to Chicago.

The Greyhound hit a pothole, jarring me back to the present.

A bead of sweat rolled down my neck. In those days, Greyhound buses had no air conditioning. This didn't present much of a problem on the highway with the windows open and a breeze blowing in. But stopping at what seemed like every little rural community in Eastern Michigan and Northern Illinois left a lot of time spent sitting without air movement as more passengers entered or disembarked—some youngsters, others grandpas and grandmas. After each stop, the bus rumbled on and bumped along pitted roads, quickly filling with the smells of ripe fruit and half-eaten sandwiches that someone else's mother had made. We sweltered. The closer we got to Chicago, the muggier and more oppressive the air grew.

I couldn't help thinking, "Maybe this woman just happens to have the same name as my mother. Maybe it's a scam. But what if it's true?" That last question kept me in my seat.

Finally we pulled into the Chicago bus station.

Peeking through a half-opened window, I searched the faces of the people waiting to greet loved ones. A tall, sandy-haired man who wore a suit and bowtie stood at one end of the gaggle. A businessman come to pick up his son or daughter? An older couple stood near the businessman. The husband sported a dark green shirt, and the wife looked lovely in a matching dress that touched the ground as she moved. I had seen European immigrants before and guessed they were German or Polish.

Three people down from the older couple stood a squat, overweight, bowlegged woman attired in a crumpled dress that she must have pulled from a chair next to her bed. She concentrated on the faces at the windows of the bus. Her hair was a mess. And I had no doubt: my mother.

Alive.

Were those tears or small drops of sweat that rolled around her reddened eyes? She wiped the moisture away, straining to get a good look at each passenger exiting the bus.

As the Greyhound's motor idled, awaiting its getaway, I thought to sit back down and go on to its next destination. But I was already in the aisle, being pushed from behind. Too soon, my turn came to exit and, as I did, I wondered and feared. *Is it too late to put the pieces back together? Can we be a family again?*

My story began nearly a century ago. Maybe some of the details are not exactly as they happened, but following is what I remember.

On my father's side, we can loosely trace our roots back to Charlemagne. Yes, the guy who once ruled most of Europe, the king who brought Christianity and goodwill to his people, is in my lineage. I liked learning that part of the story.

My great-great-great something or other grandfather Jonathan Wood was the first to come to America. According to family lore, he sailed across the Atlantic in 1798 and settled in Little Compton, Rhode Island. Many Woods made their homes in that neck of the woods back then, so it's impossible now to figure out exactly who was who.

The history is even fuzzier on my mother's side. All I know for sure is that my parents married and bought a small plot of land in upstate New York. Their meager farm lay on the outskirts of a town called Carlton, just a stone's throw away from Lake Ontario. In those days, the center of town was called Carlton Station. I was born there on May 3, 1924, the fourth of five Wood children.

Lake Ontario is a blustery expanse of water, vulnerable to hard-hitting gales. In winter, cold west winds draw the moisture from the lake and blanket the land on the south and east with snow high enough to lose a horse. On the rare clear day, you can look northward and almost see Canada across the lake.

Today a four-lane parkway begins near Carlton and stretches east along the waterfront toward Rochester. The paved road winds through gorgeous green hills and over blue rivers. But in 1924 those roads were dirt and narrow, and bridges few and far between.

Like my own path.

This path I followed was neither straight nor without serious missteps. Ease never entered into my journey, and I always felt like an underdog. Many choices I wish I could make again. Too many words crossed my lips that I wish I could take back. I made mistakes. I hurt the people closest to me. I hope I helped a few folks too.

A lot of what I remember now seems like a dream; in certain places it played out like a nightmare. But eventually I found peace, more than I believe I deserve. And I was able to, at least in a small way, keep my word to my father. I will tell you about that promise as my story unfolds, but for now know that I carried that commitment with me for my entire life.

It will be helpful for you to know something about my father, the one to whom I made the promise. He was a farmer. So were our neighbors. They talked farming, lived farming and died farming.

In those days, apple orchards stretched as far as the eye could see. There's even a story about the daughter of a local homesteader who planted the first apple tree in Carlton. It is probably exaggerated, but makes for a good local legend.

I do know that Carlton's citizens were rugged people who wrested life from the rocky ground below and the unpredictable sky above. My earliest memories are of neighbors like the Dunhams and Swetts who rode up and down on their luck. I also remember how hard work and perseverance stuck to them like the soil they tilled. Although the times were hard, most families had sufficient provision for their needs.

Not so in the Wood household.

It seemed the harder my father worked, the more we fell behind. The more we fell behind, the more determined my mother became— or was it desperation? When I was barely five, she put a short tree branch, line and hook into my hands and sent me to fish along the stream at the south end of our property. Each day she kissed my cheek and said, "Lowell, try not to come back without something to put in the frying pan."

Day after day I sat under a hot sun, the waters of the cool blue stream twisting around my feet and coursing over slippery moss-covered rocks. My mother gave me chicken livers to use as bait, hoping to attract catfish. But mostly I came home with bullheads—snarly catfish cousins with sharp spines that, if you weren't careful, sliced your fingers. I learned to respect the fish, and the hard work it took to secure them. The meat of the bullheads was paltry but still filled empty places in our stomachs.

I had an older brother and two older sisters, but our income was small, and the fishes were few. One by one my older siblings had to leave.

My sister Millie married at an early age and moved to Michigan to help an aunt with household chores—she's the one who answered the phone on the that fateful day. I can still picture Millie and her new husband, Gordon, rolling out of our driveway on an old Harley-Davidson motorcycle. For some reason a picture of the bike's teardrop gas tank stuck with me.

My sister Lillian went to live with an uncle who needed her help every minute. She did his housework and cared for his ill wife. I have only the faintest memory of her.

My older brother, Elmer, got a job with a local farmer. The pay was low, and the work was hard. Elmer eventually signed on with Franklin Roosevelt's Civilian Conversation Corps, a job that paid him enough to live on.

And then—surprise!—after the older children had left home, we got another Wood mouth to feed. My brother Dick was born in 1928. After Dick came into the world, my mother seemed to spend more time away from the house than in it.

Maybe it was the poor quality of soil my father was working, or maybe it was the coldness developing between my father and mother that eventually did us in. Either way, when the Great Depression fell on the world in 1929, our family was pummeled even further down. The bills for seed and fertilizer came due. To make ends meet, we took on a boarder.

Stanley Marks seemed like the perfect fit, at least at first. He was a drifter who had found temporary work in Carlton. Tall, sandy haired, and well built, he baled hay at a neighbor's farm. The crop had to be taken in before the first snow fell. Stanley needed a place to stay--so he moved in.

Stanley arose and left early each morning returning every afternoon. Dad got up early too, but worked his own land and rarely came in before sundown. This situation often left Stanley in our home when Dad was not. And on some of those afternoons, Stanley sent me to the store in town for treats. I had plenty of time to daydream as the walk took me about half an hour each way.

Sometimes I pretended I was the shortstop for the Yankees. I'd never been to a game, but everyone had heard of Babe Ruth. He played for the Bronx Bombers in those days and hit 714 home runs—a record that lasted until Henry Aaron broke it in 1973. During other walks to the store, I tried to figure out how to catch more fish so all the Woods could eat. A few times I was tempted to pick apples from other farmers' trees—but I resisted.

Then, just as suddenly as Stanley appeared, he disappeared. Something bad must have happened because our mother was gone too. Dick and I thought she had died. That's what Dad told us. In hindsight, it was strange, because there was no funeral, and the minister from the small Methodist church never came to our home.

I admit, I cried. Tears helped, but red eyes weren't going to bring our mother back or put food on our table. And it wasn't just my stomach that was empty. Even with my limited time on the earth up to that point, I knew I'd lost something and felt the dryness in my spirit left in its absence.

After my mother disappeared, I grew closer to my father. I prepared his food before he left for the fields and I washed the dishes each night. I was a perfectionist even then, so I scrubbed until I got every speck of dirt off every plate and bowl.

One morning when he was about to leave for the fields, Dad said to me, "Lowell, you give me hope and a reason to go on. I love you!"

"I love you too, Dad. Just tell me what you want me to do, and I will!"

All he said was, "We're gonna see better days."

Before any better days came, there were lots of worse days. The winter of 1931 saw Dad overworked and always worrying. He became ill with pleurisy. The local doctor heated his chest with hot mustard pads in an effort to dissolve the congestion in his lungs. The burning sensation was supposed to make it easier to breathe, but it didn't help. Dad's breathing became more and more painful. The hands that held and protected my brother and me fell limp. They could not shield us anymore.

Between coughs, the last words he whispered to me were, "You're a good boy, Lowell. Take care of your little brother."

Dad's death was like a limb torn off my body. No child should have to go through such a thing. I pushed against the grief. I gritted my teeth, held back tears, and fought this new calamity. My father had a last request, and I had promised to fulfill it. I had my little brother to care for.

But I had no one to take care of me.

Our brother Elmer came home to take charge of Dad's funeral. They arranged the coffin in the front parlor of our soon-to-be-vacated home. The once-white walls, now gray, were stripped of any pictures of places that we might have longed to see and of every photo that had ever been taken of the family.

Neighbors came to the house to view Dad's remains. In the small dark hallway, our friends turned their backs to talk to each other. But we still heard them.

"What's going to happen to these two kids?"

"Who's going to pay me for that seed and fertilizer?"

"Where is the mother?"

"The house needs to be sold to pay the bills."

"The kids need to go to the orphanage."

Dick whispered, "What's that?"

"I'm not sure what an orphanage is," I answered, "But maybe we can get something to eat there."

A young minister from the United Methodist Church joined us in the house. He said a few words about Dad and what a hard worker he had been. He told how Dad had "endured and triumphed" like Jesus. That is all I can remember. At the time, I had no idea what he was talking about. Yet I listened closely because the minister was a man of God and therefore deserved respect. After speaking, he led us in singing a few hymns. Then he prayed some words I did not understand and left.

I felt crushed and abandoned, as helpless as one of those squirrels in our fields when a strong wind shook their tree down. But, for Dick's sake, I stayed strong.

Dick asked, "Where's Dad?"

"He's gone."

"Gone where?"

"I dunno. But it's someplace we can't go now. We're gonna have to stay here. But don't worry, I'll take care of you. We're gonna see better days.

Chapter Two
LIFE AS AN ORPHAN

The Virgil Bogue Home in Albion, New York, was the best place in the world and the worst place in the world. Elmer brought us there since no one else could keep two young boys. That made it the best place, because we needed some place to stay. Dick was only three, and I had just turned seven.

"I'll come by to see you whenever I'm able," Elmer said.

We wanted to believe him. Oh, how we wanted to believe. We *needed* to believe—he was our flesh and blood. But deep down, I had a feeling his visits would be few. As we watched Elmer leave, it felt as if we'd said good-bye.

Dick clung to my waist as if to say, "You better not leave me too." Stares of the other children settled on us, so I pushed Dick's arms down, grabbed one of his hands, and marched us through the front entrance.

The Bogue Home quickly turned dreary and foreboding—we immediately felt abandoned. We called it the "Bug" home. A dull gray adorned the outside. The white paint inside let everyone know this was an institution or jail. Not one picture hung on the walls.

The first week we were there, Dick cried all the time. I kept a tight grip on his hand, comforting him the best I could. I shook all over and wished I had Elmer or my dad to hold my hand. Where was mom when I needed her most?

Despite my pain, I tried to act grown up—I had to—for Dick. Whatever it took, I would do what my father had asked of me. I had made a promise.

Elmer did come to see us, but he couldn't come often. When he visited, we'd run down the stairs and throw ourselves around him—giving him huge hugs. It felt as if Dad were with us.

"You two seem lively. Are they feeding you well?"

"Elmer, don't leave us! Please take us with you. We can help you. We don't eat much."

But each time we begged, Elmer said, "I want to, but I can't. Not yet. I don't have a place of my own. Maybe later. Now, Lowell, you take care of Dick."

Why did he say that every time?

Dick and I held tightly to Elmer's arms, and when he got up to leave, we wrapped our legs around his legs. Elmer disentangled himself from us and then quickly left. We saw his eyes were red and wet with tears, no more than our own. Every time he left, it felt like the last time we would see him. the only real family we had.

The Bogue Home was a typical Depression-era "home," an orphanage where the kids attended school in town alongside children from intact families, with parents who loved them. But as Bogue Home children, we had to work to help support the place. We performed various jobs, always menial labor, depending on the season and the need. Our "pay" was the "privilege" of living in the orphanage.

At apple harvest time we rode in the back of an old black Chevy pickup, sitting in the slime of decayed apple pieces. The driver dumped us off at an orchard and left us to forage for ourselves. Some of the younger boys stretched on their tippy-toes to grasp the apples that weighed down branches of the trees; older boys had to pick apples that had already fallen to the ground. Rot and worms beat us to many apples, but we were told to collect these too as, according to the orphanage director Mrs. Bronson, they made good applesauce.

So whenever we had applesauce, I checked for insect parts before swallowing. I assumed they didn't get all the worms out—maybe on purpose, to get meat into our stomachs so we wouldn't want more. Maybe this was just my imagination. Probably they pressed those fallen apples for cider, maybe hard cider for the Bogue Home working crew.

We were driven to other places in a small bus with the name of the home painted on its side. When the bus passed through the small town of Albion, the town kids yelled at us, called us names, and offered gestures which I will not describe. Later, when the adults weren't around, we fought these kids. I developed a quick temper. Though I was a scrawny boy with bowlegs, I was scrappy.

One time three of those town kids started following me—talking out loud so I could hear them: "He's an orphan kid. His folks threw him and his brother away. Ugly as horse manure." They kept it up until my neck muscles strained.

I turned and rushed at them, knocked one over, and jumped on top of him, punching his head over and over until the others pulled me off. I must have seemed like a demon to them because all three of them ran off.

Now I had to go back to the house to explain to Mrs. Bronson how my shirt got ripped and my pants got so dirty. "Just tripped on a rock." I don't think she believed me, but there was no one to dispute my story. And those other boys didn't want anyone to know that one scrawny "orphanage kid" had gotten the best of them.

Another of the Bogue child industries involved caning chairs. I was eight years old when I was recruited to do this. Dick, at four, served as my assistant. It was not easy work, especially for children. Dick wet the strips of cane, and I wove them into seats and backs for chairs. I always had to be careful not to put kinks in the cane straps. After only ten minutes, tying knots in the cane grew excruciating. My fingers hurt constantly until they became numb. After work, the pain came back even worse. Some nights, the pain in my hands kept me from sleeping. I hated it.

And there were other things I hated, like Mrs. Bronson.

Standing almost six feet tall, and around fifty years old, the woman always dressed in brown—brown dresses, brown shoes, and brown hats. Even her hair, hanging loose over her shoulders, fit the monochromatic spectre.

She kept a close eye on the bottom line, and the children at the home felt sure her heart lay somewhere in her pocketbook. We never got new clothes to wear. And she knew just how much each of her wards should eat. I can hear her as clear as day, even now. "Lowell, you've had your glass of milk today. That's enough!"

While the frugality of Mrs. Bronson could probably be counted a good characteristic for someone in charge of a charity, her good works sometimes made things worse for us. You see, she collected used clothing from families in Albion. Remember, our school lay a mile down the road, in Albion. Whenever Mrs. Bronson brought in a new bunch of used clothes, we sorted through the new stash to see what fit—or sorta fit. I found a couple of shirts I liked, but most things always seemed too big for Dick.

We wore our recycled clothing to school, of course. Some days one or another of our classmates would notice a shirt or pants or shoes that had been his. This brought their laughter and yelling and mocking. Anyone looking on probably thought my red face came from embarrassment. A closer look in my eyes revealed the boiling anger within. Why would they not want to share? Why couldn't I have a family like theirs? All I wanted was to be normal, to fit in.

From yet another new stash, Mrs. Bronson pulled a pair of used brown shoes and presented them to me. I guess they were a little big, but they were better than the ones I had been wearing, so I thanked her and took them.

Inevitably, one of the town kids recognized them as his old shoes and pointed. "Look at those old smelly shoes! My mom threw those in the garbage, and now you're wearing them."

Dick said, "Let's just get going."

But my eyes narrowed. I yanked the shoes off in the middle of that dirt road and, with all the force of anger inside me, threw them at the jeering boy.

He jumped at me and caught my left eye with his fist, turning it blood red.

Something within me snapped. I could hear Dick yelling, as if from far away, "Back off, Lowell!" But I rushed back at my tormentor and pushed him over a mound and into a culvert filled with water and mud.

That's where I left him.

I walked in my socks all the way back to the orphanage.

That night Mrs. Bronson heard about the skirmish from the snot-nosed kid's mother. As punishment for throwing the shoes back at him, Mrs. Bronson locked me in the dirt-floored basement for twenty-four hours. It really was like solitary confinement. With only bread and water to eat, I sat, cringing, in a dark and damp corner. Bugs skittered across the dirt floor, and mice ran along the walls. Biting my lower lip until I could taste my own blood, I refused to cry. That night alone in the cellar convinced me I could not stay at the Bogue Home.

Sometime later at our dinner table, the other orphans were complaining about our dinner: cold potatoes and tough pieces of meat Mrs. Bronson called "beef." That old hag lost her patience that night. In a rage, tears coming down her reddened face, she yelled at us, "No one else wants you! You're lucky to have a place to sleep and eat!"

That wasn't first time she had pierced us with those degrading words.

My hot anger morphed into cold rage, settling like a knot into my tired spirit, and I readily received it. I grew jumpy, on edge, and felt caged—like the one pet we had at the Bogue Home, a young ferret Mrs. Bronson had caught. That ferret spent every hour of the day searching for a way out of his cage.

I knew exactly how he felt.

Chapter Three

TIME TO RUN

Taking care of Dick topped my life of concerns. I *had* to keep my word to my father. But how? One day in late September 1935, after Dick and I had lived five years at the Bogue Home, Mrs. Bronson came down hard on Dick for the stupidest thing. Again, it was over food.

"Eat those boiled onions!" Mrs. Bronson screamed.

The other children's eyes went wide with fear. Whimpers escaped across the lips of the smaller ones.

"The cook spent a lot of time cleaning and boiling these onions so you could have something to eat!"

"No! Mrs. Bronson, I hate boiled onions. They make me sick." Dick tried to talk through wet sobs and coughs. "Please, don't make me eat them. I won't!"

I stood up to get between Mrs. Bronson and my little brother.

"Let him alone! Who cares if he doesn't like the onions?"

The old matron went berserk.

She shoved me out of the way, then grabbed my little brother by his arm and pulled him from his seat. Dick wriggled his way to the floor and refused to move.

"You ungrateful little throwaway!" Mrs. Bronson boomed. "No one wants you. I'm stuck with you, and you'll do what I say."

I rushed at her, arms and fists flailing, trying to push her away from Dick. "I'll kill you if you touch him again!"

Ah, the look on her face. She recoiled in shock.

I yelled over and over, "I'll kill you if you touch him again!"

The cook rushed up from behind, wrapped her heavy arms around me, and dragged me away. Dick was hauled off to the basement "prison." There was nothing more I could do for my little brother that night.

Amazingly, Mrs. Bronson did not stick me in the basement with him. Maybe she thought we'd be dangerous together. Head down, teeth bared, I trudged back to the dormitory, bitter over my failure to rescue Dick. I sat on my bed long into the night, arms crossed, and planned what to do next.

Lloyd, a boy Dick's age who had been his friend, walked over to my bed and stood there, waiting for me to say something. I hesitated, certain he would report whatever I said to the old matron. Lloyd had been left on the doorstep of St. Mary's' church; he grew up at the Bogue Home and actually liked living there. Three or four other curious kids crept near to see what would happen.

Finally, through clenched teeth, I said, "I'm leaving."

I saw no way to help Dick if I stayed there, and I was miserable. If I could get out and make some money, then maybe I could get my brother out of this damned place too.

"Anyone want to go with me?"

One of the boys I liked most, a boy named Ralph, said, "Wow. You mean it, Lowell? Are you sure? Maybe we should all go!"

Marshall was interested, but couldn't muster the courage. "Where would we go where?" he asked. "There are creepy men out in the woods behind the house. What about the cops?

Ralph balked. "I don't want to get caught and then locked in that basement. You can do it, though, Lowell. You're smart. You go! Or are you too scared?"

A cold dread in the pit of my stomach held me back. I'd seen those shadows of men walking in the woods. But I'd also heard Dick's cries. I spit it out again, "I'm getting out of here."

Ralph and Marshall and the others were now too afraid to be around me, and they backed away. A nervous urgency filled me because I thought someone, probably Lloyd, would rat me out. I had to act fast.

I wrapped a toothbrush, comb, and some clothes in an old shirt then tiptoed to a first-floor window at the side of the orphanage. With Mrs. Bronson and the cook nowhere to be seen, I pushed open the window and dropped my belongings to the ground. Putting one leg over the window ledge, then the other, I sat there for a few moments, then let go and dropped about ten feet to the ground.

I righted myself, grabbed my old shirt and started to run.

———————

As the September sun slipped beneath the horizon, the western sky faded from orange to gray. I raced across the road then through a field and into the woods. Under the cover of leaves, the woods loomed darker and colder than the road.

What had I done? I had no money. No map. No plan. No food. No one with me. Nowhere to go.

I kept running hard, looking back every few paces to see how many Bogue employees were following me. No one.

I stopped at a nearby creek, knelt down, and put my face in the cool water to drink. I felt the emptiness in my stomach and plucked several apples from a shadowy tree. The night grew darker and darker. All alone, suddenly aware of what I had done, I broke down sobbing.

Footsteps crunched through the brush—louder and louder. A ghost-man, like the ones I'd seen from the window of the home, appeared. He stepped my way.

I jumped up to run—but where?

"What's the matter, boy?"

I froze, half fearful, half curious.

"I heard someone crying. Are you lost? Don't worry. You're not alone." So, he wasn't a ghost.

"I'm Missouri Drew." He stepped closer. "And I'm on my way back to our hobo campgrounds. I've been helping farmer Joshua Grimes bring in the hay his cows'll eat this winter."

I knew that farmer. He owned the apple trees we picked from for the home.

"Grimes paid me a fair wage." He paused as he looked me over. "You got someplace to stay tonight?"

My fear of the dark outweighed my suspicion of this creature. "How far is it? Do they allow eleven-year-olds in the camp?" I stepped toward him. "What's a hobo? I don't have any money. Does that make me a hobo?"

I followed him back to the camp. A rising September half-moon cast a dim light on the rough path.

Missouri Drew educated me. "Hobos aren't tramps, who work only when they have to. And we aren't bums either, deadbeats who never work. We travel around looking for work. Right now the farmers are bringing in hay. That's why we're here. But that's mostly ended, so I'll have to start to go down south. What about you?"

"I'm . . . I'm . . . I guess I need to be a hobo too. I've been in prison—or something like that—the orphan kids' home in Albion." I thrust out my chest even though he walked ahead and couldn't see me. "It's time for me to make money so I can rescue my younger brother."

Drew just kept walking.

"He's still at the orphanage, and I have to find a treasure, or at least earn a living to get him back to normal life. Our father died, but before he died, he gave my little brother to me. That was five years ago."

The moon climbed higher and lit a clearer path to the hobo camp. Missouri Drew accepted my words with silence.

Soon we arrived at what Drew and the other hobos called their "jungle." It sat near the creek in a meadow not far from the road. Campfires crackled and sparked. One or two of the old men in the camp played a harmonica. I smelled the hobo stew before I saw it cooking over a fire. Even if it were boiled onions, I wanted it. The

24

music, the talking, everyone staying up and going to bed whenever they felt like it—I believed I had died and gone to hobo heaven.

"Missouri, who's this *angelina* [hobo for 'punk or road kid']?"

"Where'd you find him?"

"What's he carrying in his shirt? Got any food?"

The men introduced themselves: Boxcar Mick, Fry-Pan Jimmy, Lil' Big Man Max, Billy Creak Knees, Andy the Dandy. Everyone had a strange name, but I liked them and wondered what my hobo name would be. I felt as if we were instantly family.

Missouri Drew's campsite was under an old elm tree, and several of the men lay their sleeping rolls under it. Laundry hung from the lower limbs of trees and across bushes. Some of the hobos had already gone to sleep by the time we arrived, a hard day chopping wood or baling hay doing its work to take them to dreamland. Their snoring harmonized with the sound of the water bubbling over rocks in the creek—the same creek, but just a little downstream from where I had caught fish for Mom.

My mouth watered. "Missouri, you think I can I get some of that stew?"

"What do you have to contribute? Everyone who can work has to put something in the stew pot."

"All I have is an apple I took off that tree when you were coming up on me. It doesn't have any worms."

"Give it to me." He cut the apple in small pieces and slipped it into the boiling mess. Then he took a large ladle and, taking care not to spill any of the stew, put some of it into a bowl and handed it to me. No onions—phew!

We sat and talked, or he talked, sharing his "wisdom of the road."

"When you set out tomorrow, Lowell, watch out for white cars. They're the police. Make your way up this side road and head north for about a half mile. You'll run into a larger road, it's paved. That's the Ridge Road, and it's the main road through farms in this area.

"You can go to the back of the farm houses you come across and ask if anyone needs help. Find a good stick because each farmer will have at least one dog. Don't beat the dog—he's just doing his duty.

But if you wave the stick, generally he'll stay back until you get off his property."

I took in every word, cementing the things in my mind. Through the night I lay awake thinking, not able to sleep much. What was my little brother doing? Was he afraid? Crying? Was Mrs. Bronson punishing him because I broke the rules? For a long time afterwards I choked back tears, thinking about Dick and how lonely he must have been at the Bogue Home without his older brother.

Chapter Four
ON MY OWN

Lying near the roots of the big elm, I awoke to the soft cooing of mourning doves scraping for seeds and insects. The sun lay just under the horizon, and many of the men were already up. Some washed themselves at the creek, while others relieved themselves farther downstream. The soft sounds of groans, scraping feet, and clinking pots brought the camp to life.

But then a sharp realization prodded me fully awake—*what now?* I had no money, no one to contact, and police from the towns around were probably looking for me.

Maybe I should just go back to the Bogue prison.

No! I have to keep going.

But first I had to pee.

I forced myself to eat some more of that stew, still boiling but thinner than the night before. Who knew when I would have a next meal? In the still-sleepy dawn, I made my way to the side road above the camp and started to walk in the direction the hobos had advised.

I wanted to hitchhike, but every time I saw or heard a car approach, I concealed myself until I could see the car's paint. In fact, not one white car passed, but neither did any of them stop for me. After a while it occurred to me that maybe no one cared that I had left. They probably thought it was good I ran away—one less troublemaker. One less mouth to feed.

Finally I made it to the mostly paved but not a well-kept thoroughfare of Ridge Road. After a while, farmhouses began to appear on either side.

I first came upon a dustry, two-story white wood house—a lot like where I had grown up—that looked as if it were trying to be more than its creator intended. A fence surrounded the yard of almost-finished-blooming yellow asters, white cosmos, and pink roses. The back opened up to acres of cornfields, now brown stubble after the harvest. I scanned the curtain-less windows and found the back door. Then the farm dog found me.

She was a medium-size black dog with nipples hanging down, heavy from milk—and she probably cared more about protecting her pups than the family inside. With no stick in hand, I pressed my back against the side of the house, inches from her ferocious barks and snaps. Suddenly an older-looking "Mrs. Bronson" swung open the screenless door.

"Lady! Back! Down. It's all right. Calm down!"

Lady stopped barking, but her tail kept wagging as she paced in a defensive position.

"Don't mind her, boy. She's crazy about those puppies you were about to step on. I suggest you come inside pretty quick."

No argument from me. Inside, a round polished oak table with an orange oilcloth covering held court in the middle of the kitchen. A cross hung out of the way on one wall, a radio below it. The stove still glowed hot near a sink with a glittery towel draped over the edge. Two wooden chairs at the oak table provided the only seats.

The lady talked fast, her sentences all running together as if she had a million chores to do.

"Hungry? You just get to town? Passing through? We have no work right now. Hay is in. Corn done for the season. But maybe I can fix you something. Earl is with the hens, gathering their eggs. You look like you could use some fattening up. Had lunch yet?"

"No, Ma'am. I haven't even had breakfast. But I don't have any money to pay you."

"That's all right. The Lord has blessed us greatly, more than most. At least we eat three times a day. I'm Eleanor Lilley. My husband, Earl, and I lease the farm from someone who lives downstate. Our son, Emerson, works in town. He's an accountant. We see him on Sundays at the Methodist Church." She began to re-stoke the fire in the stove, putting in some twigs then a few small logs. "Now let me fix you something. How old are you?"

My, she talked fast.

"I'm eleven, Ma'am."

Mrs. Lilley did not at all remind me of my own mother. This woman was taller, about five-foot-eight, thin, with straight legs. She smiled too. The apron she wore fancied three large fish. Walleyes, I figured. As she lit a match and restarted the stove fire, she asked, "What are you doing out on the road? Your parents know where you are?"

"Both dead, ma'am. I'm the only one left in the family. I couldn't pay the bills or work the farm alone. So here I am. You sure you don't have any work for me? I helped my dad a lot on our farm."

"What's your name, son?"

Should I tell her the truth? No. Not worth the risk.

I fell silent for a few moments, probably long enough for her to recognize the lack of truth in my next words.

"Billy Burrows." I don't know where I got that. "From New Jersey." I had heard that was farming country and that they grew tomatoes there.

"Never been to New Jersey. What's it like, Billy Burrows?" Her voice carried a hint of skepticism.

"About like here. Say, can I wash my hands? I've been sleeping outside."

"Water closet is on your left. Don't forget to put the lid up. Don't want no pee when I have to sit."

29

When I came back to the table, Mrs. Lilley had already begun sizzling eggs in a black iron skillet.

Just then an older man who appeared to be in his sixties came in, calming the puppies' mother as he closed the door. "Who's this youngster?"

"He says his name is Bill Burrows, from New Jersey somewhere. I told him I could give him some lunch. He keeps asking if he can work for us. You got anything?"

Earl shook his head. "No. Too late in the season. Enjoy your meal, boy. Then be on your way. You might find something though in Hartland Corners. There's a feed store there. Jim Heyman, the owner, he knows everything that goes on around here. Jim might know someone who needs help."

Now I felt almost more eager to leave than eat the lunch Eleanor slid in front of me. I did my best to use the manners I was supposed to have learned at the Bogue Home, but gulped it down fast. "Thank you, Mrs. Lilley. I sure enjoyed those eggs and ham. You are a wonderful cook. Wish I could have done something to pay you. Someday I will. Promise!"

Knowing I shouldn't pass up any potential opportunities but keeping the image of that mama dog in my mind, I stopped at several more farmhouses after arming myself with a stout stick. That stick came in handy more than once. All the farms had dogs, just like Missouri said, but none had work. No one needed another young boy to take care of.

Then I came to a widening in the road that signaled the presence of a town. A flimsy wooden sign read: HARTLAND CORNERS, POPULATION: 78. They must have all been on vacation in New Jersey because I saw no one when I walked into Mr. Heyman's feed store. I had traveled more than twenty miles from that hobo camp. Exhaustion bore down on me, hunger snapping at its heels and chased by the fearful knowledge that I had no place to sleep that night.

"How can I help you, young man?" Mr. Heyman leaned his elbows on the wooden counter and looked up from reading a newspaper. Posters advertising horse feed, cattle feed, and chicken feed dominated the walls. The store did not just sell animal feed, though. It had enough rakes and hoes and other tools to equip an army—along with two child-high shelves sparsely stocked with candy. Heyman himself had thinned hair and looked as thin as the rakes rising from a barrel next to the counter. I guessed he was in his fifties. From the muscles in his arms, I'd say he probably maintained a large garden of his own.

"Mr. Heyman, I'm looking to earn my keep. I need to make money so I can—" I almost said rescue my brother. "So I can eat and have a place to sleep tonight."

Heyman put down his paper and came around the counter. His brow furrowed, but his face smiled. "You may be in luck. You're kind of small and scrawny, but I do know Rah Munzel needs someone. Amma and Rah are immigrants from Germany. Not everyone in these parts trusts them Germans. But the Munzels have always been honest with me. They had a boy working for them, but he just took off. Probably headed south to work in the fields that still need picking.

"Listen closely. The Munzels have a small boy living with them, their son's child. His name is Billy, and he's sick, can't take care of himself. They need someone to care for him, along with the ordinary chores around a farm. You'd have to stay in the area for a while."

"Mr. Heyman, I would love to do this. I have a little bro—I mean, I have some experience caring for younger kids. Please tell me how to find them."

Chapter Five
A SAFE PLACE

The New York autumn wind held a winter chill and a light rain began to fall off and on. I walked more quickly. The drops dampened my clothes and the roadside mud caked my shoes and spattered on my pants. I didn't present a well-kempt sight when I knocked on the door to which Mr. Heyman had directed me.

Could this be the start of reuniting with my brother? Or will it be a dead end?

I wanted so badly to take care of Dick as I'd promised Dad and to be in a normal family again—maybe even find a way to get back with my older brother and sisters. For this to happen, I had to earn money, probably a lot of it. But standing in front of the Munzel farm, I didn't think my prospects looked promising.

The house resembled the Lilley place I'd visited earlier in the day, minus the fence, flowers, and dog. The stone steps leading to the house were swept, and the farm gave off a strict, no-nonsense cleanness. Nothing lay around unused. A not-so-old Chevrolet sat parked on the gravel driveway. Several elm trees stood watch around the house, shedding their leaves the way the winter sky would soon shed snow. A creek running behind the trees at the back of the house reminded me of the hobo camp. I preferred not to go back there.

I knocked on the back door.

Amma Munzel pulled the curtains from the gray, glass windows of her door. She slowly opened the door part way. "Yes? How can we help you?" Her voice carried a German accent: quiet, kind, and reserved.

"Mrs. Munzel, my name is Billy Burrows—wait—no, it isn't. My name is Lowell Kenneth Wood, and I need work. Mr. Heyman at the feed store said you might need some help, maybe especially with your grandson. I was born on a farm, spent my first six years there. I had—I have—a younger brother about your grandson's age who's in an orphan home, and I've had experience taking care of someone that young. Can I please come in and talk with you?"

The chill of the darkening sky bit at my body, and I twitched. The kind lady opened the door. "Wait here in the kitchen. I will find my husband."

Her oak table sported a dull gray oilcloth table covering, along with the ubiquitous wood burning stove. No cross on the wall here, but the requisite radio sat on a long-legged table.

The six o'clock news murmured low through the room when Rah Munzel came in. His eyes widened. "Who are you?" His accent matched hers.

"Lowell Wood, Mr. Munzel. I can help you, I know I can. I, um, would like to make a proposal. Will you listen to it?"

"Why are you here? Where did you come from? Who are you?"

"I can explain all that. But first will you listen to my plan?"

"This better be good. We may be immigrants to America, but we are not stupid." He fixed his eyes on me, waiting.

"Mr. and Mrs. Munzel, I will work for you for free—take care of Billy, and do chores around the farm. You give me a room to sleep in, even if it's with Billy—I'm used to that. But you have to allow me to go to school. There must be one near here."

"Go on."

"You have to let me work for pay for other farmers. I need money. Someday I want to help my family come back together." I paused to make sure I hadn't forgotten anything. "Okay, that's it."

Mr. Munzel stared at me, motionless except for his blinking eyes. "Yes, we do need help with the farm, and also with our grandson, as Amma says Mr. Heyman told you. The doctors say our grandson has a weakened heart. Our daughter-in-law passed away while she was in labor. It caused our son too much pain. He will be back, but for now he is in Buffalo. He wants nothing to do with his son."

The man pressed his lips together and looked down.

I dared not speak until he said whatever was on his mind. I knew how it felt when someone you loved died. And I knew how it felt to not be wanted.

Mr. Munzel drew a long breath. "I have to say your proposal is interesting. Let Mrs. Munzel and me talk about this. Decisions made quickly are never good decisions. My father used to tell me, 'The longest distance between two points is a shortcut.' He laughed to himself. "But at least for tonight you should stay here. Right, Amma?"

"Of course, Rah. I would not send the boy into the dark alone. We will talk, Mr. Lowell Wood, but tonight can I fix you dinner? I have some chicken and boiled potatoes."

"That sounds wonderful."

The plain-looking grandfather clock in the sparse living room softly chimed seven times, but a long day of walking had made me weary. My head nodded several times at the dinner table.

Mrs. Munzel said, "Okay, now you go upstairs and sleep."

The Munzels gave me my own room next to their grandson. I had not met Billy Munzel yet. He was already sleeping when I finished supper and lugged myself up the stairs to find a room with a black metal heating grate in the floor. Warm air from the basement furnace kept the space warm enough to calm the ache of chill gripping my bones. The only decoration in this bedroom was the head of a small deer that stared at me, unblinking.

I pulled the heavy covers over my head and fell asleep.

Chapter Six

HARD WORK AND BILLY

I woke up to the sound of footsteps going down the stairs. Darkness still lay on the room.

Should I get out of bed?

Maybe it was a burglar. Or a detective from the Bogue Home who followed me to the Munzels. I slid from the warm bed and hid behind a chest of drawers. Dressed only in my underwear, I started to shiver.

The living room clock chimed six times.

Then, muffled voices.

I heard parts of a conversation, but they were speaking German. Mr. Munzel kept saying something that sounded like "young," and I took that to mean me. Mrs. Munzel kept responding, "kuh melken," which sorta sounded like milking a cow. Later I learned that "Junge" is the German word for "boy" and "kuh" is the word for "cow," so my guess was close. But beyond the basics, I couldn't understand a word they said.

Okay. . . . I took a deep breath and set my thoughts straight. The Munzels must get up and start work before even the sun shows itself. I didn't care what work they gave me—milking, sweeping, pulling rocks from the fields, or cleaning cow manure from troughs in the barn. Whatever the task, I would do it.

I pulled on the same clothes from the day before and trotted down the squeaky stairs. Mrs. Munzel stood in the kitchen, alone.

"Where is Mr. Munzel? I'm ready to help him."

"He is out in the barn milking the cows. But I have something to tell you. My husband and I discussed this last night, and we want you to stay and help us, at least for a while. We want to try it for a few days, then make a decision. Okay?"

A smile welled up inside me. I might have a home, at least for a while.

"We agree with your plan. No problem with that. But if you do stay, you will have to work, no playing or goofing off. You work for us first, then you can study your school stuff or work for the other farmers."

"Okay, but let me think about it for a moment. Quick decisions are not good decisions." I let my smile out.

She looked away as she seemed to suppress her own smile, then cleared her throat. "Mr. Munzel will be back soon. Now I must wake up Billy."

We walked up the stairs and into a small bedroom where a small boy lay with his eyes closed, breathing heavily. Mrs. Munzel said the doctor told her the boy had a bad heart. Hmm. No mother, no father. Without his grandparents, Billy could have been in the Bogue Home like me. Maybe what he had was a *broken* heart!

Mrs. Munzel sat on Billy's narrow bed. Outside the window the dark sky began to glow as a sallow sun poked its head over the horizon. The boy started to move. One eye opened and gazed directly at me. "Oma, who is that?"

"This is Lowell, Billy. Lowell Wood. He may be staying with us for a week or so. You remember Henry, who used to help you? He had to leave us to go south for work. Lowell is going to help Opa and me with the farm just like Henry did. He even slept in Henry's room last night."

Billy took to me immediately. I liked that. He turned his head toward me and asked, "Lowell, when I get up, can I show you my spider collection?"

Mrs. Munzel jumped in, "Billy, you clean up and get dressed. Lowell can stay and help you. After that, you can both have some breakfast. Then you can discuss, *uch*, spiders."

Billy needed help getting going in the morning and he had a million questions.

"Why do I have to wear shoes?"

"Who says you're supposed to wash your hands after you pee?"

"Can I wear my red shirt?"

But other than not running everywhere once he was up, he reminded me a lot of Dick. I accepted that as both a blessing and a regret.

"C'mon, Lowell. Let's go outside. I'll show you some live spiders."

When he finally came back from the barn, Mr. Munzel insisted on calling the Bogue Home to tell them where I was. I think he had an immigrant's fear. He didn't want to get in trouble with the sheriff if they ever found out where I'd landed.

My heart throbbed as he picked up the telephone receiver hanging on the wall.

For a moment, I thought of running out the door. Back to the hobo camp. Then the operator connected him with the Bogue home, and there was no turning back.

"Hello? Is this the Bogue Home?" He nodded to Mrs. Munzel, who stood stiff with clasped hands. "Mrs. Bronson, my name is Rah Munzel. I live just north of Gasport. I am calling about a boy named Lowell Wood."

My feet angled toward the door, ready to escape.

"He is here on our farm. We would like to try him out. . . . What is that? . . . Oh my. We will keep an eye on him. . . . Really? Well, if you say so. . . . "

The conversation lasted only a few minutes, but seemed like forever. Finally, he hung up. My feet stayed.

Mrs. Munzel leaned forward. "What did they say?"

Mr. Munzel looked at me. "Well, they said they were glad you found a new home because they were not going to take you back, ever. A Mrs. Bronson told me you were trouble, and that you could not come back even to see your brother." He sighed and kept looking at me.

I dutifully bowed my head. But the words burst out of my mouth, "I wouldn't go back to the Bogue Home even if they begged me."

"I see." Mr. Munzel paused. He must have been thinking hard about what to do with me. "I still would like you to stay and see if our arrangement can work, but that is up to you."

I lifted my head. "Really?"

He nodded.

"I'll do everything I said last night. I need to earn enough money to get Dick out of that place."

I was immediately assigned chores in all the Munzel commercial enterprises. The first week passed in a blur of milking cows, moving rocks out of the now barren hay fields, getting signed up at the Gasport public school, and coming to know the Munzels—whom I came to call Rah, Amma, and Billy.

The work was hard and there was so much more to do here than there had been at my dad's farm, but at least I had a dry place to sleep and more than enough to keep me busy and not think too much.

Work filled even the nights. We candled eggs—hundreds of them. All of us, even Billy, put in time in the cold basement by holding eggs in front of a candle, searching for cracked shells and broken yolks before putting the good ones into cardboard cartons.

"Lowell, I heard a car horn," Amma said one night. "Go see what they need. We still have some apples besides these eggs. Remember, six cents a dozen for eggs, four cents for apples."

"Yes, Amma. Right away." I was happy to have a reason to get out for even a short time. The man in the car wanted a dozen large eggs. On my way back into the house, I met Rah coming in from the barn.

"Rah, it's already after eight o'clock. I have homework."

"You Americans. If you want to get ahead, you have to work, day and night! Do you have a full crate of eggs yet? You should go back down and finish working like the rest of us."

If all Germans worked the way he did, I wondered how they ever lost the Great War.

"After that, we need to talk to you."

After I filled the crate with eggs, it was more than relief that brought me back up the stairs. Survival is a powerful attraction.

"You're a skinny little guy, and we need someone who can pick up bales of hay. You know nothing about how to lead or milk my cows, and the hens want you nowhere near them. You are not really the kind of help we need. But . . ." He sighed. "Billy likes you, and you're smart. We think you can be taught to give us the help we want. So if you are willing, we may continue this experiment."

And we did. For two years I worked with the Munzels, until at thirteen years of age I graduated from the high school. During that time, I hadn't saved a nickel, and I needed to get Dick out of the Bogue Home. It was time to renegotiate my contract with the Munzels.

"Rah, I need to make some money, not just work for room and board. I have another proposal."

"Lowell, you don't have to leave us. Let's hear your idea and work something out."

I didn't want to leave, but I had not forgotten about getting Dick out and bringing our family back together. I had found our sister Millie in Michigan and had been in contact with her. We both wanted to reunite the Woods--at least, what was left of our family.

"How does this sound?," I asked Rah. "I'll pay you eight dollars a week, and I will milk the cows. For that, you and Amma give me room and board. But I want to work in Lockport, too. I am too young to drive, but Mr. Stack drives his Chevy to work in Lockport every morning and he told me a factory that makes gears needs help. They want someone who can handle a six-pound hammer to pound numbers into the metal gears. If I can lift heavy egg boxes, I can lift a six-pound hammer."

Rah gently nodded his head.

"And there's the kosher turkey processing plant in town—they need help on the weekends. I've seen the place. It isn't heavy work, but it is messy. I can do that work. A rope circulates through the plant, with loops hanging down. You grab a turkey from a cage and ease the rope around its neck. They have rabbis who use straight razors to efficiently do in each turkey. Messy, but the money is good."

I renegotiated my contract with the Munzels. I paid them eight dollars a week and milked their cows. They provided me with room and board as long as I worked in Lockport. Mr. Stack and I drove back and forth to Lockport five days a week for about a year. On weekends I dispatched turkeys from their lives on this earth and did other odd jobs. Even though I paid the Munzels, I managed to save enough money to move on to stage two of my little plan.

REUNITED WITH
MY BIG SISTER

I had come to the Munzel farm in the fall, and four autumns later my time with the Munzels came to a close. The mature corn and hay had been taken from the neat-rowed fields that we'd cared for all spring and summer. A new chill crept into the air and left hoarfrost that slept on the gray grass at night and disappeared under the midmorning sun.

I will always be grateful for what I learned from Rah and Amma about working hard and, above all, what it looked like to be a family. They gave me the gift of living with people who cared deeply for each other and cared exceedingly for an invalid grandchild. Something kept them from consigning him to the care of strangers—a decision I wished Elmer and my sisters had made for Dick and me. Unlike my own family, I experienced from these two humble people something supremely important: compassion.

Yet my appreciation met limitations. I admired compassion in others and happily received it, but more and more it came to live outside me. Compassion lived with me like honey—sweet, but I couldn't afford it. I saw only one path to success, and dollar bills paved it.

Right from the beginning of my letter correspondence with Mille, she encouraged me to come to her home in Jonesville. The big motivation for me to leave the Munzel farm, besides being with my sister, was the opportunity to drive a car at fifteen; that was the age at which you could get a license in Michigan. The way I looked at it, having a car would enable me to get more jobs and earn more money.

Restoring the family motivated Millie, but in her situation it would also help to find someone who could make some money help pay the rent. After all, we were in the midst of the Great Depression. Helping out felt fine with me, although I had to use some of the money I'd saved to buy a one-way Greyhound bus ticket to Jonesville.

My mind reached a decision, but my heart had a more difficult time. Rah shook my hand goodbye, holding on longer than was comfortable. Amma's big farm arms held me too tightly. Billy's tears at my going were the toughest. They tugged my heart and brought to mind how I had abandoned, and in a way was again abandoning, Dick. I had enough money to get myself to Jonesville, but not enough to bring Dick along with me.

I pulled away from the Munzels feeling badly for everyone. But, as I marched to the bus station carrying one small bag, my thoughts shifted. For the first time in my life I consciously acknowledged that sometimes getting ahead in this world simply requires sacrifice. I left Dick in the Bogue Home, and turned my back on the family that had adopted me. I did not know for certain if my action should be deemed good or bad. Deep down, to be shamefully honest, I felt exhilarated.

Bigger things waited ahead.

My thoughts of what might be grew as the bus bumped along somewhat paved roads between New York and Michigan. I didn't sleep a wink for ten hours—too busy dreaming up how everything would be perfect once I got to Millie's.

I finally arrived in Jonesville at 11 p.m. on a Friday. Cool Michigan air and a coal dark night devoid of streetlights greeted me. You know what didn't greet me? Or, I should say, *who*? Millie. Nor anyone else.

I got off the bus alone, carrying my small bag. The bus driver, trying to keep to his schedule, quickly departed. As the lights of the bus disappeared down a lonely road, loneliness surrounded me as I stood in front of a low-lit old brick station.

What to do?

My first thought was to look for someone official. Maybe a policeman or security guard. Then, from inside the station, I heard what at first sounded like loud snoring. When I pushed open the door, I saw no one, but I heard groans coming from a dark back room. Worried, I pulled back a curtain and surprised two figures who frantically disentangled themselves. From the metal star on the shirt lying on the floor, I surmised I'd found the security guard. A dark brunette slipped through the rear door while vainly attempting to secure some undergarment.

What an auspicious welcome to my new hometown.

"I don't know what you *think* you saw." The man glowered at me. "But if you want to live a longer life, you will remember it as a strange dream."

"Yes, sir."

Apparently assuming that his badge provided all the protection needed, the guard shifted into a more relaxed mood. I told him my name and that I was looking for my sister, Millie Baker.

Surely with a town as small as Jonesville, I thought, he'll know where everyone lives and what they're up to.

I was right. The now-more-composed officer gave me instructions on how to find Millie. He also informed me that the previous day Millie had given birth to her firstborn, a boy, whom she named John Robert Baker. With her absence satisfactorily explained, I thanked the guard, filed my "strange dream" away in case I ever needed to recall it, and headed toward Millie's.

Following the security guard's instructions, I came to a two-story wooden house marooned at the end of a street. No lights shone from the windows, but I heard an infant crying inside, then someone talking baby talk to quiet him. I knocked softly and called in a hushed voice, "Millie? It's me, Lowell."

I didn't wait long until the door opened to reveal Millie and my new nephew. A stern look on her face greeted me with, "I thought you were coming tomorrow morning."

This reception just got better and better.

At least I had a place to sleep—in a strange little town, in a strange state, with people I did not know. At fifteen I was starting life with a third family.

I woke up early the next morning to the sound of a baby's cry. I'd been given a room in the basement, not far from the old coal-burning furnace. At least it was warm. The cold fall nights in Michigan were only a prelude to the winter. As is typical in Michigan in November, grayness shut out the sun all around. I climbed the old wood basement stairs to greet my sister, her husband—and a new life!

"So it's 10 A.M., and you finally decided to wake up." Millie blew a long bang of hair out of her eyes as she rocked the baby in her arms.

Great. The non-wonderful reception continued.

"I've been up for hours with Robert here. And my husband, Gordon Baker, is at work."

"I'm hungry, Millie. It was a long, rough ride. I'll be glad if I never feel another pothole for the rest of my life. I'm sure that driver aimed for every rock and every ditch on the way from New York."

"All I have is mush," she warned. "That's what we all had this morning, except for John Robert, of course. He sucked me dry."

"Okay, I'll have the mush. Please change the subject."

"Did you know our mother's sister lives near here? Three miles away in a small town called Hartland—yes, there is a Hartland in Michigan, too. She pays me to wash and iron. It's a lot for me to do, but with the new baby we need the money. Besides, she knows all the family skeletons. I know there are some secrets she's keeping from me. Maybe that's because her husband is the sheriff in Hartland."

Why was she telling me this? I'd had enough drama. I just wanted to earn money.

A restless and interrupted night had left Millie tired, but I needed to know everything about Jonesville. And I wanted her to know about where I'd been.

As I shoveled in the mush, I launched into it.

"What kind of work can I get?" Then, before she could answer, I threw in the important part. "I need a driver's license. How do I get one?"

She dutifully answered. I went on. "We have to get Dick out of the Bogue Home. Let me tell you about that place, and my hobo friends, and the Munzels . . ."

She could see I was all wound up; she could not know how I felt fearful at having spent months of my hard-earned money to get to this place. I knew that money is power—or at least I knew the lack of it was the lack of power. And I had exhausted most of my money. A driver's license would return at least some power.

I tried to explain that having a driver's license would help us all. I laid out my ideas. "With a license, I could work two jobs, one away from here, maybe in Hillsdale at the college, or in Jackson, or even Fort Wayne—and get back in time to work another job and . . ."

After a while, Millie's eyes began to blink and shutter. When her head fell to her chest, I realized I should probably take a walk. This gave me a good chance to discover what might be in my new neighborhood. With Millie and Robert both sleeping, I headed off to take a look around.

Chapter Eight
A GIRL NAMED BETTY

While there weren't a lot of citizens in Jonesville, the ones who made this town their home also extended a friendliness to newcomers. Red maple trees lined its narrow streets, their leaves brilliant shades of crimson.

I was not outside long before I saw a pretty blond girl in a bulky brown sweater and green skirt jumping rope in her driveway across the street. She looked to be about my age.

I walked over to her.

She kept jumping.

"You need help with your jump rope technique." In fifteen years, I had never jumped rope, but that didn't stop me from pretending I knew what I was talking about. "Hold your hands lower to the ground. That will give you more speed."

She tried doing that. Somehow, it worked. Whew.

She finally asked, "Who are you? I saw you come out of Millie's house."

"My name's Lowell."

"I'm Betty Swope."

With the jump rope in each hand, would she shake mine? I held out my hand.

She paused, took both rope ends in one hand, and shook mine.

Then her mother stepped out. A scraggly, gray-haired battle-ax, she bellowed, "Who are you and what are you doing badgering my daughter? You're trespassing on my driveway."

Before I could answer, Betty grabbed my hand and shouted, "I'll take care of him, Mom!" She pulled me out to the sidewalk and around a bush, out of her mother's sight.

I liked this cheeky girl more every second.

"Sorry about my mother," she said in a lowered voice. "She's usually upset about something, but so far today she's been in a really dark mood."

I peeked around the bush as the mother went back inside.

"What about you? Where are you from?" Before I could answer she asked, "What were you doing at Millie's house?"

She lowered her shoulders, apparently calm and ready to listen. My answers flowed like a soundtrack as she led us around the small town. She introduced me to neighbors and storekeepers along the way and became my first Michigan friend—and then my best friend. I could tell Betty anything. She told me things she wouldn't have told anyone else, especially about other boys, and especially to her mother.

"Lowell, Freddy Schmidt wants to take me to the movie house in Jackson, the one with the balcony. He says the best place to watch the movie is from the balcony, but Jenny Lockhardt told me not to go with him unless I bring handcuffs. What did she mean?"

"Let me talk to Freddy Schmidt. Then if he still asks you to go to the movies, you won't need any handcuffs."

We were just friends. We walked, we talked, and when the seasons turned warm, we swam together—even skinny dipped together—like buddies. Neither of us ever thought it would be more than that.

One afternoon Betty came to me, head down, eyes puffy, and asked, "Lowell, can I tell you something, and you won't get angry at me?"

I nodded.

"My boyfriend, Jimmy Constantine, and I were fooling around. We didn't go all the way, but we did go too far. We're in love, Lowell, but neither of us is old enough to be married. Then last night happened, and I was amazed at how wonderful it felt—I mean when we had done it. But later I felt really guilty. I went to ask my mother. Big mistake."

Betty held her hands to face, tears streaming, nose running. "What does God think of me? Will I be punished?" She looked up, her face a wet mess. "I know God forgives everything, but when I tried to talk to my mother about what I felt, she covered her mouth, then she cursed me."

"What'd she say?"

"'You'll be damned by God, you fornicator!'" Betty burst into more tears.

I sat wide-eyed, clueless.

"What did she mean?"

No comment from me.

She kept crying.

I knew why she was telling me about the experiences with her boyfriend and her mother. We talked about everything. Never held anything back. But why ask *me* about God?

She whimpered again.

"Who is God?" I asked. "I haven't met Him. You can't prove Him. He was never there for me. He wasn't there for my father or my little brother either. Maybe He just created us then walked away."

She blankly stared ahead.

I took a deep breath. "I haven't had much church education, but it seems to me if you create a person, you should take responsibility for them. I can't see that God has done anything to make my life profitable."

Betty's tears stopped. "Lowell, I believe God brought you to Jonesville, maybe just to be my friend—to sit here and when I need it, to calm me down. You are a good person. But not me. I can't forgive myself. I let God down. I drove my mother away. She can't stand to look at me, and I despise her. What will my father say when he finds out?"

She once again burst into tears.

"Betty, I'm not your best-informed source of information about God. And I think your mother is nuts. But I do know one thing—you are a beautiful person. God—if you believe in that kind of thing—must have made us to feel love, not just think about love or talk about love. He wanted us to experience it, and not with just our minds but with our whole bodies. You love this boy. That's what happened."

I had no idea what I was talking about.

She lifted her face to look at me. "You're my best friend, Lowell. I will always think of you as my best friend."

Chapter Nine
HITCHHIKING AND BREAKING HORSES

Kiddie Brush & Toy Company stood as the tallest building in Jonesville. They manufactured metal toys, and they needed young men to work in apprentice positions.

With wars starting in Europe and Asia in 1939, most people in Michigan (including me) believed it wouldn't be long before the United States would be pulled into the fighting. That meant more manufacturing—and Michigan had both experience and production capacity. It would also mean we'd most likely lose many men who could run those machines. All of that came together to open up a job for one eager fifteen year old: me.

"Mr. Camp, just tell me what you want me to do. I'm ready for anything."

"You ain't ready for nothing. Pay attention, or you'll lose one of those scrawny fingers."

"Why are you so crabby all the time? You got extra help, the best help of anyone here—me. Just tell me what to do."

"I can't tell you. This isn't school learning. Tool-and-die making is a skill. It has to be observed. Then comes hands-on learning, the best kind there is." He glared at me to make sure I got the message.

I got it. And I was glad he didn't kick me out for being so intentionally cheeky.

"When you're ready, I'll show you how to square a block. That's the first thing you'll learn how to do. If you don't square the block, nothing turns out right after that. For right now, shut up and watch."

I did. Eventually I learned to square a block and use heat-treating tools. I wanted to be the best tool-and-die maker in the plant. I also wanted to go further than that and improve my skills. So, after working eight hours a day with cranky Mr. Camp, two days a week I hitchhiked the five miles to Hillsdale College.

Besides money being power, I also heard that knowledge was power. So of course I wanted to learn more in order to make more money.

I did whatever I could, suffered any abuse, and swallowed a lot of my own words, some that should not be seen in print. I felt driven to it. Prayers of contrition filled each night spent away from my brother Dick, not to God but to my father. I prayed to Dad for forgiveness.

I determined to rise out of my curse of poverty. I longed to not only gain the ability to bring my family back together, but also become somebody to be taken seriously, to be admired.

So, I took on more work.

John Tillman had a ranch near Hillsdale where he raised cattle and horses. Mr. Tillman kept a lookout for young guys crazy enough to try their hand at breaking horses, an art that is part knowledge and part intuition.

"How much does it pay, Mr. Tillman?"

"Ten cents an hour—and nothing for bandages or crutches."

"I'm your boy. Let me at 'em."

There are many approaches to getting a horse to accept a rider, but the basics are the same. First you have to have a way with animals, which I seemed to have. From there I perfected my method. I'd get to know the horse, develop a relationship with him, and get him to trust me. Then I lay across the horse, gently so as not to spook him. Then I laid a saddle pad over his back. Then a saddle. Gradually. It took time.

Next I would slowly and gently place my left foot in the stirrup and swing my right leg over the horse's back, putting my other foot in the right stirrup. At this point I had to stay low, because if a horse sees someone on his back, it spooks him. I'd hold tight to the saddle with my legs but not grip the reins tightly, because if I the horse bucked me off, a jerk on his reins would spook him even more.

After a while I became fairly good at breaking horses. This helped me to know a lot of the local farmers, ranchers, and businesspeople, as well as a good number of horses.

I also got very familiar with first aid boxes.

In between tool-and-die making, hitchhiking to Hillsdale College, and breaking horses, I found work some Saturdays dispatching chickens the way the rabbis had cut the heads off of turkeys. If it paid, I came ready to work.

But then I figured something out. Why did I need a middleman when I could be my own boss? So in 1940, at sixteen years old, I started my first business.

Carlton Station may have gotten more snow than Jonesville, but the snows came earlier in Jonesville. The calendar says winter begins on December 22, but Jonesville had a leg up on the calendar. In October the blue skies fade to gray, and the sun sits so low in the morning that it needs a wakeup call. All of this leads to early snow and plenty of it, which means people needed help to dig out sidewalks from the thick white blankets.

To me, the snow might as well have been white gold. I learned how to go door to door, selling my snow-shoveling services. I recruited some local kids to shovel snow for families I signed up. Betty was taking a drawing class in high school, and she helped me design posters to put up in the local stores, even as far away as the Kroger Market in Hillsdale. After a while I had so much work, I had to hire kids from town to work for me.

"Mrs. Henry, I see your sidewalk is covered with snow. Can my 'Wood Shovels Team' handle that for you? Only twenty-five cents for the whole sidewalk. Another five cents to open a path to the back of your house."

"Aren't you Millie's nephew, that orphan kid?"

That orphan kid. I hated that phrase. I would do anything to never be called that again.

She raised her eyebrows, apparently waiting for a response.

"Yes, I'm Millie's nephew." I paused, put on a smile. "And I'm ready to work."

"Okay. I need the front and back done. But do the front first so I can see what kind of job you do."

Rah Munzel's wisdom came back to me. *Any job worth doing is worth doing well.*

"Mrs. Henry, if you don't like what we do in the front, fire us. And I won't expect a penny from you."

We did such good work, and the business became so successful, I decided we should branch out. Houses in Jonesville were heated by coal, but burning coal left ashes that had to be shoveled out of furnaces and carted away. So the Wood Shovels Team got into ash removal as well. At last I was making enough money to expand my world.

And that meant applying for a driver's license.

Chapter Ten

ONE STEP CLOSER
TO FREEDOM

Though my sixteenth birthday crept ever closer, I still didn't have my driver's license.

To get the license a person had to be fifteen years old, pay a $10 fee, and drive himself to City Hall to take the test. The only person in town I knew who had his own car was Jim Schroeder, the night watchman, the same *didn't-see-him-with-the-woman-but-only-dreamed-about-it* watchman from the night I arrived in Jonesville. Jim adored his 1937 Ford Deluxe Tudor Sedan. If you bought that car from a dealer, it might cost $750. That's pretty steep when the average income in Jonesville only hit about $1,400 a year. But Mr. Schroeder had a friend at the Ford Motor plant in Detroit, so everyone assumed he paid a lot less.

Still.

I found Jim late one afternoon down by the bus station. The afternoon sun blanketed our crisp and chilly May day. Mr. Schroeder was sitting on the front porch of the station, jacket buttoned up tight, his watchman's badge reposed on his chest, and his antique-looking pistol peeking out of a holster on his right hip. Just then a Greyhound bus pulled up and began disgorging passengers. Most stretched their legs and stayed near the bus for re-boarding. Only one or two, if any, had reason to stay longer than a few minutes in Jonesville.

"Nice afternoon, Mr. Schroeder. Hope things are peaceful here today. No riots or anything."

He looked up from studying the mob threatening his town.

"How come you're not hanging around Betty Swope's house and bothering her mother?"

"Betty and I are just friends. You know that. But I have a favor to ask."

"What kind of favor?"

Deep breath. "I need to borrow your car."

"Pffft! What are you talking about? That car's just two years old. You don't even have a driver's license. And even if you did, I'd be crazy to let a young jackass like you drive my car. Get out of my sight and let me do my job in peace."

"I need to borrow your car so I can take the driver's test at city hall, Mr. Schroeder. You're the only person I know who owns a car. Mind if I take a look inside the station? Last fall when I came into Jonesville, I had a peek, and I remember you had a back room. Just wondering if the layout is the same."

"What do you mean, you scrawny nitwit?'

"I need to borrow your car. And I can keep secrets real well, or I can drop some hints here and there about a certain watchman and his late-night habits."

Schroeder dropped his right hand to the old pistol. His eyes darted from me to the passengers – witnesses – all around.

No need to push my luck.

"I just need the car for one hour," I said. "I'm willing to arrange for the ashes from your furnace to be carted away every week for a month. What do you say? If any harm comes to the car, you can shoot me."

His brain appeared to be working so hard I thought I could smell the grindings burning off, just like in the tool-and-die shop.

"One hour. And if you're not back by then, I *will* shoot you. You can come around tomorrow afternoon to shovel the ashes. Hasn't been done in two months, so you'll have a fine job to do. When do you need the Ford?"

"Tomorrow morning's good enough."

"Boy, you better never get into any trouble around here. There will be no mercy from me. You get what I mean?"

I noted the passengers re-entering the bus.

An appropriate time for me to leave.

———————

Jim Schroeder reluctantly met me at 10 a.m. the next day in front of his house. I eyed the Ford sitting in the driveway.

"You've got an eighth of a tank of gas," Jim said. "Enough to get you to City Hall and back, so don't think you're going to drive this car all over the country. Be back here by 11 a.m. or I will come and find you."

"Yes, sir."

I drove myself to City Hall to take the test. The driving inspector started as I expected, with a question. "Do you have a car to drive?"

I showed him.

His eyes widened, then narrowed. "Hey, this looks like Schroeder's car."

I nodded.

"That guy is a pain in the ass. How'd you get him to let you drive it? I never thought he'd let anyone touch the car, let alone drive it. What you got on him?"

If only he knew. "Mr. Schroeder is a dear friend of mine. He just wanted to see his friend succeed in life, and part of that is getting a Michigan driver's license."

The inspector shook his head. "I don't believe a word of it." He looked over the beautiful vehicle before him. "But you *do* have a car. Now let me see you drive the thing around the block without killing yourself and then prove to me you can park it."

I managed to drive the Ford around the block with no fatalities. And, since this was one of the few cars in Jonesville at that time of day, parking was easy. I got my license.

As I slid back behind the wheel, new license in head, I thought about the few blocks separating me from the high school right—and Betty—right now.

Since I had the car, along with forty-five minutes left in my one-hour allotment, it wouldn't hurt to just drive past there. The first time I drove around the school, I saw no one outside. But after I passed it by several times, some students stuck their heads out the windows. My fourth or fifth time around, Betty and some others came outside for a school break. They cheered and waved.

I waved back, first with one hand, then two hands—just to show my dexterity driving a car. The car careened left, jumped a sidewalk, and into a field of mud. A brick wall with the words "JONESVILLE HIGH SCHOOL" surged toward me. God, or someone on my side, must have reached in to help me avoid the wall by inches. Unfortunately, the shiny Ford now had mud splattered up to the door handles.

With the thought of a bullet riding shotgun, I got the car out of the mud and began the drive home. However, a few feet from Schroeder's driveway, the eighth of a tank of gas became an empty tank of gas. The powerless vehicle drifted to the side of the gravel road and stopped. I checked my watch.

Twenty minutes left. Glancing around and seeing Mr. Schroeder nowhere, I ran up to his house and dropped the keys in the mailbox. Then I hitchhiked to Hillsdale, the better to stay out of that old grouch's pistol's range. We could take care of his furnace the next day, or the day after.

For about a month, Betty and I found it better to do our talking out of sight, on the wooden bench under the willow tree in Millie's backyard. When at last I gave Millie three dollars to pay for the gas and a dollar for cleaning up the Ford, I felt free to go back out in public.

Chapter Eleven
MY FIRST BUSINESS

The ability to buy back my abandoned brother and bring him to Jonesville drew tantalizingly close. For nine years, I'd prayed to Dad and worked every job I could. Dick spent those nine years waiting. I couldn't fathom him turning thirteen in that place and dug even deeper to get him out before it happened. We needed funds to pay for his transportation to Jonesville and for his food and other needs if he was going to stay at Millie's house. And I had to keep paying my own way and help out my sister. Remember, the entire country battled daily to survive The Depression. Times were tough. My income had to grow for me to be able to rescue Dick. That driver's license broadened my universe; it also opened up new possibilities for me to earn more money.

Charley Haines, one of the "Wood Shovel" kids, asked if I would drive him to Fort Wayne one Saturday night. He had a cousin whom he really wanted to see.

I did not own a car, but thought I could probably borrow one from among the tool-and-die makers at Kiddie Brush and Toy. Of course I'd have to pay for gas and for wear and tear. That meant I *could* drive Charlie, but it wouldn't be easy on my funds.

"Why should I pay money to borrow a car to drive you to Fort Wayne on a Saturday just so you can visit your cousin?" I said.

Charlie twisted his face and kicked his toe on the ground. I waited out his silence.

"Okay, Lowell," he said. "I can trust you." He cleared his throat. "Have you ever heard of *The Beautiful Body*?"

"Huh?"

"It's a film about sex hygiene."

"What's that got to do—?"

"They show it at a burlesque theater in Fort Wayne. The theater's called the Scarlet Fever. I hear that film shows *everything*. According to my cousin, a third of the guys in Fort Wayne have seen it, and some have gone back several times."

I stared at him, unsure what to say.

"Have you ever been to a burlesque show?" he went on. "My cousin is a doorman at the Scarlet Fever. I can get you in for free."

I had skinny dipped with Betty Swope, but that ended a while back and we were kids. Never had I seen a full-grown naked woman, although I'd thought about it countless times. Charlie's proposal tempted me; I only needed a vehicle to make it happen.

I negotiated a deal with one of the Kiddie Brush and Toy workers to rent his automobile.

That Saturday, Charlie and I set out to drive the eighty miles to Fort Wayne. Charlie talked even more than I.

"Lowell, I've been thinking about my life, what I want to do. It was all right shoveling snow and ashes as a kid, but I want something more. I'd really like to get away from Jonesville. Maybe I'll get a job in one of those sex movies! What about you? What do you want to be?"

"Rich," I immediately replied. "I want to be rich. If I had all the money in the world, I'd be happy and wouldn't have to worry about anything."

He nodded and hummed in agreement.

"And I tell you what," I went on. "I would use my money to keep my family happy. Charlie, there isn't anything more important than family. My father wasn't able to keep us together. He wanted to, but the times came against him. I haven't told many people, but I have a younger brother back in New York. He's in an orphanage now. Before my father died, he asked me to take care of my brother Dick, but I couldn't help him back then. I finally ran away and left him. It's a long story. Too long for this car ride, and way too sad."

A road sign said were entering Fort Wayne.

"Remember this day, Charlie. You'll see. Someday I will be rich."

Fort Wayne had grown up as an Army and trading post, next to two major rivers. Peace reigned until they built the Wabash and Erie Canal, connecting the Great Lakes with the Ohio River. Then the railroad arrived and made Fort Wayne a population center.

The burlesque theater sat in the older part of town, but it wasn't the seedy place I expected. The town enjoyed financial ease, living on good salaries from the factories that ground and whistled and hummed day and night.

Workmen came from the farms all around northeastern Indiana. Some of the men worked in the factories during the week and went back to help their families on farms through the weekends. But not all the men left the city on weekends. The Scarlet Fever Burlesque Theater seemed to some a good place to spend a Friday or Saturday evening.

As we arrived in Fort Wayne, I began to get nervous.

"You're sure we don't have to pay anything?" I said. "I have enough money to buy gas to get us back to Jonesville, but not much more."

"Don't worry," Charlie said. He pointed toward the theater. "There's my cousin, waiting for us next to the theater door. Come on, park the car—quick, before his manager sees him standing there."

I parked my rented car on a side street, away from brick walls. The theater was impressive—a brilliant white marquee, all lit up, with the words THE SCARLET FEVER written in red, flashing on and off.

Charley's cousin's real name was Claude, but everyone called him Clicks. I found him to be an all-right guy, and really funny. When he started talking fast, his jaws twitched, and he ended up making clicking sounds—the by-product of getting his his jaw dislocated in a fight long before. Those clicks made him sound even funnier. Because of this, the theater manager gave Clicks a short spot now and then on stage, in between the more well-known acts. Clicks claimed to be a rising star on the click-humor circuit. I got the impression they'd let anyone jump in and be part of the show.

Pictures on either side of the lobby showed gorgeous gals standing in front of white clouds with almost enough clothes – scarlet red, of course – on their bodies. Betty Swope would have died if she had seen this.

Clicks led us to a place behind the spotlight in the balcony. When the show began, the heat from the spotlight warmed the left side of my face as it followed an emcee by the name of Lou.

Lou grinned at the audience. "I thought of investing some money in a burlesque theater, but then I thought better of it. It was too risqué."

Groans filtered through the theater. Lou was not terribly funny. Then some scantily clad women came to dance. One of them went by the name of Miss Stake; her face couldn't be described as very pretty, but the rest of her hit the impressive list. Seeing it made my whole face hot.

And then came *The Beautiful Body* movie. I saw more parts of beautiful bodies than I knew existed.

I knew right then what I wanted my next job to be.

"Clicks, I wonder, what would someone need to do to become an emcee at The Scarlet Fever?"

"You're a fast talker," Clicks said. "Yeah, you could do the job. But you're only sixteen. If you really wanted the job, you'd probably have to shoot Lou, the current—*click*—emcee. He's the owner's son-in-law."

"I'm not really one for shooting people."

"Better yet, get a picture of him coming out of Miss Stake's place at three in the morning. He tells the owner—Jake Wescott, his father-in-law—that he's going home. And he tells his wife, Jake's daughter, that—*click*—he had to stay late." Click's eyes widened at me as his head moved up and down in silent expectation.

"Not my way to do things. What else might work?"

"Let me think on it."

We went to a restaurant on West Jefferson Street. The three of us shared a club sandwich while Clicks regaled us with stories of the dancers and the emcees, which made me all the more eager to get a job at The Scarlet Fever.

"Clicks," I said when he'd finished another story. "Introduce me to Mr. Westcott and I have a five-dollar bill for you."

"For a five-dollar bill, I would introduce you to—*click*—Santa Claus. Next Saturday, show up at the theater around 1:30 P.M. Rehearsals will be ending. Jake likes to relax before a show at—*click*—Mickey Finn's, the bar next to The Scarlet. I'll introduce you as a radio disc jockey from Detroit. That could get you an invitation to lunch."

Back home that night I was too excited to sleep. Millie and Gordon regularly listened to the *Make Believe Ballroom* radio show on their Philco table radio. In the few times they did this and I happened to not be off working, I listened along. I knew all the songs. Why shouldn't I introduce show tunes in Fort Wayne?

The next day I met my shovel crew. "Charley, I'm going back next Saturday. What about you?"

"No, can't go. But I know what the outcome of this is already. The way you looked when you were in The Scarlet Fever, I could see what was coming next. When you throw yourself into something, everyone else needs to get out of the way. Bring me back a feather from one of those girl's headdresses, will you?"

When I throw myself into something . . . Yes! Thank you, Charlie. Everyone, get out of my way!

Chapter Twelve
VAUDEVILLE NIGHTS

The next Saturday, in the same rented car, I arrived at the Scarlet Fever at 1:30 p.m., just as Clicks advised. Clicks stood outside talking with an older man who looked about four feet tall, stomach falling over his belt, bald, half a cigar clenched between his teeth. This must be the impresario of Fort Wayne flesh.

"Here he is, Mr. Westcott" Clicks said as I approached them. "The kid from Detroit I told you about—Lowell Wood. Has his own program on the radio in Detroit. Only twenty-one years old, and he's already famous."

"Hello, Mr. Westcott."

"Afternoon."

"Hey, have you heard about the instructions that guides give to hikers in Alaska?" I said.

"What are you talking about, kid?"

"They tell hikers to wear bells on their clothes so they don't surprise bears. And they tell them to look for signs of bears along the trails, like bear droppings. But one hiker asked the obvious question, 'How do we know if they are bear droppings?' The guide answered, 'They're the droppings with bells in them.'" I smiled.

By myself.

"Who is this guy, Clicks?"

"I'm Lowell Wood, Mr. Westcott, and I have a hundred more of those jokes. I'm tired of radio and thought I could get *more exposure* in burlesque. Get it?"

"Mr. Wise Guy. How is my good friend George Shorts at WWJ? Is he still married?"

Who is George Shorts? "Yeah, he is, Mr. Westcott. And his kids are fine."

"Get the hell out of here, whoever you are. George Shorts was never married and he died two weeks ago."

And that was the end of my interview. No lunch either. Mr. Westcott stomped off.

Well, I came all the way to Fort Wayne, why not stick around? "Clicks, can you get me into tonight's show?"

"Not any more. Westcott knows who you are. And where is that five-dollar bill you promised?"

I parted with five hard-earned dollars just to get kicked out of a profession I hadn't even started. It was worth it though to stick around for the show, even if I had to buy a ticket.

The show began at 8 P.M. I got there at seven to stand in line. I bought my ticket, but because the doors hadn't yet opened, I stood in front, studying the photos of Miss Candy Cane on the theater's bulletin board. That's when a commotion erupted from inside.

"You ungrateful idiot!" Something crashed, probably broke. Yelling and cussing. Then three men appeared—Mr. Westcott and another guy dragging out Lou the emcee.

Mr. Westcott's face was red and bulging. "Miss Stake? *You* made the mistake, Lou. Get out of my sight before I break your other arm." Lou hobbled down the side alley.

Mr. Westcott turned around and saw me watching it all.

"What are you looking at, you bow-legged runt?" He turned toward the door and then stopped. "Hey, you're Click's lying friend from Detroit."

"I am indeed. And that's no lie." *Hmmm. That wasn't bad, Lowell.*

"I need an emcee for tonight' show. Get your butt in here if you want the job."

Wow. "Sure, Mr. Westcott, but first tell me what the job pays."

"You can't be serious. I'm hiring you off the street to emcee a first-rate theater production."

"Then pay me first rate—five dollars an hour."

"Are you crazy? Maybe I'm the one who's crazy. I can't believe I'm bargaining with a dishonest kid for a top spot like this. Three dollars, not a penny more." He chewed on that cigar so hard it broke in two. Ashes fell on his clean white shirt and nearly burned a hole in it. As he swatted the ashes away, I made my counter offer.

"Make it four dollars, or I'm gone." I turned to leave.

"God Almighty! Okay, four dollars. Now get in there; the show is already late getting started."

In truth, I would have paid *him* to let me get up in front of that crowd. What a break! And I made good on it, renting that car every Saturday. Even made the car's owner happy.

Crowd participation at The Scarlet was a given. Crazies and drunks, and guys too young and stupid to behave themselves, always filled the place. But emceeing those shows taught me to be comfortable in front of all kinds of audiences—a skill that would benefit me all my life. Besides, I got fringe benefits, like meeting Henny Youngman and Jimmy Durante when they came and performed in the theater. Millie loved it when I brought her their autographs.

But the main benefit of working ten to twelve hours on a weekend came in bringing home forty to fifty dollars each time. All that helped pay the rent. More importantly, along with my other businesses, I had enough to accomplish my goal. With my new income, we could finally afford to pay for Dick's transportation to Jonesville and to clothe and feed him at Millie's house.

Dick was twelve years old, and he had been in the orphanage for nearly a decade. I hadn't been allowed to visit him in all that time— only Elmer got to see him. But we had been writing to each other.

I had Millie call Mrs. Bronson—who still ruled the place—and tell the old woman she wanted to bring Dick back to his family. I asked Millie after her talk with Mrs. Bronson if she could get Dick on the phone so I could tell Dick myself.

"Hello?"

The sound of my brother's voice nearly did me in.

"Dick, it's me, Lowell. I am so sorry it took this long, but we finally have the money. I've been saving it ever since I left. I saved it so the family could get back together."

As Dick replied, my eyes welled with tears.

"Lowell, I've thought of you every single day since you left. I ask Elmer whenever he comes how you're doing, and he's told me all along how you've worked and wanted to get me. I did feel abandoned and lonely . . ."

I think we both choked up at the same time.

"But I understand why you left—and how Mrs. Bronson wouldn't let you come back."

I let the tears stream down my cheeks.

"So I'm not angry. You don't have to say you're sorry. Just bring me home."

And we did.

Dick would go on in later years to become a successful businessman. We stayed close throughout our lives. After I moved to St. Louis, I visited the whole family from time to time. I didn't go often, but they all knew that if they ever needed anything, I would be there to help them. You owe your family a debt of concern, even those you think do not deserve it. There is nothing more precious than family.

But I'm getting ahead of myself.

Chapter Thirteen
MY UNDEAD MOM

Sometimes in January the gray winter overcast lifts and reveals a brilliant blue sky and the stark, cold Michigan winter landscape turns blazing white. The days do not immediately become warmer because in Michigan the arrival of spring is counted in months, not days.

In March 1941, with Dick settled in, happy, and going to school, we began to believe the warmth might also return to our cold family.

That is, until late one Saturday afternoon.

I had just come back from the Tillman ranch, sore all over from trying to ride a stubborn black-and-white Appaloosa. This time the horse had won.

The phone rang.

I picked it up. A woman asked for Millie. "Millie, it's for you."

I thought I recognized the voice on the phone as that of our mother's sister, the one for whom Millie did the wash. The aunt in Hartland. The one who knew the skeletons in the family closet. She had never called *us* before.

Millie took the phone. "Yes? . . . No, I can't sit down. I'm holding the baby, and he has to be changed . . . What? Okay, now I'd better sit down."

She fumbled with one hand to turn a chair. "Lowell, take the phone. You'll want to hear this—or maybe you won't." She handed the phone to me and sat with a blank stare, as if seeing something from a far distance that did not look quite real.

I took the phone. "Hello?"

"Lowell, this is Lowell? Haven't seen you since you were a baby. Anyway, we thought you might like to know. It's about my sister, your mother. We're pretty sure she's in Chicago somewhere."

No. She didn't say that, and I didn't hear it. Couldn't have.

"Are you there?"

"What?"

"Your mother."

"She's dead. My mother's dead."

"No, Lowell. I'll say it again. We think your mother's in Chicago."

"Is Chicago somewhere on the other side of heaven or hell?"

"Achhh. You can ask Millie about her. You're old enough now."

I felt as if a train were zigzagging and crashing through every corner of my head.

And—just as if we were having a normal family conversation—the aunt continued. "Anyway, some northern Illinois crime news comes through the sheriff's office every week, and we think—we're afraid—your mother's husband is in jail. Your mother's made some poor choices, but she's still my sister and—"

"Wait a minute. Back up. My mother who was dead isn't dead? She's alive? Living, you think, in Chicago? And she's married? My mother is married? And her husband may be in prison? Is that what you are telling me?"

"We're not sure."

I wanted to kill someone right then, but I didn't know whom.

The aunt fell quiet.

I should have screamed, but I simply asked, "How do we find out?"

"We were thinking about that. Johnson Hobbs may be able to help. He lives in Jonesville. You probably know him. And he's taken some courses at Hillsdale College, wants to become a private detective. We thought if you were to talk to him, he might do some research. Of course, you'd have to pay him. But frankly, no one here has the time to dig around the mess that is the crime world of Chicago. "

Now *I* needed to sit down. I pulled over another chair, and Millie sat Robert down, then leaned in. I tilted the receiver so she could hear, too. "Are you sure about all of this?" I said.

"Pretty sure. Sure enough to call Millie and you. How is Dick, by the way?"

Do you care? "Dick is fine. We're going to have to discuss this some more. Ask Johnson Hobbs to call us."

I hung up.

Unbelievable.

Tears coursed down Millie's face.

"For most of my life until five minutes ago, I was an orphan," I said. "Now I'm not?"

Gordon came into the kitchen. "What's happening?"

Millie, not yet able to talk, pulled another chair around and motioned for Gordon to sit.

Then Dick came in. The four of us sat on hard chairs around a chilly table. How appropriate.

I was the first to speak. "Millie. Please. Tell us what you know. Is our mother dead? Or not? And why are we hearing about it this way?"

Gordon went to the sink to get a glass of water for Millie. Finally, barely composed, with her face wet, red, and puffy, Millie sipped some water and tried to talk. At first her words came in a jumble. But as she faltered in circles, she calmed down and started to speak coherently. And she told Dick and me what we never expected to hear.

"Yes. We knew she was alive." She swallowed and took a deep breath.

I pressed my lips together to keep anything from screaming out.

"Ran off with Stan Marks, that laborer our father let stay with you."

So of course there was no funeral.

Of course no one talked about it.

Of course that grease ball left around the same time.

"We never thought we'd hear from her again. So embarrassing—her leaving your dad and the two of you. You were too young. You wouldn't have understood." She started crying again. "Now you know."

I sat dumbstruck.

Dick spoke first. "All right." Then he didn't seem to know what to say. He looked around.

No responses.

He pushed himself to continue. "What are we supposed to do? Do we really want to see her?"

The kid had guts to just come out and say it.

He went further. "I'm just feeling settled here at Millie's and at the high school. What would we do, visit her? Bail her *husband*—" he stopped and sighed, "—out of jail?" He leaned back.

I still didn't know what to say.

"This is making me sick." Dick stared blankly at a wall.

Millie went to get the crying baby, still in his soiled diaper. She calmed the baby down while the rest of us sat in silence.

As she changed Robert's diaper, she spoke slowly and deliberately. "She is our mother. She did an evil thing leaving the three of you. Who knows why anyone would leave her own children and husband, especially when they needed her so much. But if we don't try and help her now, we are no better than her."

That did it. I couldn't help myself. "All this time I've been with you, you said nothing! And now you talk like you're Reverend Millie." I seethed. "She abandoned us! Left a baby. Left me and our father. I am not about to forgive her. And I am not sure I want her back in our lives. She's made her bed—let her sleep in it."

"Lowell, you're angry now. But remember, she's still your mother."

"Still my mother," I muttered with as much sarcasm as I could muster.

Millie turned away. I hoped out of shame.

I don't know why, but my immediate thought was of the black dog at the Lilley farm. To protect her young pups, she'd cornered me, an

74

enemy much larger than she. And I'm sure she did it without stopping to think.

What lack in our mother allowed her to abandon us so easily? The dog had better character than that woman.

Then Millie's words worked their way through the crust of my anger. If we ignored her hardship, were we really like her? I did not want to inherit that evil trait. It would get in the way of everything I wanted to be.

Chapter Fourteen
DETECTIVE WORK

The phone rang again. Hobbs, the guy practicing to be a detective.

Millie shook her head, picked up the baby, and handed the phone to me. That baby really came in handy for her.

I listened to his self-introduction and to what he knew so far about this supposed mother.

"Yes, Mr. Hobbs. A real shock. What can you do for us?"

Johnson Hobbs lived in Jonesville but served as an assistant sheriff in Hartland. We all thought him to be a squirrely kind of guy. When he looked at you, you had the sense you had done something wrong. He had seen an advertisement in the Hartland paper, *The Livingston County Press*, for a course that when completed would sanction him as a private detective. He offered us a deal—fifteen dollars and he would find our mother within a week.

"And if you don't find her in a week?"

"Sorry. That just covers my expenses. So no refunds."

What a lousy deal. "My family will talk it over."

Now we had to decide: Could we afford this private eye, plus the trip to Chicago, plus whatever costs might hit us there? In 1941, fifteen dollars plus the rest amounted to no small chunk of change. But each week I had put aside some money. Fifteen dollars would use up some of what I'd saved, but we could do it.

The bigger question was *should we?*

Millie and Dick had composed themselves now. What little composure I'd found crumbled with the news of the fifteen-dollar cost. We didn't take a family vote or anything. We just came to agree it was the right thing. We needed to know if our mother was in trouble, and if so, how we could do what she had refused to do—find a way to make our family whole.

We gave Mr. Hobbs the green light. He never told us how he found her, but within two days he came back with a phone number for me to call. He said to ask for "Mrs. Firrone." Not wanting to add to Millie's phone bill, I collected change and found the one public phone in town—the one near the bus station. Good old Jim Schroeder. At a time on Thursday morning when Mr. Schroeder was not on duty, I arranged my change in order on the phone booth shelf and dialed the number.

"Who is it?"

"I was given this number and told to ask for Mrs. Firrone."

"What do you want?"

"I am looking for Hazel. Used to be named Hazel Wood, but I'm not sure what her last name might be these days."

"Are you kidding me? You the police? Who gave you my number?"

I couldn't say an assistant sheriff studying to be a detective provided it. Suspecting I might be intruding on the world of criminal activity, I decided to do the only appropriate thing.

I lied.

"I owe Mr. Firrone money, and I can't be late with payments. He was supposed to meet me but never showed up. When I tried to find out what to do, I was given this phone number and told to ask for Hazel. Now, are you going to let me talk to her?"

"Hazel's my daughter-in-law. She doesn't live here, but I can tell her where to meet you, so you can divest yourself of your burden. That's the only way you'll get to see her. You okay with that or not?"

I struggled to even imagine someone talking to me this way about my own mother.

"Tell me quick or I'll hang up this phone."

"Mrs. Firrone, don't hang up. I lied. I don't owe Mr. Firrone any money. Hazel is my mother. I last saw her in Carlton, New York, about eleven years ago. I do have some money, if she needs it. I want to help her. Her sister in Hartland, Michigan, told us she was in Chicago."

"Well I'll be damned. I knew she had family in Carlton, but I didn't know she had kids."

What?

"We're in real hard times right now, with my son Earl, her husband, in prison.

Didn't know she had kids?

"If you really want to see her, come to Chicago on Thursday. I have a sister in Hillsdale. The last time she came to visit, she took the bus from Jackson, Michigan, that arrives in downtown Chicago at 4:17 P.M. Be on the bus, and I'll make sure Hazel is there waiting for you."

The phone buzzed, and I shoved in another nickel.

"I can't promise what she'll do after she sees you. But we have a debt with an attorney who says Earl ain't going nowhere until he gets paid. Says he needs fifty dollars for Earl's lawyer."

My heart jackhammered in my chest, draining my body of all energy.

"Are you there, young man?"

"Four of us."

"What?"

"There were four of us kids."

"My word." Now it was her turn to be speechless.

"Tell my mother I'll be there."

Chapter Fifteen
RENDEZVOUS IN CHICAGO

At an average forty miles an hour, along with stops, the trip to Chicago took ten hours. My legs swelled and my back ached. Riding so long on that Greyhound bus, even a comfortable position, soon became uncomfortable—no matter how many stops. My mind fared no better. I went over and over what I might say to her. Millie and Dick thought I should act interested in what had brought her to this bad place in her life. What was she thinking?

Of even greater concern to me was, how would I know her? It had been eleven years. I'd been four years old when she left us. I had an image in my mind, but it got mixed up with fishing poles and arguments and Stanley Marks. Where did Firrone fit in? I looked out the bus window at the houses and more houses and brick buildings crammed together, straining to imagine my mother.

At last the bus made its fitful entry into the Chicago bus depot, a potholed place on a worn street in downtown. I peeled my body out of the cramped seat and my fellow travelers jostled and pushed out of the Greyhound.

Coming down the steps of the bus, I took another look around.

"Get going, kid. You're blocking the way."

But with that quick glance, I saw a short, fat lady standing half behind a column and looking at each bus passenger as they came down the steps. It wasn't until I was out and away from the bus that I could get a better look. She had bowlegs, just like mine. I stared, and in that moment my mother fixed on me with a smirk.

Mixed feelings—not at all love, mostly a sense of inquisitiveness summed up by *why?*—drew me to her.

At first she said nothing, just looked me up and down. She smelled like old tires and, wearing a baggy, ill-fitting dress, she looked like a bag lady.

"Which one are you?"

Which one?

"I'll bet you're Lowell. You have the money?"

What?

My mind went blank, probably out of self-preservation.

I was dumbfounded. I was disgusted. I was so angry I couldn't speak. I tried to swallow the hard lump in my throat.

After all these years, all she cared about was: Do you have the money?

I swear, I was ready to jump on the next bus back to Jonesville. Instead I grimly followed her to an empty wooden bench inside the station. After all, she was the only mother I had.

She saw my confusion, so she continued her chatter. "Guess you're wondering what happened."

Uh, yes.

"Your father was a good man, just not good enough to make a decent living. I didn't plan it, not at all. Stanley Marks offered me hope, a way out of a depressing life I knew wasn't going to get better. I made a choice. Stan had prospects in Chicago. Should I stay on that deteriorating farm with no hope for change, or leave with someone who had ambition and prospects for a better life? Besides, he was such a good-looking man."

My mouth went dry. I felt my fists clench. I knew it, it was Stanley Marks!

She must have noticed. "Lowell, grow up."

Grow up? Me? Grow up?

"You only have one life to live on this dirtball planet. As I see it, you can choose to stay trapped in your circumstances, or you can do something bold to make a better life for yourself. I figured out a long time ago that there are no great gains without great sacrifices."

How noble.

"I chose a better life. Besides, I was expecting Stanley's child and didn't want to do a lot of explaining when, you know . . . I suppose deep down I was afraid to face your father."

Now I wanted to kill her.

I held back my fists and finally spit out, "Stanley's child? Are you kidding me?"

"I'm not kidding, Lowell."

"You left us! We thought you were dead. For eleven years, I wondered where your grave was, so I could go there and say goodbye to you. Instead I find out now that you just left."

"My sister in Hartland—your aunt—picked up news of all of you from Millie. Millie knew or suspected what I'd done, but she never knew where I'd gone. My sister told me about Frank's passing and how you and Dick went to the Bogue Home, and how you ran away and left Dick there because *you* wanted a better life."

As if my running away could have any similarity to hers.

Another bus pulled into to the station. The place grew more crowded. An elderly woman that had been sitting near us on the bench moved closer. I didn't care what she heard me say.

"It wasn't the same thing! That Mrs. Bronson who was in charge was more like a witch. She didn't love us, and she never tried to make the place decent. We *inmates* all worked hard but had nothing to show for it. The food was terrible, and we had to wear clothes cast off by families in town while their kids made fun of us for it. I left so that I could make a better life for Dick."

Her face was grim, but unrepentant.

"Do *not* act as if it were the same," I warned her.

"Let me just say that things didn't turn out the way I'd hoped. Stanley Marks couldn't find a decent-paying job here. But we had to have income, and he found it getting involved with the Firrone Gang."

"You left us for a guy who joined a gang?"

"They'd been experts in bootlegging and making bathtub gin, but more and more their livelihood came from stick-ups, scams, and running basement gambling houses—and some other things."

I shook my head. This was my mother saying this.

"Then life took another mean turn. Four years ago, Stanley got cancer and died two months later. If there is a God, He is cruel and nasty."

"Don't blame this on God. *You* did this." I didn't even believe in God, and here I sat defending Him.

"Okay, God may not be to blame, but He sure is laughing right now."

"And you deserve it."

I turned for a quick look at the elderly woman next to us on the bench. Her eyes were wide open, missing nothing. My anger didn't allow me to care.

This mother, or whatever she was, sighed. "Well . . ."

"You left Dad and Dick and me."

"As I said—"

"I don't care what you said. You did everything wrong."

"My, aren't you the judge?"

For the first time I truly understood how a son could actually feel like strangling his own mother. Then it got worse.

"The police have been trying to shut down the Firrones for years. Before he became ill, Stan was working a scam with the gang when the police caught onto them. He was driving a truck for the Salvation Army, picking up furniture. You know how they do it, they collect furniture, cart it to their store, sell it, and the money is supposed to go to help poor families and to reform drug addicts and alcoholics. Well, Stan picked up the furniture all right, but the best of it found its way to the Firrones' resale furniture store. The poorer furniture he delivered to the Salvation Army store."

Unbelievable.

"The cops weren't interested in Stan or me. They went after Earl Firrone, the leader of the gang. But they did want me as a witness against Earl. Now Stan and I never did marry. So when the police arrested Earl Firrone, the only way to keep me quiet was for Earl to marry me."

I tried to process this. I couldn't have made up such a story if I'd tried.

"It was soon after this that Stan died."

"How convenient for you."

"I guess it was."

I glared at her.

She looked back as if we were having a normal conversation.

"What else *aren't* you telling me?"

"Would you like to meet your three other brothers?"

The elderly woman jumped up and put her hands over her ears. Her purse fell from her lap. She picked up the purse and practically ran out of the station, looking over her shoulder as she left.

I wanted to go with her.

"Lowell, don't look so angry. I never did marry Stan, but we had two boys."

"This just gets better all the time."

"When I look at them, I sometimes think of you and Dick."

"So thoughtful."

"Then Earl and I have one son."

I wanted to throw up.

It was now late in the day, a day I suddenly wished had never started.

This woman with the label of mother had hair like a rat's nest. Her eyes drooped, and her speech came slow. Everything coming out of her mouth I did not want to hear.

I looked at the bus schedule for a bus straight back to Jonesville. Unfortunately there weren't any more that day.

"With the police getting on us, we don't have any income. I'd like to get us all into the apartment I found. But Earl is in jail. The boys aren't even with me. Stay with me tonight, and tomorrow I'll introduce you to those new members of your family."

Did I really want to meet these people?

Though fury coursed through me, I also felt concern for the children relying on this woman. Maybe because of what I'd been through. I had little choice anyway. I went with her.

We traveled twenty minutes by city bus to an apartment house on the south side of Chicago. The neighborhood was blue collar—nothing fancy, but not a place where you'd be afraid to walk alone at night. We climbed two flights of stairs, and as we went up, we passed people lounging on the stairs, laughing and yelling in another language I supposed was Italian. A distinct smell of garlic came from the flats on the second floor. I had to go slowly behind my mother, who stopped every three or four steps to catch her breath. Inside the apartment, the furniture looked like one might expect from the small size and plainness of the rooms. It seems Earl had taken the best furniture that good old Stan had delivered.

The whiteness of the kitchen walls contrasted with the dirty yellow of the rest of the rooms. My mother pulled a pot from underneath a wood counter and began to boil water on the electric stove. Out of sheer exhaustion my headed nodded, and my eyes kept closing.

Spaghetti. With no sauce, no meatballs.

"Lowell, tell me about Millie and her new baby."

"Not much to tell. John's a good baby. Dick's taken a liking to him. Did you know Dick moved in with us at Millie's place?"

She nodded.

I could hardly eat the dry noodles. "So, where are my new brothers? The ones you told me about earlier."

"With Earl in jail, it hasn't been the easiest time for any of us. They're being taken care of. I'll explain all that tomorrow."

Fine with me. I had all I could do to make it onto the couch, where my mother laid some well-worn sheets and a rolled-up blanket inside a pillowcase. It was only seven o'clock when I fell asleep, but I didn't wake up until the next morning.

Chapter Sixteen
A NEW FAMILY

My mother found some biscuits in the back of the old Sears and Roebuck refrigerator. When she heated them in the oven, the smell overcame my initial reluctance, which stemmed from what looked to me like wormholes in the biscuits. It could have been my imagination.

"Should I call you Hazel or Mother?"

"When you were young, you called me Mom. You were so active. Remember when I used to take you fishing?"

"No. Well, maybe you did, but I don't remember. I do remember when I was about five you sent me out to fish alone."

She didn't respond. It was already 8:15. Where were these new brothers of mine?

"Mom—" That felt weird. "Can I meet my new family?"

"Not your new father, Earl."

My new father. The criminal. "He is not my father."

She paused, a biscuit halfway to her mouth. She set the biscuit down. "I can't get in to see him until Friday."

"Fine."

"We can visit the three-year-old, Bobby—Earl's and my son. He's in the Mercy Hospital. Brought him there yesterday before you arrived. I think there's something wrong with his hearing, or maybe his brain. Whenever I tell him to do something, he stomps his feet and says no. If I try and make him do it, he poops in his pants. This isn't the first time he's had to go to the hospital. Maybe this time, those stupid doctors will find out what's wrong with him."

Yes. Certainly blame it on the doctors. The kid's behavior couldn't possibly have anything to do with his mother.

We finished our biscuits.

"And what about the other two? Where are they?" I feared her answer even before she spoke.

"It's like this. When Stanley died, I couldn't take care of the two children. Gene is nine, and Stanley Junior is ten. I had to leave them at the St. Vincent DePaul Home."

My breath stopped. Dumping her kids in orphanages was like a habit for her.

"Broke my heart."

I'll bet.

"I'm only allowed to see them once a month, but with you being in town for a short time, I'm sure the nuns will make an exception. We should get going if you want to see them before your bus leaves. Did you say you had some money for me?"

That shook me back. Her main concern.

She put on an imploring look.

"I've got several hundred dollars saved in Jonesville. How much is the bail for Earl?"

"One hundred and ten dollars. But I could use some help right now. The lawyer says I have to pay him fifty dollars right away. Earl's trial is coming up in sixty days. They can't put him away without my testimony, and I don't have to say anything. He'll get off, and then we'll need to leave Chicago."

"I see."

"These hustlers with tin badges will never leave us alone if we stay here. I was able to keep them away with some of the profit from the furniture store. Now that Earl's in prison, the store had to close. I am not giving them one more nickel!"

Hustlers with badges? Coming from her?

Kids in orphanages and the hospital, husband in jail—running away with Stan Marks did not make her life easier. Or anyone else's.

"Let's go see your sons. Then we can talk money."

Mercy Hospital stood within walking distance, so we went there first. The streets on the south side of Chicago in 1940, once filled with Irish, Italians, and Lithuanians, were increasingly occupied by black immigrants from the South. I breathed in the foreign smells from the restaurants we passed.

My heart pounded. A sense of excitement coursed through me. I surprised myself by how easily I took to this big city. I'd never seen such gargantuan buildings. And I'd never seen a hospital as big as Mercy Hospital, not even in Fort Wayne. We stopped at the desk to ask for the room number of Bobby Firrone. Room 212, Pediatrics. My mother breathed a weak sigh of relief—only one flight of stairs.

The hospital was clean but worn. Yellow walls, marble floors—at one time it must have been a real gem. Wrought iron railings lined the stairs, and crucifixes lined the hallways. In a room with ten beds, we made our way to a boy bouncing on his bed while looking out a large window. The other children lay still and stared.

The mother, or Mom, stopped and leaned toward him. "Bobby, Bobby, look at me." She pointed. "This is your brother Lowell. I'll explain it all later, but he has come just in time to help us. Stop that jumping!"

"You mean he brought us money?"

I could almost see dollar signs form in the six-year-old's eyes.

"How much you got, Lowell?"

Yesterday's feeling of throwing up returned to me.

The kid didn't stop. "How did you find him, Mom? He's got funny clothes. Looks like a farmer." He gazed at me. "You have cows?"

I refused to answer.

"How old are you? Where're you from?"

"I live in Michigan, outside of Detroit. How old do you think I am?"

"Like Mom says, 'old enough to know better.' You gonna get my dad out of jail?"

"Maybe. But I want to see your brothers, and I have to get on a two o'clock bus back to Michigan. Can't stay long."

It seemed to me that Bobby Firrone had inherited a few too many things from Mom's side and stood a better than even change of sharing much of his father's fate. I felt ready to leave. "Hope you feel better."

We walked outside into the morning sun. With my eyes closed, I turned my face to soak up its warmth, the same one I'd felt across so many years working farms and small towns. The heat replaced what had drained from me in that hospital room.

I slowed because at that moment, I knew I could never experience warmth with this woman or this child. "Lowell, come on. Step it up. We have to be there by 10 a.m. if you want to see the other two. Then maybe you can buy me some lunch before you leave."

How thoughtful.

The Vincent DePaul Home was farther away. My mother got us on the public bus we needed to take, but it took over half an hour to get there.

Visiting hours had ended.

Chapter Seventeen
ANOTHER ORPHANAGE

Even though it was March in Chicago, perspiration trickled down the small of my back as we walked toward the brick building where my younger brothers now lived. I had not been to a place like this since I fled the Bogue Home. This orphanage was far bigger. To me, that meant far scarier. Images from the past flooded back into my mind—lying awake in the boys' dormitory, working until I ached, fighting with the town kids, and Mrs. Bronson--the etched-in memory of Mrs. Bronson.

I followed my mother up five steps and past two huge weather-beaten wooden doors into the orphanage. By the time we got inside, my mother was coughing badly.

A large crucifix greeted us in the lobby—a crown-of-thorns Christ looking right at us. One of the sisters who ran the orphanage strutted our way, smiling at us brightly. At this point, I never knew I'd be in such need of a smile.

"Sister Charity, this is Lowell, one of my sons from my first marriage." My mother made the introductions.

A look of fear swept over Sister Charity's face.

"My first husband died of pleurisy."

This news brought the sister some relief, and she extended a comforting arm around my shoulder.

I guessed the cherry-faced nun to be six feet tall. At that height, her flowing gowns made quite an impression.

"Sister, I'm sorry we're late, but Lowell has to be on a two o'clock bus back to Michigan. Can we still see the boys?"

The Sister displayed a stern look but let it melt into a shrug. She let us inside.

Smells of incense and bacon and eggs wafted our way as we walked down a long marble hallway. We never had bacon and eggs in the Bogue Home. And Mrs. Bronson never burned incense.

Unlike the Bogue Home, this place had paintings hanging on the walls. They really seemed to like saints around here. The guys in paintings all had heads surrounded by halos, and they were dressed in bright red-and-blue flowing robes. One painting showed Jesus with arms stretched out to young children. I could have used that image to inspire me at the Bogue Home.

By a door to what looked like a dining hall sat a large and finely crafted woodcarving of a bunch of guys sitting around a table, eating. I wondered why anyone would make such a carving.

The children surprised me most. As we passed them, they were laughing and smiling. I had never imagined such a thing to be possible in an orphanage.

We stopped outside a large auditorium, a classroom, while the nun went in to get Stanley and Gene.

"How much do you have to pay to keep them here?"

"Lowell, if I had to pay, they wouldn't be here."

Of course. Why did I even ask?

"Earl and I are members of St. Vincent's Church. Earl's family has been one of the mainstays of the parish for decades. One year Earl and I donated $1,000 to renovate this building."

My eyes must have given me away. Was it because I couldn't believe she and her gangster husband went to church, or because I couldn't believe she'd ever give anyone $1,000?

"Don't give me that look! The money of sinners has the same value as saints. Here they don't discriminate on the basis of sin or where money comes from."

Ah, I hadn't even considered this third outrageous thought.

"I don't pay anything. The church is taking care of the costs for the boys. In some ways, it's better for them. This way, they can't skip school."

If they skipped school because other kids laughed at their charity clothes, I would understand. But I doubted that was the case. And if Jonesville had church schools, which they didn't, I doubt they would have taken money from the likes of Earl and Hazel Firrone.

As I contemplated all this, Sister Charity returned and introduced me to the last of my newfound brothers. Half brothers.

Our mutual mother smiled and talked as if she did this sort of thing every day. "Boys, I never told you this, but this is my son from a former marriage when I lived in New York. His father died, and his older sister—your sister—took him in to raise him because I had to move to Chicago."

Had to. I stared at her and said it out loud, *"Had* to?"

She ignored me. "There's more to the story, but this is a good place to begin."

She forgot the orphanage part, of course.

Sister Charity stiffened and looked as if she would faint. She steadied herself with a hand on the wall and coaxed us into an empty classroom down the hall.

Little Stanley Marks—part of the reason our mother left—was thin as a rail; his hair the same sandy color as his adulterous father. He stood a little taller than his brother. Although our fathers were different, Gene Marks reminded me of my father.

Despite my dislike of the six-year-old earlier in the day, and my misgivings about meeting these two, my heart started opening to them. They couldn't be held accountable for their situation—just like I couldn't for mine. No matter what my mother had done, or would do, these boys were my brothers, at least by 50 percent. Even the six-year-old.

"What's your name?" Stanley asked.

"Lowell Wood. And I live in Jonesville, Michigan. I must tell you two that I'm as surprised as you must be right now. My little brother and I had to live for a few years in an orphanage. Do you like it here?"

They both stared at me. Stanley responded. "We're okay, but it would be better if we could be in *our* house. Don't get me wrong, they treat us okay, but we miss our dad—and mom—don't we, Gene?"

"Yeah, we do. Sister, you know us, we like you and all, but we'd rather be back in our house. We know there isn't room in the apartment where our mom is. But maybe if we were with her, we could help her out until our dad comes home."

As kind as she'd been, Sister Charity had an impatient look on her face. She glanced at the door, as if to say, "I did you a favor, now I have to get these children back to their teachers."

I had to say something before she ushered us out. "Boys, I know a lot has been taken away from you. In some ways I understand. A lot was taken away from me." I avoided looking at my mother. If I did, I might have gone into a rage.

The boys stood still, attentive.

"I'm going to talk with your mother about an idea I have to help you get back to the family. I'm really sorry to have to rush off now. I must get back to my house in Michigan. But I promise I will not forget you."

The nun nodded in agreement--to what, I wasn't sure. I needed to touch the boys before they left, at least shake their hand. Stanley took my hand with a firm grasp, but Gene ignored my gesture and rushed to wrap his arms around me. "Hope to see you soon, Lowell. I like being your new little brother."

That did it. I had to get them to stay with us. Regardless of this mother.

I put my hands over his little arms. Then Stanley reached his arms around us both.

The nun whisked them back to their class.

As we left the Home, the wind picked up, as it does in Chicago in March. The temperature dropped quickly, and the coat I brought with me didn't give enough protection. Shivering at the city bus stop, I spoke as the adult to Hazel Firrone.

"I'll give you what cash I have now and send you the rest next week. You'll have what you need to get Earl out on bail." I cringed at the thought of how hard I'd worked for that money and where it would be spent. "I want to talk to Millie about how to bring you, Earl, and the boys to Michigan. I'm sure Millie will want that. I'm not sure about her husband. I'm bringing in enough to support us all, or at least I can afford to get the boys out of the home and bring them down right away. You and Earl can do what you have to do here and then follow later. That's all I have to say."

She was quiet.

And without speaking, we rode the jostling city bus through the South Chicago streets. A grimace contorted my mother's face. It seemed to me she was turning this over and over in her mind—and her heart, or whatever part of it could still feel.

Whatever she thought, I had doubts she could raise the boys to be responsible people.

Finally, she spoke. "I don't want to lose a family again, Lowell. Once was too much for me."

"Me, me, me." I shook my head. "Mom, this isn't just about you."

"Well—"

"And you didn't *lose* any family. You walked away from us. You *ran*."

She looked the other way.

We rode silently for a while.

Then I said, "Those boys need a place, and I think Millie will agree to care for them until you can move someplace near us. That's the truth."

"I'm tired, Lowell. I've been tired for too long." She stopped.

I waited through her silence.

"I'll talk to Earl," she said. "Yes, send me the money. I'll get Earl out. We can't leave for a while, at least until the trial is over. About a year from now, I suppose."

As if waking up, I suddenly began to fear I had acted too quickly. I had never met this Earl Firrone, and wasn't sure I wanted him or this meandering mother back in the family.

"In the meantime, you talk with Millie. If she agrees, we'll take the boys out of St. Vincent's, and they can go live with you. Are you sure about this?"

Maybe not about her and Earl, but I knew those two boys should come live with us. I spoke without looking at her. "Yes. I know just how Stanley and Gene are feeling right now. I wish I could take Bobby too, but that would be too much for Millie. She doesn't have the space. Or the strength. You and Earl are another story. Maybe you can go to be with your sister. I believe she has room at her place."

We arrived at the bus station with no time for me to buy my mother lunch, which did not bother me. I pulled out the sixty dollars I'd brought along on the trip just in case I needed it. Despite all my feelings, getting this long-lost mother food in her apartment and money for the city bus so she wouldn't have to walk everywhere—all of that constituted an emergency. Not to mention bail for Earl.

"This is all I have with me. Take it."

"This isn't much, Lowell. Is this all you came with? Are you sure you don't have more? You wouldn't cheat your mother, would you?"

"Augggh!" I almost took it back. I turned my back so I wouldn't have to see her.

What was I expecting? She was the same person.

At least now I knew the whole story. And now I had three more brothers.

THE WAR

Chapter Eighteen
THE BIG DECISION

Tongues wagged all over Jonesville. Would we help the British in the war? Then December 1941 brought the outlandish news: the Japanese bombed Pearl Harbor. Newspapers everywhere printed stories about the ambush on the US fleet and the abominable atrocities committed by Germany and Japan upon their neighbors. You couldn't say the words Hitler or Hirohito without someone cursing.

Why did our president wait so long? Couldn't he see war coming? Or maybe he didn't *want* to see, just like I didn't want to see the bill for the clothes Dick, Stanley, and Gene needed for school, or the grocery bill to feed this big, happy family.

Millie and Gordon worked all they could. Millie's laundry business grew. She expanded her customer base beyond the family. Gordon's work constructing houses slowed down, so he took a position at the Kiddie Brush & Toy Factory. The factory had a contract with Ford Motor Company to manufacture parts for the new tank Ford was building for the Army.

Still, Millie worried over our finances. Rent, food, utility bills—the unending bills created a precarious state. "Lowell, can't you get more time at Kiddie? We could use about ten more dollars a week."

"I tried that, remember? If I work more at the factory, I'll have less time to break horses. Tillman pays me ten dollars for every horse I break. The factory only pays fifty cents an hour. Weekends I'm too busy with the vaudeville work in Fort Wayne."

She shook her head. "Well, we have to have more income somehow."

The three Firrones moved in with my mother's sister in Hartland, the aunt who knew everything. I sent them money for the bus ride, but refused to support them. That didn't stop them from asking for help from Millie. This added to Millie's anxiety, and to her litany of woes, like: "Mom and Earl aren't contributing anything. Earl is supposedly looking for a job, but they spend all day at her sister's house doing God knows what. That child of theirs is a handful—skips school half the time. Anyway, we need more income."

"I'll talk to George Camp. He's a supervisor now at the factory. Maybe he can suggest something."

I wanted not to care. But I couldn't escape a relentless drive from deep within me to bring the family together, no matter what, and to make it happy and good. In a way it even defined me, even though I'd never needed to think it through.

And looking at poor Millie, what else could I do? Millie's house was bursting the walls with her toddler and all of us "borrowed" offspring. I appreciated Gordon; he remained understanding about it all. John Robert was now three, and Dick spoiled him by being too quick to pick him up or grab a milk bottle or sneak him one of the chocolate chip cookies Millie baked.

When Stanley and Gene came to live with us, John became intolerable.

"Hold me."

"Play with me."

"Stanley, come here."

"No. Gene, you do it."

"No, I want Dick."

100

When the three school-age boys weren't around, he pouted, waiting at the door until they came home.

I hardly ever stayed home. Trying to support all these dependents stretched even what I could earn. That's why I had to get help from Mr. Camp.

I approached him with a plan.

"Mr. Camp, I need some advice." I'd learned that if you're going to ask someone for something, it helps to first ask their opinion.

"What is it now, Wood? I don't have time for any stupid questions or pranks." Camp was still the same old no-nonsense grump. But he cared about people—you just had to create the opportunity for him to show it.

"You probably know that my sister has taken in three children not her own, four if you include me. We need more income. Do you have any ideas about what I could do to earn more money?"

He didn't hesitate. "I signed up and served in the Army for four years when I was your age. Ever think about joining up? Pay's not so bad, and maybe you could earn your stripes, get promoted and earn more. You're cocky, but you're smart, Lowell."

In the midst of the clanging, hissing machinery, I could hardly believe what I heard.

"We'd miss you here, but you wouldn't have to work so many different jobs. Plus you'd get your clothing and food paid for, and you'd see more of this world, get to Germany or Japan and finally teach those fellas a lesson."

This made sense to my seventeen-year-old mind. Plus, Millie would have one less person in the house. I imagined leaving the family to keep it together. Uncle Sam would feed me and give me his uniforms to wear. Everyone knew danger stalked the U.S. so long as the war continued. Maybe I could help. I had no idea where Germany and Japan were, but I felt eager to get overseas and kill those Germans and Japs.

"How do you do it? Sign up, I mean?"

"There's a military recruiting office in Jackson. Just go there and they'll do the rest. If you want, I'll take you. It's a smart decision for a young guy like you, and it's your patriotic duty."

Truthfully, I was not entirely committed to this solution for keeping the family financially viable. I'd never fired a gun. But fighting didn't frighten me—I had been in enough fights at the clubs in Fort Wayne. "Don't back down from a bully. They'll never leave you alone." That's the advice I got from Westcott, the manager of The Scarlet Fever. Germany and Japan had shown themselves to be bullies; they needed to be stood up to before they got to the shores of the United States.

I talked myself into it.

"Okay, Mr. Camp. When can we go?"

Chapter Nineteen
MR. CAMP'S WORLD

The next morning, George Camp picked me up in his ratty Ford Coupe and drove us to Jackson, Michigan. It was March 1942. We had to time this right, so we would be back before the afternoon shift began. He talked all the way about his service in the Army, which began *after* WW I ended. He had stories about the time he served in France, mostly stories about the girls and the taverns. That got my interest, but that wasn't all he talked about.

"Wood, you need to think about what you are doing. You're young. You haven't seen men die. I came close to it in Europe, but the fighting had been over for some time. I still saw the destruction. And the graves. Miles and miles of crosses at a place called Romagne-something-or-other in France."

I tried to imagine that many crosses, or even a cemetery that big. All the graveyards I'd seen were small with weather-beaten gravestones.

"I will never forget the graves. Over 14,000—fourteen thousand!— young soldiers, most not much older than you, asleep forever in the cold dirt, just in that one cemetery."

I kept trying to imagine.

"Why? Because they loved their families and their friends. They cared that much. They gave everything."

That rang like a bell inside me. I could do that for my family if I had to. Even if I died, they'd be together. And they'd remember me as a hero.

"Lowell Wood, don't you just sign up to see the world or to get money. This is serious."

I felt it. For the first time I felt moved beyond earning money in order to lift myself up and reclaim my family. Mr. Camp got me to think about a whole commitment beyond that.

He looked at me for a response.

"I'm not afraid to die, Mr. Camp. But I am scared about coming home crippled, maybe losing a leg or an arm. That's what I'm really afraid of."

Mr. Camp, a Michigan Lutheran, was not impressed. He took a while to consider what he felt he had to say. "Most of us believe there is a hell and a heaven after you die. But one place in the Holy Bible, the Lord says, 'Do not fear those who can kill the body but not the soul. Be afraid of the one who can kill body *and* soul in *hell*,'—or something to that effect."

That scared me even more. Especially if the Lord existed.

"Plenty of soldiers come home having sacrificed a piece of themselves for the sake of their country and loved ones, and they live meaningful lives. They make significant contributions. But once you're dead, all that comes to an end. There is no more contribution you can make, not to your country, not to your family."

I did not like this.

"Son, you also could become fuel for the flames of a very unpleasant afterlife."

And this sounded worse. What was he, a secret evangelist?

"Am I scaring you, boy? I hope I am. What you are about to do is maybe the most important thing you will ever do in this life: Defend your country, your home, and your family. Yes, it's dangerous, but who else is going to do it?"

His words brought me full circle, as if he'd taken me on a frightening roller coaster ride and brought me back to the starting point. The whole idea connected with something deep inside and galvanized my commitment—my need—to become a soldier.

We arrived at the enlistment center. A very serious sergeant met me at a serious-looking steel desk. The interview was brief.

"What year were you born?"

"1924."

"How old are you?"

"Seventeen."

"Sorry, son. Come back next year after you turn eighteen."

On the drive back to Jonesville, I thought Mr. Camp would yell at me for being a year too young. But he maybe figured he should have known, because he treated me to more stories, this time about Germany.

"I got to Germany in 1937, my last year in the military. Hitler was building a hotel set between a beautiful freshwater lake called Chiemsee, in the southwestern part of Germany, in a place called Bavaria. I had never in my life seen country so beautiful. They turned that lovely hotel into a rest camp for German officers—who are now turning the world into a bloodbath.

"I had a date with one of the local girls, and we ate at a restaurant perched on the side of a mountain. We could see the whole lake and valley. Afterwards . . . Why am I telling this?"

"C'mon. Finish the story."

"It doesn't have an ending."

I stared at him.

"Why the Creator allows war in His world I will never understand. What I *do* understand is that the flaws in our human nature—pride and selfishness—will someday mean the end of us all."

The fields and cow-studded pastures passing by felt normal to me. The world revealed in his stories seemed so much more.

"Maybe we weren't meant to understand it," I said. "Maybe we were meant to make it right. Do you think my serving in the Army can make this world a better place?"

"Better you find out for yourself. When is your birthday?"

"May third. I'd like you to bring me back then. I have to get away from Jonesville and into the Army. I can send my paycheck home to Millie, and I can see more of the world. I want to serve my country, make my contribution."

If only I could get rid of the fear that seemed permanently knotted and stuck in my throat.

Chapter Twenty
IN THE ARMY NOW

A year went by as John Robert got bigger and Dick excelled in school. I got more hours at the factory and still kept my schedule at the ranch. But our finances kept as tight as ever, as Millie and Gordon tried to support youngsters growing into teenagers and young adults. Shortly after my eighteenth birthday I received greetings from Uncle Sam. The terse letter told me to report for induction to a camp in Rochester, New York, on September 10, 1942. I would become a soldier in the U.S. Army.

I felt sure I'd be sent immediately to combat the enemy hordes.

I then found that the Army doesn't work that way.

First, I was shot with needles. Then they beat me into passable physical shape. Then I took all kinds of tests.

"Private Wood, I need to see you. Alone."

"Yes, Sergeant Venzke."

He led me to a small office away from the testing rooms.

"You are one smart son of a gun, Wood. You have a great future in the military. Our tests say your IQ is off the charts—187. We have big plans for you."

"Yes, Sergeant!" I grew nervous. In my brief experience, no one in the military ever complimented a private. I must be in trouble.

"You, Private Wood, are on your way to Miami. Your train leaves in five hours. Get your gear together, and get your butt over to the Sergeant at the train station. Good luck."

"Sergeant, may I ask what I will be trained for?"

"Son, you are not going to be trained. You are going to train. You will teach soldiers judo and knife fighting."

My mind went blank. No category for this. "Sergeant, I know nothing about judo or knife fighting."

"Miami is a beautiful place, Private Wood. You will love it, and you will train soldiers to fight with a knife and employ judo in their defense. One more word from you, and you will be looking out from inside my stockade's iron bars."

"Yes, Sergeant." Lesson one: Do not argue with your sergeant.

The train to Miami was a crowded twenty-hour ride. But for someone who had only been to upstate New York, Michigan, Fort Wayne, and Chicago, the sights along the way amazed me. We went through forests, over mountains, and across rivers until we crossed the border of Georgia into Florida. The flat and mostly undeveloped landscape of Florida in 1942 provided an ideal place for military installations. Thousands of soldiers and sailors went there for training. Pine trees gave way to palm trees as we came close to Miami.

Miami in September is great – if you have air conditioning. Privates like me had none. I perspired so much that my shirt always stuck to my back. When I wore my cap, perspiration ran into my eyes. The heat made it nigh unto impossible to sleep.

The sergeant in charge of fighting skills development welcomed me to my new assignment. "Private Wood, you have been promoted to corporal, and you have been assigned to teach judo and knife fighting. You will have the lives of hundreds of recruits in your hands. To help you, the Army has prepared a manual on knife fighting and judo. Study it well. Tomorrow you begin."

Though I'd learned not to argue with a superior officer, I still thought he should have the benefit of knowing my total ignorance about either of these subjects. "I think the sergeant should be aware I have no skills in judo or knife fighting and no preparation to teach these to other soldiers."

"Is that so, Corporal Wood? Are you questioning the wisdom of the Army in giving you this important assignment?"

So, should I speak my mind, or should I just shut up and do what I'm told?

"Sergeant, I just think the sergeant should know that the soldiers might not be well served by an inexperienced judo and knife fighter teaching them."

"Corporal Wood, I did not ask you for your opinion about your fitness for your assignment. You are making a big mistake if you think I care one whit about what you think at all."

I detected no kindness in his voice. "Okay, Sergeant, have it your way."

"Have it my way? I will, Corporal. My way is that your pay will be docked this week to teach you an important lesson. My way is the Army way, and you shall not question it. Now get out of my sight, and learn that training manual!"

The skin on the back of my neck tightened under the perspiration already resting there. I wanted to suggest to him what he could do with his Army manual, but it would have only gotten me into more trouble.

Losing that week's pay would hurt my family in Jonesville. I had to write to Millie to let her know she would miss a week of my pay. Her letter served as a cold reminder to keep my mouth shut.

The manual made the basics of knife fighting and judo clear enouh. I taught the class what I had read the night before and had enough sense to ask a couple of the soldiers who had the skills and the time to come and demonstrate for my amateurs, including me.

One of my amateurs was Clark Gable. Yes, the movie star. His wife died in a plane crash while selling war bonds, so he enlisted in honor of her. Imagine that. He was quite a guy. They shipped him off to Germany to fly combat missions. I don't know if he ever used his judo or knife fighting skills in the Army or in a movie.

Chapter Twenty-One
WHERE THE ACTION IS

Though Miami was nice, I didn't join the United States Army to teach judo and knife fighting to new recruits.

"Sergeant!" I almost shouted. "This corporal very much desires to join the fighting Army. I want to go to where the action is."

"Then put in for another assignment, Corporal."

"I have, Sergeant. Several times. I would like to go over the ocean to fight Germans or Japanese."

"You don't know what you're asking, Wood. You are young, and you are stupid. Most of my soldiers would love the assignment you have."

"I know that, Sergeant, but I've been here three months. I want to be a part of the real fighting."

"All right. Let me see what I can do."

The sergeant delivered. One week later orders came for me to become a radio gunner on B-17 and B-24 bombers. At last I would be trained for war! Scott Army Air Base outside of St. Louis, Missouri trained all the gunners. I prepared to leave right away.

Miami in December has some of the most pleasant weather in the world. I arrived at St. Louis Union Train Station on a December night during an ice storm. What had I asked for? Ice made Market Street, in front of the train station, slippery and dangerous. Thankfully, the bus that would take me to Scott Field, an hour southeast of the city, sat waiting.

The driver of the military bus slumped sideways in his seat, facing the door, his head thrust into a copy of the *St. Louis Globe Dispatch*. I stowed my duffel bag and climbed into one of the few empty seats.

"Thanks for not leaving without me," I said.

"You're welcome, Corporal, but we weren't waiting for you." The driver didn't even look up from the paper. "If I try to drive on this ice now, we'll end up in a ditch. Just have to wait until the roads are better. Make yourself comfortable. We may be here a while."

Thankfully he kept the bus running and the heat on. I put my head against the back of the seat and fell deeply asleep.

I'm not sure how long we waited, but when I woke up, we were driving across the Eads Bridge, over the Mississippi River, and into Illinois. We moved slowly, but on the way, our driver kept some of us awake by giving us his version of the air base's history.

"Soldiers, you should be aware that Scott is one of over thirty Army air bases started after World War I when the military realized the potential of air power. The base is named after Corporal Frank Scott, one of the first enlisted men killed in an Army Air Corps crash. Two one-mile-long runways were just built, and . . ."

That's all I heard. My eyes closed again, and I didn't awake until I felt our bus jostling into a parking spot inside the base. We slowly exited the bus and stepped around patches of ice to make our way to a sturdy, low building. Our bunks waited inside.

I remember nothing after I lay my head on the hard Army pillow.

———————

Early the next morning, the reveille bugle called us out of our sleep and into what the military considered "new opportunities."

I looked out our barracks window to see the light of a new day shining on a silvery white landscape. Millions of ice crystals reflected and magnified the rays from an anemic sun. Ice sparkled on the trees, the grass, the buildings, and the B-17 bombers. The storm of the night before had let up long enough for us to make our way safely to the base, then the relentless ice reasserted itself, lashing until dawn. After a hot shower, I got dressed and went to the mess hall.

"Attention!" An unidentified sergeant made himself known in a proper sergeant voice: full roar.

"Men, you will finish this beautiful breakfast of biscuits and gravy, and in exactly twenty minutes, you will present yourselves to be educated at the building immediately to the south of this mess hall. Carry on."

The soldiers arriving at Scott for radio gunner training were a select group. The officer who welcomed us to our first training session made that clear.

Lieutenant Schroeder was assigned to get us ready for our class. He looked younger than I, but he was stiff-necked and wore an ugly scar on his cheek. He kept rubbing that scar like a badge of honor. Either it hadn't completely healed, or he felt it necessary to show us recruits that he'd already seen action in the war.

"Welcome to Scott, soldiers," he said with a confidence that matched his scar. "You are among the few privileged to be here. Soldiers chosen for this duty are required to be between eighteen and thirty years old, have at least an eighth-grade education, be no taller than five feet ten inches, and no heavier than one hundred and seventy pounds. You had to have gotten a one hundred percent on the classification test."

The test score seemed like the only selective part. Luckily or unluckily, I met all the requirements.

"You will hone your skills as airmen in the Army Air Corps. Any questions before we begin?"

This time no one had given me a manual to read. If they had, I'd have studied it, maybe even memorized the whole thing. But I had one pressing question.

"When do we get to kill our enemies, Sir?"

"When we're reasonably sure you won't kill yourselves, Corporal."

The twenty or so others sitting in the classroom laughed. No one could figure out if I meant my question as a true inquiry or as a test of our new lieutenant.

Or if I was just being a pain in the neck.

I wasn't quite sure myself.

"All of you jokers in this class are here to learn to be radio gunners," the lieutenant continued, not missing a beat. "The radio gunner is an important part of the crew of any Army bomber plane. As the name suggests, when on a bombing mission, he is the member of the crew responsible for maintaining continuous radio contact with his air base and the other airplanes in his squadron. Communication will take place mostly when the aircraft is flying to and from its target."

I grew bored listening to him go on and on. *C'mon, let's get to the training!*

"But because the enemy will protect his troops and facilities, you should expect to be frequently shot at."

Now he had my attention.

"When under attack, the radio gunner will fire his machine gun and destroy any enemy pilot foolish enough to approach his airplane."

We spent the rest of the day studying the intricacies of the .50 caliber machine gun. Later we learned about and took turns operating the radio—an instrument I would get to know well during numerous practice flights. Eventually, I learned to take apart the machine gun and the field radio and to put each of these back together again, blindfolded.

Two landing strips at Scott allowed us to take off at all hours of the day and night. During that time, I learned an additional skill.

"Corporal, is that beer still cold? Pass one up here."

"Yes, Sir, captain. Right away."

On these B-17s and B-24s, beer bottles fit best in the space where the radio gunner sat. I had to open them before we took off, though. If I tried to open one at high altitude, the carbonation of it would explode and spray all over. As the one responsible for the beer, I had the privilege of dispensing it to the rest of the crew.

Let's just say I always got my fair share.

I had been on my way to becoming a sergeant, and it would have happened, if not for my short fuse. That scrappy orphan kid, so hurt from being abandoned, so determined to overcome, still lived inside me. The shame of wearing castaway clothes and getting ridiculed by the town kids never went away and got resurrected every time someone made fun of me. I couldn't shake it. The feeling—the rage—was so deeply rooted.

Counselors would have invited me in for therapy.

The Army sent me to the clink.

Lieutenant Schroeder warned, "This is the third time you've been locked up. Keep this up and you will be court martialed right out of this Army,"

"Sir. I should not be punished for the fight. I was not the one who started it."

"Doesn't make any difference, you little screw-up. How would your mother and father view that?"

"Father's dead, Sir. Mother's a bag lady in Chicago, Sir."

"Well, thanks for that positive piece of information, Wood. Today you return to the privileged rank of private."

Chapter Twenty-Two
DANCING WITH SHIRLEY

During the six months of training at Scott, provided I avoided trouble with the sergeant or lieutenant, I spent weekends in town.

Girls in St. Louis were friendly to soldiers, especially if he made it known he'd been ordered to fight overseas. Fighting orders proved alluring—romantic in a scary way.

Brawls broke out often in the city bars and parks; once or twice the military police carted me away. Each time, I woke up back in the Scott Army Base stockade, my pass for next week cancelled, my future as a private prolonged.

At first when I had time off, I tried to find clubs like the ones I had gotten to know in Fort Wayne in the area around The Scarlet Fever. Being in those places led to trouble, though, and they cost too much money; I was still sending what I could back to Millie.

The government operated USO clubs. The lower costs made one in St. Louis particularly good. I met some good-looking young women there.

"Care to dance, Soldier?" A girl who couldn't have been more than sixteen asked me.

"If you insist." I smiled.

"How nice of you, big shot. What's your name?"

"Lowell Kenneth Wood. My friends call me Woody. What's yours?"

"Shirley. Shirley Schuelte."

"Where do you live, Shirley Schuelte?"

"I should be asking you that question. Let me guess. Chicago, right?"

I shook my head.

"No? Well, some place in the Midwest then. Am I getting warm?"

"You are definitely warm. I'd say you're hot."

"Are you flirting with me?"

"Of course. And I'm from the Midwest, a small town outside of Detroit you've never heard of: Jonesville, Michigan. What would you say if I asked you for a date?"

"I'd say I have to ask my mother first."

"Ask her!"

Shirley smiled. "She'll want to meet you."

"I'd like to meet her too. If she's half as pretty as you are, I might ask *her* out on a date."

"My father wouldn't like that. But he might like you if you watch your mouth, smart guy."

"I think I'm in love."

"With whom?"

"With Shirley Schulte."

"You don't know me, Lowell Kenneth Wood. I think you *haven't* fallen in love. Seems to me you're mired in lust."

"Maybe. But I'd still like to take you out on a date."

I'd nearly come to the end of my six-month radio-and-gunnery course, but I still had time to get to know Shirley. I told her I planned to come to St. Louis the next weekend and asked if I could meet her at the entrance to the zoo in the city's Forest Park. She thought that would be okay, and said she'd ask her parents about my stopping by to meet them.

Thankfully, Shirley's father, Gus (short for August) turned out to be a friendly guy—when given the opportunity. This usually required his wife shutting her mouth. We didn't get to see Gus' friendly side often.

May Schulte dominated the family. She made all the decisions and then told everyone how to carry them out. Seemed like what people called a "matriarchy."

I can just imagine how the conversation between Shirley and her mother went:

"Mother, I'd like to bring to the house a boy I met at the USO Saturday night. He seems really smart, and he has a good sense of humor. He asked if I would meet him at the zoo Saturday. He wants to take me out on a date alone, but I told him you'd have to meet him first."

"You met him at a USO dance? So he's a soldier. You know how I feel about soldiers. No one loves those heroic boys more than I do, but Shirley, you are too young to be going out by yourself on a date. How old is he?

"I don't know. I didn't give him the third degree."

"Well, seems that you got to the first and second degree since you're asking us to welcome him in our home. Where's he from?"

"A small town in Michigan. Jonesville, I think he said. He was really polite, Mom, and he is so good looking. You know only the smartest young men are allowed into the Army's Air Corps; I think he has good prospects. That's what you usually ask, right? 'What are his prospects?'"

"These young guys don't stay at Scott very long. I guess it's okay. Ask him if he'd like to come for dinner after church Sunday. Gus, what do you think?"

"Sure, May. Whatever you say. At least Shirley's being up front with us. It would be good to meet the young man."

The last weeks at Scott were among of the best of my life. The Schultes cared about each other, and they stayed together. Unlike my family. Shirley and I saw each other often. On weekends I even got to stay over in a spare bedroom at the apartment of one of her aunts who lived nearby. The Schultes took me to church with them.

Church services at Our Lady of Sorrows were a new experience; a lot of mysterious Latin mumbo-jumbo went on at this Catholic church. And who would give that kind of name to a place? Seemed that you'd be obligated to get depressed every time you walked in the door. The priest seemed happy, though. And he took an immediate interest in me. Whenever he saw me, he thanked me for serving with the Air Corps.

The easy growth of my relationship with Shirley did not please Momma May. It frightened her.

"Shirley, watch out," she would warn. "These young men have only one thing on their mind. I like this boy, but you don't have a dress large enough if things between you and him go too far. Don't act as if you don't know what I mean. Remember, he's a soldier, a soldier who wants to go where the fighting is. Getting involved with him before he goes overseas would be a mistake."

"Mother, why do you always think of the worst that can happen? Can't you just be thankful I'm going out with a great guy, someone who's smart, who is supporting his sister, someone who wants to do the right thing and serve his country?"

The warning from Shirley's mother rang in our ears when I received word to move out. Not to China or Germany yet, though. Just Reno, Nevada for more training.

I never thought it would be hard to leave St. Louis and its ice storms, but I had fallen in love with Shirley. When I was with her, I became a blabbermouth and told her everything of my life. I told her about Carlton and my mother's abandoning us, then discovering Mom in Chicago.

I recounted my pilgrimage at the Bogue Home, running away, life with the Munzels, the move to Jonesville, even about Betty—though I left out the skinny-dipping part. I also confessed my employment at The Scarlet Fever. Shirley just listened, and I suspect she quietly marveled that I had lived so much life in a relatively short time.

Little did I know then that I had just begun. Bigger stories were yet to come.

Much bigger.

Chapter Twenty-Three
PRIVATE WOOD, AGAIN

May of 1942. Scott had been a good learning experience, especially with Shirley nearby. Now I sweated in the desert near Reno—where I couldn't believe they gambled out in the open, unlike our backroom huddles in Fort Wayne. Here the Army gave me still more gunnery training, this time in gunnery and Morse code. After this I hoped to join a bomber crew and get into the fight raging overseas in Asia and Europe.

The Army had a different idea.

They always had a different idea.

As our gunnery and Morse code courses finished up, the other soldiers received assignments. Some to Asia, others to Europe, a few to Africa. My name never appeared.

Trying to get overseas, I applied for every job posted on the bulletin board. I wanted to see the world. I knew I had the training and aggressiveness to make a difference in the fighting. That scrappy orphan kid still lived large in me and itched for a worthwhile fight.

At last—finally!—the Army came to the same conclusion: I would be prepared to go overseas. But not in the way I had expected.

Of course.

After all my training in gunnery, radio operation and Morse code (and, of course, beer dispensing), the Army now intended to train me as an officer. An *officer*? Maybe this had something to do with my high scores on the aptitude and IQ tests. For the first time in my life, I wished I were dumb. The first time around, they didn't give me any training; now they gave me too much. Long live the Army.

Out of all my assignment applications, the Army chose a spot for which I had no aptitude. Again. I reviewed the orders sending me to ASTP, the Army Specialized Training Program. Then, I went to my commanding officer.

"Lieutenant, what's the idea? I have been trained and am ready to do battle in an airplane, with bombs, a machine gun, radio, and Morse code. I am a radio gunner par excellence."

"Private Wood, you will go where you are told. The Army wants you in Athens, Georgia, where you will attend the Army's program to train men who have graduated from high school but have had no college experience. There you will learn to become an officer and, I sincerely pray, a gentleman. Along with this assignment, you will be given the rank of corporal."

I was so angry I could spit. "Lieutenant, this is a clear case of mistaken officership. I kindly request that you change the Army's mind."

"Keep it up, and you will not only lose those new stripes on your arm, you will lose your freedom. I'll have you put behind bars."

I took the evening train to Athens.

The Army Specialized Training program in Georgia was designed to last two years. But eagerness to finish and get to where I could make a difference, not score another notch in my army belt, pushed me to move more quickly. I requested, and received allowance, to overload my course schedule and decline breaks between courses. But all this became too much, not on my ability but on my emotions. My rank as corporal did not last long.

The MP stood over me as I sat on a curb outside the Paws Bar. "What's with you, Private Wood? This is the third time you've gotten into a fight. These college boys get your blood up?"

I tried in vain to speak clearly. "All I did was . . . put my arm around this cute thing at the bar. She didn't . . . mean a thing to me. Someone should have told me that girl's . . . boyfriend was there." I stupidly started to cry. "I miss Shirley, my beautiful girl in St. Louis." Tears of a soldier with whiskey on his breath, who'd been away too long from his girlfriend, from his family, from his home, leaked out.

Then a miracle happened. This MP had pity on me. "I'm going to leave you here. Do not get into more trouble, okay?"

"Ummm . . ."

"Okay?"

"Sure. I'm really . . . a good guy once you get to know me."

Someone, somewhere, with some sense realized I would never be an officer. This required another change in the plan the Army had for me. The next day Sergeant Freitag called me to his office.

"Private Wood, you have been selected to volunteer for the IC."

"Forgive me, Sergeant. What are you talking about?"

"The IC is the Intelligence Corps. You will be a part of an elite team to root out corruption and theft, vices that are weakening the war effort."

"Sergeant, does that mean this soldier will be a part of the police?"

"Even better, Private Wood. You will be one of our undercover detectives. A spy for Uncle Sam, a member of G-2."

I didn't even want to ask.

"As soon as you finish preparation for your new assignment, you are to report to Reno, Nevada. And for this you will be given the rank of corporal."

"I do not believe this."

"That is what is so brilliant about your new assignment. Neither will anyone else."

I was stunned, angry, and ready for another fight. Even with the sergeant. As I burst out of the sergeant's office I rushed passed a second lieutenant.

"Soldier, you forgot something."

He was a superior officer.

"Corporal! You forgot to salute."

I had no patience for this. I saluted him all right, with one centrally located finger. That cost me the new stripe before it even got re-sewn on my sleeve. Back to my default position—Private Wood.

It didn't matter. Millie would have to get along without the extra few dollars. By now she'd grown accustomed to it.

Chapter Twenty-Four
UNDERCOVER OPERATION

I returned to Reno in January 1943, ever more frustrated at not having gone overseas. More galling was that they were training me to be a stool pigeon—an investigator, going under cover, with false identities, finding soldiers stealing goods to put on the black market. I tried to rationalize my assignment by saying to myself that rooting out thieves and traitors contributed to the defeat of our enemies.

My first assignment did not require dropping bombs on Berlin or gunning down Jap Zeros in the Pacific. Oh no. My assignment instructed me to deal blackjack in Reno at the Palace Club Casino. My military service: dealing cards. I couldn't believe it.

The card dealers could tell when someone came into the casino with a big wad of cash. But none of them knew I the Army put me in the casino to find miscreant military types with a lot of dough on hand. In a short period of time, I identified a number of military deserters, thieves, and swindlers. When I found somebody, I alerted my supervising officer, Lieutenant Locano, who sent the information to the Military Police.

After I'd been in Reno for two weeks, serving my country amid cards, dice, and flashing lights, the lieutenant called my private phone number at my apartment.

"Private Wood, we believe some of the women dealers are offering our soldiers more than card games, and they may be taking more than money. One of our soldiers was accosted after being in the home of one of those women, someone named Laura Wiley. Says his wallet was stolen. Get to know this Miss Wiley and find out what you can."

I knew shy, young, attractive Laura. She and two other female dealers lived in a rented house in Virginia City, about a half-hour from Reno. Petite, golden-haired Laura had serious skill for spotting cheaters at the blackjack table. She taught me a thing or two. In fact, I had thought of asking her to go out with me. I now had the perfect excuse.

Later that afternoon found us dealing for the high-roller blackjack tables. During our first break, I approached her.

"Laura, I see you're not on the work sheet for Friday night. How about us going out to dinner?"

"That's sweet of you," she said, "but the girls and I are having a few of the servicemen over Friday night."

I stood there, eyes down.

"Want to come along?"

Virginia City had been a gold mining town, but the population declined as quickly as the gold depleted. In 1943, not many people remained. The neighborhood reflected a dying town—a shuttered restaurant with paint peeling and weeds filling the parking lot, a church with a door half off its hinges, and a few lights on here and there in small houses far apart from each other. I'm sure the daytime offered great views of the mountains. But with no streetlights and an almost-new moon, at night it felt like entering a dark closet.

The Army supplied me with a Chevy as part of my cover—I loved it. For the first time I felt as if I had my own car. Made me feel like somebody.

The closer I got to Virginia City, the narrower and more deserted the roads became. Following Laura's directions, I took thirty minutes to finally find her place. As I pulled up to the two-story wooden structure with wraparound porch, I wondered why these young women lived so far from work.

My headlights caught the shapes of two other cars parked close to the house. I knew one to be Laura's; the other I didn't recognize. I parked and got out.

A thin sliver of moon just above the roof of the house competed with the light coming from inside. The closer I came to the house, the louder the music inside became. They must have had some kind of Victrola going because no radio signal could come in that loudly and clearly this far from civilization.

No need to knock; the door was open. A bar was set up near the front, and four middle-aged men, along with three young and very good-looking women, stood around. The women I knew; they worked in the casinos. The men I hadn't seen before.

"Woody, you made it! What took you so long?" Laura walked over and put her arm around my shoulder. An almost-full glass of whiskey sloshed in her other hand. The rest came off her breath.

"Katy and Andrea you already know. The guys are just passing through on their way to San Diego." She pointed to each. "Lloyd, James, Hank, and William. We met them yesterday. They were thinking about leaving this morning, but we convinced them to stay another day. They're supposed to be getting ready to go somewhere overseas—something important, I'm sure. But they can't tell us."

It looked to me like the four guys were further along with their drinks. Empty and near-empty glasses sat by or in their hands. The women's glasses looked nursed—fingerprints all over, glasses half full.

Hank approached me. "Woody. That's a strange name. Do you have a family tree?" He turned to see the others laugh; they didn't. "C'mon, have a drink. Katy, get Woody some booze. Looks like he needs it. Don't he, fellas?" Now they laughed.

For my professional role, I could suppress the scrappy kid in me.

Hank spilled his drink. "Uh oh! Got some on the couch, girls. Maybe I should go upstairs and change?"

The girls didn't respond, and the other guys seemed too drunk to follow his lead.

But that's how I'd expected the girls to be making extra cash out here. Strange.

Instead, Andrea touched his shoulder. "Hank, first tell us some more about your time in the war. And where you're going next."

"None of your business, girlie."

"Then whose business is it?"

Lloyd's whiskey glass was empty. No telling how many drinks he'd put down. Now he jumped in. "Gonna be the business of them Japs when our carriers bring those fighter pilots closer to Hirohito's house." He steadied himself. "Heard something about a lot of us closing in on New Genie, or something."

James shoved him back. "Shut up, Lloyd! You ain't supposed to talk about that."

The girls just kept smiling and pouring more whiskey. Maybe their interests weren't what I originally supposed. My ears started ringing as my blood pressure shot up. Spies with this kind of knowledge could have a disastrous effect on the war in the Pacific.

"Lloyd," I asked, "how much did you win at blackjack?"

"Win? I won nothin'. Not a damn thing. Lost almost everything I had. I was gonna send money home to Nancy. She's saving for when I get outta this sailor suit. She's working so hard, and I go and lose a month's pay."

The women stared at me and shrugged. Laura stood up, went over to Lloyd, and took him by the hand. "Hey, I want to show you that letter I got from this admiral who stayed at the Palace Club a few weeks ago. It's upstairs."

Now that's what I'd expected earlier, but at this point it seemed to carry a different purpose.

"Hold on." Hank hauled himself up. "It's too late for that. We have to get going early. Thanks for the drinks, girls. C'mon you guys, before I drag your butts out myself."

Lloyd needed a little more encouragement to leave than James and William, but they all staggered outside.

I followed right behind them. "Looks like the party's over. Nice evening, Laura. Hope we can do it again sometime."

When I got back to Reno, I called Locano. A week later Laura had a visit from a detachment of Military Police. After some searching, they discovered Laura's brother in the German army. Eventually all three women were arrested for stealing military secrets.

Maybe the Army had me doing something useful after all.

Still, not exactly what I signed up for.

Chapter Twenty-Five
A "DEAR LOWELL" LETTER

Lieutenant Locano recommended me for promotion to corporal. I had been this route before, but, what the heck, if someone wanted to give me an increase in pay, I'd take it. Might as well see the glass half full. After six weeks or so in Reno, I received assignment to go undercover. Someone in the 14th Armored Division in Fort Campbell, Kentucky, had apparently stolen truckloads of shoes. The only good thing I saw coming out of this was that to get to Kentucky, I had to go by train through St. Louis. Shirley Schuelte.

In fact, I'd been saving money to buy a ring to give to Shirley.

We wouldn't have much time together when I stopped there. I sent her a telegram, asking her to meet me at Union Station. All the way to St. Louis I dreamed of a time after the war, when Shirley and I could start a family of our own. We'd live in a two-story white house with a lush green yard, flowerbeds, and a picket fence. I'd drive her around town in my own car, a Cadillac. And kids—I wanted one, two, three, four of them! We'd have the happiest family ever.

Travelling overnight, I reached St. Louis at 3 p.m. The fact that Shirley was still in high school never concerned me. In my life I'd never been too young for anything, whether I liked it or not. She skipped her last class to meet me at the station. Snow fell in big fluffy flakes, and there she stood bundled in a white cloth coat that came down to her ankles. She looked like an angel.

"Shirley! I've dreamed about you every night. Only you."

"Mom and Dad send their affection. How long can you stay?"

"Not long. My train leaves in two hours. I'm on my way to Kentucky to find whoever's stealing the Army's shoes. We can't have guys going into battle barefoot. But never mind that. Where can we go to talk?"

"Everything here is too hectic. We can walk a few blocks to Macy's. They have a restaurant, and it won't be crowded at this time on a cold day like this."

It was twenty-three degrees, so instead of walking we took a cab to Macy's department store and found a cozy seat in a corner of the restaurant. The clinking of plates and conversations carrying on around us sounded like background music to me.

No one had ever taught me social graces or finesse. I figured Shirley would have plenty of time to do that in the future. For now, I just did things.

First, I took a big breath.

"Shirley, we don't have time for me to beat around the bush." I fumbled in my Army overcoat pocket and extracted a small box with the ring inside. "I want to marry you." I gave her the box.

Shirley was speechless. Tears welled in her eyes and ran down her cheeks. She wiped them away with the back of her sweet white hand. She took the ring out of the box and slipped it onto the wrong hand. We both laughed. I took it off and put it onto her left ring finger. Then we sat there holding hands, smiling and laughing.

She was The One. I felt grateful to love someone who would never abandon me, who would stay by me and raise a family together.

"I love you, Lowell. I wish Mom were here. I'm scared of what her reaction will be. Daddy will be pleased. If you could come to the house right now, I know she'd give us her blessing. Do you really have to leave right away?"

"Wish I didn't. But the sooner I leave, the sooner I'll be back. This war can't last forever. Maybe after this cockamamie assignment, they'll give me a week off. Then I can talk more with your mother and father. But for now let's enjoy our short time together before I need to get back to the train station."

On the train to Kentucky, I felt like I was flying on cotton clouds. I had never been so happy. Ever. I took seriously my commitment to Shirley. At nineteen years old, I decided the time had come to look at life as an adult.

I became more serious about my assignment because that's what an adult would do. I worked hard and smart, and I found the thief in only ten days of observation and conversation. Turns out he was a corporal, a little older than I. My superior officers expressed amazement at how quickly I found him, but they did not grant me any time off.

Instead I'd get a free trip to India, where I would be a radio gunner while continuing my undercover work. Then came the really good news: The Army was sending me back to Scott for still more training in preparation for going overseas. Back to St. Louis. Back to Shirley. I almost jumped into the arms of the sergeant when he told me—but I refrained. I didn't want to get demoted again.

Could my life be any better? My orders, finally, to go overseas! And a couple of weeks with my fiancé before leaving, to boot. I sent Shirley a letter to tell her my good news.

When I arrived at Scott, my half-full glass turned half-empty. A letter from Shirley, with a lump inside, lay waiting for me:

Dear Lowell, I am finding it hard to write this to you. No matter what I say, my mother insists I have to return your ring. Mother feels that at sixteen, I'm too young to be engaged—and definitely should not be engaged to someone in the service who is going overseas. She is afraid you will be crippled or killed, and it would not be fair to me to live with something like that for the rest of my life. Please try to understand, although I know you probably won't. Don't try to see me, it will only make things harder. Sincerely, Shirley.

Chapter Twenty-Six
OUT OF THE FRYING PAN

I had been moping and wanting to die at Scott Army Base for less than a week when I received another letter. This time, from my best friend in Jonesville, Betty Swope. She and I occasionally sent letters back and forth, just friendly letters, keeping each other up on our lives.

Her letter worried me.

"Lowell, I can't stand staying here with my parents. My mother tries to run everything in my life. My father, well, he's no help. There is a boy I cared for, we were really close. But I always had to sneak around to see him. Now I think he is going to dump me because of them! I'm afraid."

Way back when I first came to St. Louis, I wrote to Betty and invited her to come if she could find a way. The letter now in my hands said she would leave on Friday afternoon. If she followed through on her plan, she would reach St. Louis on Saturday, two days from now.

Now what trouble had she gotten into?

It didn't matter. I would never abandon a friend in trouble. On Saturday I took the bus to the St. Louis train station and waited. An overcast sky matched my trepidation at learning whatever Betty needed to tell me, but the sun made an appearance just as her train pulled in. For that moment, it felt like a scene out of a fantasy love story. I recognized her immediately and ran to meet her.

"Betty, it's really you! Do you have any luggage? How long are you staying?"

"I'll explain it all. It's so wonderful to see you. I missed you so much." Then she did something she'd never done before, something I never expected.

She kissed me.

With more than a friendly kiss.

A train whistle went off on another track. People bustled all around.

And I'd just gotten a French kiss.

I was dumbfounded.

I wanted more.

"I go back on Tuesday. All I have is this one suitcase."

"Wh-what's the kiss all about?"

"Where can we talk?" Her blond hair hung longer now, and at nineteen her shape had definitely grown into that of a woman.

"I didn't know how long you were going to stay, so I got you a room at a motel near the base. There's a bus leaving for Scott in twenty minutes. We have just enough time. The driver will drop you off at the motel, and I'll catch up with you later."

I was dying to know what had happened to make her upset enough to leave Jonesville and come all the way out here. And how had she done this without her mother agreeing?

What was blatantly clear was that she did not look like the young girl I had said goodbye to.

"Don't go back to the base," she instructed. "I really need to talk to you."

Plan B. We got on the bus and Betty snuggled close to me. She put her head on my shoulder. Never did that before. I could smell perfume. Another first. She searched for my hand and held it like she meant it.

My thoughts of Shirley started fading.

It was chilly when we got off the bus, but only a short walk to the motel. I carried Betty's luggage and led her inside the motel lobby.

"You go on ahead," I said. "I'll wait in the lobby while you get settled upstairs."

"All right, Lowell. But maybe you could carry my bag up to the room for me? It's kind of heavy to carry up the stairs."

The hotel clerk must have had extraordinary hearing, or he had a lot of experience. He gave me a stern look when I went to get the key to Betty's room. "Sorry. Unless you're married, one of you stays down here."

Oh boy. This was all getting away from me faster than I could keep up.

Betty quickly settled in her room and came back down to the lobby. "Let's get something to eat, and then I really want you to come upstairs to my room. There's something I want to show you."

"But the clerk said we had to be married. I don't mind getting in trouble with the military—I've had plenty of experience. But this guy could call the local police, and we'd both be in jail."

It was now 8 P.M. on a frosty Saturday night. So, we left our discussion at that and walked across the motel parking lot to the Bob Evans restaurant. The thought consumed me that the last time I'd been to a restaurant with a girl was at Macy's, with a ring and stupid, false hopes. But this time around I'd learned my lesson.

The people inside kept their coats on against the chill because of the restaurant's wartime rationing of heating oil. A waitress wearing a heavy wool sweater took our order: we each had meatloaf. I was an adult now, so I also ordered wine, merlot for me, chardonnay for Betty. We'd just taken our first sip of wine when Betty leaned across the restaurant table.

"Let's get married, Lowell."

Huh? Did she just say that?

"I've known you longer, and I know you better, than any boy in Jonesville. You know my thoughts before I know them. We've always loved talking to each other."

I think she did.

"I can't stay here for a long time, but if we get a marriage license, we could be married by a justice of the peace by Tuesday. What do you say?"

Our food hadn't even arrived yet.

I stammered, "You—you sure you want to marry a soldier? Especially one who's going overseas?"

"Not just any soldier. I want to be Mrs. Lowell Kenneth Wood."

I took a deep breath. And another.

I felt as if I were hanging on to the bumper of a speeding car.

"You know, Betty, that does make sense." My inborn, practical business acumen kicked in without my realizing it. "Millie and Gordon would be ecstatic if we got married. They'd be able to spread around those extra kids they've been caring for. You could live with Millie until I got back. Help out Millie with the kids and the laundry."

She didn't even flinch.

"But what are your folks going to do to you when they find out? They live right across the street."

"I'm through with them. I want to start my own family. And together we would do it right."

I liked the sound of that.

"Are you sure you have to go overseas?" she said. "What if we eloped and you just deserted?"

"Don't be crazy. If they caught me, I'd go to prison. I'd never get a job, and all the folks in Michigan would hate me. Besides, I can make extra money doing what I am doing, going overseas to India."

"What if you had a child? Would they still make you go?"

I sat back a little. "Of course they would. Lots of soldiers have kids."

"Oh."

"I *have* to go overseas. I've wanted to ever since I joined the Army. They finally trained me. I also need to put aside more money for when I get out of the Army."

She returned to the issue at hand. "Let's get married. And then we can discuss children and finances." She beamed and nodded her head. "We already sound like a married couple anyway, don't we?"

While I had never seriously thought about Betty the way I thought about her that night, the idea appealed. We were both nineteen, we came from the same small town, and we'd been friends for years. Who knew how long the war would last, or even if I would stay alive long enough to get back home? I wanted, *needed*, someone who would listen to my thoughts and feelings.

I wanted to be loved.

The only problem was her parents. They were a huge barrier, but I'd already overcome so many other obstacles in my life.

Mr. Munzel's advice from so long ago, about not making quick decisions, didn't occur to me at that moment. Too bad. Waiting might have helped.

Later that evening I called Betty from the base. "I want to marry you. I asked the sergeant for a three-day pass, and he gave it. We'll go to St. Louis, take the trolley and see the sights. Then I'll bring you back to the motel. We can get the marriage license on Monday. What did you bring to wear?"

"Well, just in case you said yes, for the wedding I brought my best Sunday church dress—white with pink ribbons on the waist and sleeves. For after the wedding, well, I wouldn't be able to wear it in church, if you know what I mean."

We were married near the base in a brief ceremony on Tuesday morning at city hall in Collinsville, Illinois. That afternoon Betty was back on the train to Michigan.

In my heart I felt and determined to be as true to Betty as I had ever been to Shirley.

What they say about lightning never striking twice in the same place is not true.

Somewhere between St. Louis and Jonesville, something must have changed in Betty's heart. Several weeks later, I received a "Dear Lowell" letter:

Lowell, I am so sorry. When I got home my mother went crazy. My father went to the police station and told the police I was out of my mind, that you had convinced me to run away. They threatened to have you arrested. I knew that would not be good for you, to have you in prison when I know you had your heart set on going to India. My parents insist that we annul the marriage. They've found an attorney who will be contacting you. One more thing, I found out yesterday I am expecting.

My mother and father have agreed to let me stay in the house and raise the child as if it were their own. The baby will be fine. Please, if you ever loved me, don't fight me on this. Goodbye, Lowell.

Just like that.

Stunned silence. I could not hear, feel, or think anything.

Through the rest of my time at Scott Air Base, I went through the military motions, but my mind stayed wrapped in a daze.

It took me a while to think straight, but I think I figured out what happened. I could be wrong, but it seems to me Betty may already have been expecting—*before* she came to St. Louis. I heard from Mr. Camp that Betty's boyfriend suddenly moved out of Jonesville a few days before she first wrote me and visited. I also remembered what she'd told me a long while back about how ecstatic, then guilty, she'd felt about the two of them having sex.

I felt more sad than angry. My best friend. How could she use me like that?

Was there no one I could trust?

No one?

Being abandoned as a kid is bad enough. But being betrayed as an adult felt like salt in a lacerated heart.

Betty wrote me a few times after that, but I never opened her letters.

Chapter Twenty-Seven
WAR—FINALLY, ALMOST

On May 18, 1942, the American general in charge of the Allied forces in Burma, General Joe "Vinegar" Stillwell, got chased out of the jungles by the Japanese army and entered Assam, India. He led 117 American, Chinese, and Burmese refuges out of Burma, while nineteen Burmese nurses in the group led the soldiers in singing "The Battle Hymn of the Republic." Regardless, Burma was now lost.

Even more crucial, the road from India across Burma that had been bringing supplies to Allied forces fighting the Japanese in China, the Burma Road, was cut off.

In March 1943 I received my orders: "Pvt. Wood, report to Camp Anza to prepare for embarkation to your new duty. Your assignment will be hazardous and will help determine the outcome of our war."

The action, and the sense of purpose, I'd been waiting for! But the hazardous part left me a bit concerned.

Camp Anza was a flat, dusty staging area in Riverside, California, a city of twenty thousand, halfway between Los Angeles and Palm Springs. They built it almost overnight on an old ranch. Here we received inoculations, uniforms, and information specific to our destination of war zones in the Pacific.

They readied me for "CBI," military-speak for "China, Burma, and India." I spoke with whomever I could to learn what the fighting was like in that part of the world. What I learned made me more eager to get there: with the closing of the 717-mile-long gravel-and-potholed Burma Road, the Army Air Corps now assumed responsibility for getting supplies to the Chinese. It would be the largest supply mission ever carried out using airplanes.

Before this, the Army Air Corps bombed and strafed and did reconnaissance. Air Corps planes had not been tested as a way to move significant amounts of war material. Many military and civilian leaders doubted the mission could succeed, among them General Stillwell. I would be part of the effort to prove them wrong.

One day the ground shook. I heard stuff crashing inside an office and felt thankful to be outside. The local fellows didn't react much, but the earthquake scared the heck out of me. I thought my heart itself would leap into my throat. Here I was, eager to fight a war in China but terrified that the earth jiggled in California.

Though Camp Anza was flat, dusty, and boring, Riverside sat near enough to Hollywood and Palm Springs that stars like Bob Hope, Lana Turner, and Frank Sinatra came to entertain us soldiers. Even though most of us were here for only about ten days before being shipped overseas, during that time invariably some movie star or sports hero showed up to boost our morale.

In the camp I became friends with Jimmy O'Hara, another radio gunner headed for India. Jimmy was five feet tall, with orangey hair, a bit of a spare tire around his middle, and a smile always on his face. He always seemed to have money to spend, and he claimed to have a well-known cousin in Hollywood: Miss Shirley Temple. None of us believed him.

"What if I call Shirley up and invite her to go out with us?"

We doubted he could.

Just for fun, Jimmy called her and invited her to go out on a date with a couple of us. To his surprise, as well as ours, Shirley Temple actually came in a limousine that seemed as long as a football field. Wearing a provocative dress, she smoked a cigarette in a long white cigarette holder; in her other hand she held a martini glass, the contents of which she struggled not to spill.

I never got to dance with Shirley Temple. Besides Jimmy, plenty of other guys asked her for a spin around the floor. I did discover that Shirley was not the sweet little thing you see in the movies.

Chapter Twenty-Eight

ON THE INDIA FRONT

In 1943, it took four weeks to travel by ship from Los Angeles to Calcutta. Anticipation and a long voyage made the trip both exhilarating and monotonous.

On the way, the Army Air Corps pilots studied charts of the Indian Himalayas, especially the area between Assam, India, and Kunming, China, where the largest mountains sent sharp air currents thousands of feet into the sky, sure to make any flight difficult. We radio gunners practiced taking apart our radios and machine guns, as well as sending and interpreting Morse code.

Some of us formed deep friendships, especially Jimmy and me. We made plans to start a bar and grill when we were safely back in Michigan, probably in Ann Arbor so we could get to see the University of Michigan football games. But first we had this other business to attend to in India, Burma, and China.

Finally we arrived.

We arrived to a squalid city teeming with more people than I had ever seen in one place, and with more smells than I ever cared to consider. The streets pulsed with coolies pulling rickshaws alongside piles of rotting garbage, cars and buses spewing black exhaust. Crowds of people sweat in the relentless heat and humidity.

I held my hand in front of my face. "I wonder if anyone here has heard about the invention of the bath."

Jimmy shook his head. "Might not do much good." He gestured to a nearby cow. "Those wandering free everywhere, leaving their piles of poop, doesn't help much either. I could eat a hamburger about now."

"This is a strange place, Jimmy. I guess they're just doing the best they can to get through their lives the way we are with ours."

Initial word said we'd travel on the Bengal and Assam Railroad, the narrow-gauge train taking supplies to Assam, a seven-hundred-mile journey that included travel by barge and truck. The trip could take as long as our journey from Los Angeles to India. I hoped for a ride in an airplane, but taking gasoline and ammunition to the Chinese and the American armies fighting in China outranked a soldier needing transport.

The Allies needed the Chinese to tie down the million or more Japanese troops pushing Generalissimo Chiang Kai-shek's army farther and farther west. As long as we could keep the Japanese soldiers engaged in China, they could not be sent to the Pacific theater to fight our soldiers there.

We'd been at the American post in Calcutta for five days, getting our bearings. None of us looked forward to the trip over land, but neither did we want to stay in Calcutta. Either way, we would soon have to reorient ourselves to a more dangerous circumstance, flying over mountains while shooting at Japanese fighter planes intent on turning us into wreckage. I tried to keep that out of my mind.

Shipments to supply Chiang Kai-shek came into Calcutta then went to Assam. From there airmen made treacherous flights over some of the highest mountains in the world, the Himalayas. They called this trip "flying over The Hump."

"Woody, what do you know about the American General Joe Stilwell?" Jimmy said.

"Vinegar Joe? I hear he gets the job done, not always following Army protocol."

"My kind of officer. What about General Chennault?"

"Why the questions, Jimmy? Chennault's in China. Stillwell leads the ground troops, and Chennault oversees the Air Corps. I hear they don't get along well. "

"I just need to know how all this works. As I understand it, Major General Stratemeyer was put in charge of the Army Air Corps here in India and Burma. His office is somewhere in Calcutta. General Stillwell goes back and forth between India and China. Chennault pretty much stays in China."

"That makes sense, since all the supplies come in here before they go to—what's the Chinese city they fly into?"

Jimmy made it a point to learn as much as he could about the geography of where we were going and how troops and supplies traveled. "The supplies funnel into Kunming. I hear there are some pretty pricey items coming in these days. I also hear some of it gets lost once in a while."

That kind of statement could get a soldier in trouble. "Don't know about that, Jimmy. Let's get going. We only have one more day before our pleasure trip to Assam begins."

"I saw a shop a few blocks back at the Burra Bazar that sells tobacco. I think I'll go back and take a look. Maybe find some souvenirs."

"Go ahead. I'll just wander around some more. See you back at the post."

Jimmy's leaving was lucky. I'd been trying to find a way to get to General Stratemeyer's headquarters without attracting attention. Before we'd left Camp Anza, I'd been told to report to the general's office in Calcutta.

Chapter Twenty-Nine
TROUBLE IN THE RANKS

I walked into the general's headquarters. "Corporal Wood reporting for duty. I am here to speak with someone in the Criminal Investigation Division."

"Captain Vilani's your man. Wait here." The other corporal disappeared up some stairs at the end of the hallway.

At least inside the building the smell was much better. Spit and polish clean. Smelled like the same cleaning chemicals used in the barracks at Scott. My nose could relax.

"The captain says to come ahead. Up the stairs, third door on your right."

Pictures of current Army heroes lined the narrow white halls. As I entered the captain's office, I stopped. The man before me stood in front of his desk as if he had just been called to attention. A large map hung behind the desk. Official-looking papers pinned to bulletin boards and taped everywhere covered the rest of the walls. He leveled an angry stare at me.

Oh no. I must have done something wrong.

An electric fan laboriously pushed air around the room as if, like me, the air wanted a way out.

"Corporal Wood, we are in trouble."

We? Ahhh. "A lot of trouble in this city, Sir. What is it that concerns the captain?"

"Pilfering. Stealing. Burglarizing. Call it what you want, it is undermining our ability to fight the enemy. Our soldiers are suffering shortages of clothing and ammunition because criminals, both local and among our Allied soldiers, care only about enriching themselves. It is happening on too large a scale in the CBI Theater, some of it here, in Calcutta, but mostly in Kunming. You are here to help stamp it out."

I did not consider myself the most upright of creatures on God's green earth. But I could not understand how any soldier could live with his conscience and steal supplies meant to help his comrades to fight the war. "Captain, what orders do you have for me?"

"You will maintain your responsibilities as radio gunner. It is a good cover. And besides, there are fewer and fewer of you as we progress towards victory over the Japanese.

Fewer and fewer of us? I didn't like the sound of that.

"I do not need to tell you, soldier, that the trip over The Hump is dangerous. It is no picnic. Between enemy fighter planes and the treacherous weather in the eastern Himalayas, the 525-mile flight has been a path to the cemetery for many flyboys."

"Is this air supply thing worth it, Captain? Or is it just some Army Air generals trying to experiment, maybe prove a point?"

"You bet your life it's worth it."

Hmmm. At least they were willing to bet *my* life, and the lives of thousands of others.

"Our forces in China are tying down thousands of Japanese soldiers that the enemy would otherwise use to push back our forces in the Pacific. Is it worth it? Those soldiers cannot fight without a constant supply of food, fuel and weapons.

"The brave airmen supplying our soldiers in China have carried more cargo over any given route than at any other time or place in history. Even when the Burma Road re-opens—and Vinegar Joe *will* open it—even then, we have already proven we can move more war supplies faster, and with less loss of material, than could be moved using trucks and railways on a highway."

Edges and corners of papers on the walls that were not pinned or taped lilted and curled forward in the sultry heat. The map had red lines marking what I guessed were supply routes.

"Are you listening, Corporal?"

"Yes, Sir. You are moving the supplies."

"Is it worth it?"

"Yes, Sir. It is worth it, Sir." I hoped he believed me.

"Ask the Chinese holding out against the Japs. Ask General Chennault and his Flying Tigers. Without those supplies, they're dead."

"Dead, Sir. The mission is worth it."

"You got it. Those C-46s and 47s are workhorses. They are heavy and can take the turbulence from the mountain updrafts better than most planes. But updrafts from fifteen-thousand-foot mountains are difficult for any pilot in any airplane. And they do it with no radio navigation aids. Do you grasp the difficulty, Corporal?"

"I believe I do, Sir."

"Then they must safely land those birds in monsoons. You ever been in a monsoon, Corporal?"

"Not yet, Sir. But I am sure I will have the pleasure."

"Those planes have another disadvantage." He paced left then right.

I began to wish I had stayed in Florida to teach judo and knife-fighting skills.

"Because they are so heavy, they cannot maneuver well when under attack. Our gunners, along with escort fighter pilots, engage and destroy those Japanese Zeros, but they are not able to get all of them. And sometimes they get us."

He paused and looked down. An unusual display of Army humanity. "I hate the term, but that, along with flying in extreme wind and weather, is why some call our planes 'flying coffins.'"

I was impressed. A little skeptical. More fearful than anything else. "So the radio gunners can talk to each other in flight, but have no navigation help from the ground? Sir, how do they find their way?"

"They do it the old-fashioned way. They follow the rivers and get to know the mountains and the valleys. And they keep one eye on the lookout for enemy planes. Up until we arrived, Assam had no airfields. The US built those bases. This is important, Wood. It's the first test for the new Army Transport Command. But only two-thirds of our planes are serviceable at any time. Part of our problem is the thieves. That's why you are here."

"What's my assignment?"

"When you get to Assam, look for Captain Francis Fleming. He'll be your contact. The next thing you will need to do is to establish credibility. So your cover will be to fly as a radio gunner with one of the planes that supplies our forces in Kunming, Chennault's base. Do the usual. Keep your eyes open; get to know the men and how they occupy their time after duty. See who spends a lot of money, who disappears for long periods, who has secrets."

I had plenty of experience seeing that.

"Bottom line: Tell us who you suspect is in on this sorry affair and then let Captain Fleming know. He and the MPs will take care of it from there. Be careful, though. There are American, British, and Indian troops in Assam. Any or all of them could be involved. And this is not just a problem in Assam. The thefts extend all the way to Kunming."

"I understand, Captain. Just one question: how do I get to Assam? I believe it takes a month to get there by land and river."

"We need you there ASAP, Corporal. Maybe I can find you an elephant to ride."

I did not dare respond to that.

"Just kidding."

The slightest hint of a smile broke into his still-serious expression.

"I will assign a seat for you on the next flight. But you will probably have to sit on top of the bombs to keep them from rolling into the gasoline."

Maybe someone had coached him to lighten up, or maybe the heat had gotten to him. "You are very humorous, Captain. But that might be better than riding elephants and barges."

He smiled. He finally *smiled*.

And I didn't get demoted to private.

"Sir, I have a colleague who is a radio gunner. May he have permission to come along?"

"Not this time, Corporal. Too many Jap Zeros and not enough of our planes and crews to risk losing even one."

Jimmy would have to find his own way into the air war.

FAMILY
PHOTO
ALBUM

LK ready to serve his country

So many stories
to tell

Elephants
were common
transportation
while stationed
there

LK often spoke about
wanting to live in
India after the war
ended

Life lessons
learned

Buddies
depending
on each
other

Hunting for
dinner

Locals were
also personal
assistants

Yours truly
in front of
Taj Mahal,
Agra, India

Involved in
bringing
supplies to
the Flying
Tigers

It was
common
for young
children
to market
items in the
streets

LK with one
of his best
buds

India was filled with mystic and fascination

The temperature over 110 °F by day and fell low at night

LK loved his brown
wavy hair.
(In his later years he
still saw his hair this
way in the mirror)

LK's father who was a
homestead farmer

Rare photo, LK with
both of his parents

Learning to walk at a premature
age resulted in bowed legs

Always contemplating

LK with former wife Shirley

Vacationing with the kids

LK always remained close
to his sister, Millie

LK vowed to buy
the orphanage to
tear it down

LK with his son and
family pet

LK's father passed from a
case of pleurisy

LK's girls visiting Santa Claus

All of his kids together

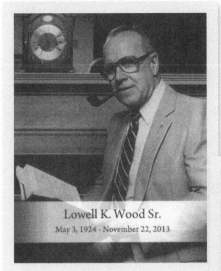

Lowell K. Wood Sr.
May 3, 1924 - November 22, 2013

Business

Very distinguished

His word was his bond

Real Estate office
on Gravois

He worked multiple jobs as he grew
his Real Estate Co.

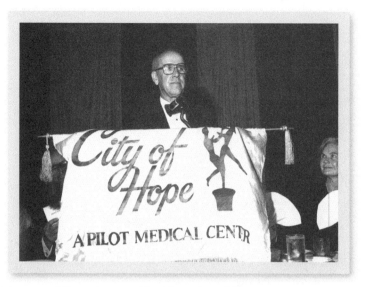

LK was honored for his many achievements...

...throughout his
business career

His years as Real Estate
Commissioner

LK was very active in the political arena

Serving on many types of Committees and Boards in St. Louis

Taking Patty under his wing, taught her and called her his Protégé

LK was known for wearing bow ties throughout his career

After moving to Naples LK was able to take a much more relaxed look at life

Being so involved in the
Gateway Arch...

...he finally made it up
on July 7th, 2013

Being a kid magnet
was another one of
his special qualities.
Granddaughter
& Great
Granddaughters

Dinner with friends from Pakistan, Naples FL

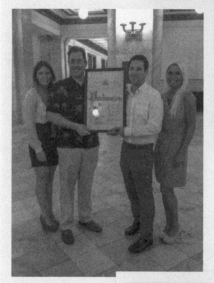

LK Wood Sr. Day in City of St. Louis, May 3, 2014 Proclamation signed by Mayor Francis Slay

10th Wedding Anniversary, Family gathering, July 7, 2010. Ritz Carlton, St. Louis

On the Allure of the Seas cruise ship, 2012

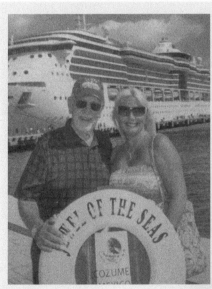

Last cruise taken May
2013. A week of Birthday
Celebration. LK's Birthday

Wedding Day July 7, 2000.
Paris Hotel in
Las Vegas, NV

Another Day in
Paradise, Naples
Beach

Always the life of the party–
"Mayor" of the Savoy

LK on the golf course
wearing his favorite hat

Chapter Thirty
TIME TO BATTLE

Captain Vilani kept his word. The very next day I received orders to report to Dum Dum Airport in Calcutta. The Army liked to control every aspect of a soldier's life, yet they adopted the strangest-sounding local names. This one sounded like part of a children's circus. A private picked me up in Captain Vilani's jeep and said we would have a brief stay in Agra, then proceed to Assam.

When we arrived at the airport, I could not believe what I saw. Definitely not a circus. Along the sides of the airfield were parked planes in various states of repair—or rather, disrepair. The planes took a heavy toll from the air war, and getting spare parts through the Calcutta port proved very difficult.

At the far end of the runway stood a C-47 with engines running. The private dropped me off just as the door shut. I waved my arms wildly in the direction of the cockpit and noticed an insignia I recognized: CBI command. Above that was painted "Uncle Joe's Chariot." The pilot ignored me at first. Guess he didn't want to hold up the flight for a lowly corporal. But then the door suddenly opened, and I ran up the extended stairway.

A middle-aged soldier stood at the door, his campaign hat in hand and no insignia at all on his uniform. The others, strapped into their seats, stared at me with raised eyebrows. The soldier at the door extended his hand to pull me in.

"Double speed, Corporal. This bird needs to fly."

Someone from the cockpit said, "General, you both need to take your seats right now, Sir."

"All right, everybody. Take your seats. Don't want to give those Jap Zeros any more of a target than necessary."

I took a seat by myself near the tail of the plane, surrounded by war supplies. I closed my eyes and prayed. At least I went through the silent ritual. I suppose I would have had to believe in God to genuinely do that. I could imagine an atheist in a foxhole, but I could not imagine an atheist in a flying coffin.

The C-47 lumbered, then thundered, down the runway, roaring and rattling as it heaved itself into the air. Once it reached its altitude, the weight of the plane made for a fairly smooth ride. At this point General Stillwell got out of his seat and made his way past other soldiers and supplies to sit next to me. No pretense about the man, though I did hear he didn't suffer fools gladly.

"I thought I saw you praying when we took off. So was I. It's all right to be scared, corporal. Only the psychotic ones are not afraid. The rest of us just deal with it."

"I guess I will deal with it, Sir. I'm a radio gunner, and I'm curious about what I should look watch out for when flying into China."

"Corporal, curiosity is good. Helps you know your enemy and your friends—who you can count on."

"Sir, I heard the Chinese soldiers we're supplying cannot be trusted, that they will turn and run once a fight begins."

"Up to this point the Chinese infantry has been poorly led, but the fighting men themselves have great courage. I fought to bring a few thousand Chinese infantrymen under my command, and I have found them to be excellent fighters, fearless in battle."

I could not believe a general had purposely come just to sit and talk with me.

"Some months back, I was flying from Assam to Kunming with some high-ranking Chinese officers and soldiers assigned to protect them. We were fifty miles from Kunming, and their top officer and I had been discussing the valor of his men. To prove the courage of his fighters, he asked that the jump door be opened. Then he ordered two of his men to jump out the open door. I thought he was just testing them, and he only told them once. Then the two Chinese soldiers jumped from that airplane, with no parachutes."

My breath caught.

"Disgusting." His face grew red, and the muscles on the side of his face twitched. "But no one can tell me Chinese soldiers aren't brave."

That was a bit beyond my level.

"When we got to Kunming, I tried to have that general jailed, but the Chinese felt they needed every officer they could muster. I'd have shot him myself if I'd had the chance."

We were getting close to Agra. The general got up to return to his seat, his face still red with anger. As he sat down and strapped himself in, I made a mental note not to get into an airplane with any Chinese generals.

Just then the pilot radioed back to us, "Five Zeros approaching from the east."

The pilot brought the C-47 down close to the ground and opened the throttle to full speed. I heard what seemed in my mind to be a tree brush along the plane's fuselage. Then we rose steeply and banked right. We would have been thrown out of our seats if we weren't strapped in. From the cockpit we heard, "Good job flying between those trees."

Then came the *rat-a-tat-tat* of a machine gun. Bullets hit the shell of our aircraft. In a hard bank left, anything not tied down crashed across the fuselage.

"Dear God, get me out of this, and I will make it worth Your while." Some men yelled prayers, others yelled curses.

Another roll right, and I found myself hanging by my straps out of my seat. Someone on the left side lost his lunch—all over the guys on the right.

A cheer rose from the cockpit. "P-40 Warhawks! Three coming from the west."

I wished I could see the fight going on outside. Our lives hung on the bravery and skill of the three American fighter pilots. "O God, give them good aim."

Our cargo plane leveled out. No more twists. No more bullets. All we wanted to hear now were the updates of the dogfight.

"Another Zero down. Middle Warhawk got him from above. Three-on-three now. Zero's turning on the middle Warhawk. Wait! Other Warhawk shot his wing off. That son-of-a-bitch is done. Other two Zeros keep circling—Nooo! Warhawk hit, diving. A ball of fire."

Then they were out of sight.

We rode in deathly silence the rest of the way.

Agra lay ahead. The antiaircraft there would provide us cover. Some might have called the landing on the improvised airfield rough; to me it was the best landing of an airplane I could ever imagine.

Chapter Thirty-One
OUR ASSIGNMENT

My first mistake in Assam State was thinking it'd be easy to find Francis Fleming, the captain in Chabua and my contact. I started in the area of the officers' tents. A lieutenant sat on a tree stump cleaning his Smith & Wesson .38 Special in the flickering light of a dying campfire.

"Lieutenant, I have been asked to report to Captain Fleming."

The lieutenant kept cleaning his gun without so much as looking at me. He hummed a tune I didn't know. As I got closer, I could see he was chewing something, tobacco I presumed. Ever so often he spit into a nearby bucket.

"Excuse me, Lieutenant?" I tried again. "I have been commanded to speak to Captain Fleming. Do you know where he is, Sir?"

"What's that? Who are you, and what are you doing interrupting my meditation time?"

"Sorry, Sir. I didn't realize."

"It's all right, corporal. I have been given some of the finest betel nuts anywhere in India. Natives pick them off the areca palm trees. They stimulate me and help me focus when I meditate. This pack cost me more than I should have paid because I'm *not* a native. You're new here. We don't have much alcohol, but wrap these nuts in betel leaves and chew them. They'll make you happy through and through. Besides, they kill worms in your gut. And they make you feel more alive."

"Yes, Sir. I need to find Captain Fleming."

Bleary eyed, he said, "You might try the Burmese fortuneteller's basha. The captain tries to find any advantage he can. I'm not supposed to tell anyone, so . . ." He wagged his finger at me.

I nodded. This was weirder than anything I'd ever seen in the Army.

"Tomorrow he flies out on a mission." The lieutenant focused on the gun in his hands while humming with the drug in his veins.

"Thank you, lieutenant. Where is the fortuneteller's basha?"

"That way." He waved with his right arm. "Just outside the post. Painted sign of a guru in a turban. Long white beard. Okay, now can you leave?"

I acquiesced to the officer's urgent wish and found the sign with the picture of the guru.

Under it was the *basha,* an old, brown, military issue tent surrounded by branches from agaru trees I'd been told about. The tent door was open, and a sweet smell emanated from a white haze drifting out from the darkness. I looked inside. The only light came from smoldering agaru branches. The smell reminded me of the incense at Our Lady of Sorrows in St. Louis.

"Anyone here?"

A petite woman who appeared to be about sixty years old emerged from the darkness in a green-and-yellow sari. . Her matted and straggly hair heightened the fire in her eyes.

In a high-pitched and gravelly voice, she asked, "How can I help you?"

Was that crazy lieutenant playing with me?

She narrowed her eyes and hunched forward. "You want to know something, something about your time in this war. . . . But I have more to tell."

"I'm looking for Captain Fleming."

"He left. Short time ago. Come in. I help you."

Why not see what the fortuneteller had to say?

We sat on a rug near the burning Agaru branches. She took both my hands in hers, palms up, and closed her eyes.

"You have come from far away."

No kidding. Why am I doing this?

"You have a secret you cannot share, a secret that will bring you much unhappiness."

Forget the secret. Will I get home alive?

She swayed back and forth. The white incense swirled around her as she moved, something I'm sure she practiced to set the scene. The agaru branches that had been slowly burning now came alive, throwing dark shadows on the smoky walls of the hut.

"As you lived for some time in an institution, you will die in an institution."

"Most people die in hospitals." But how did she know the first part?

"There is more."

I didn't want to know any more. I pulled my hands away. "That's enough." I threw a few coins at her and got out of there. I now began to dread my future in this place, where, if there was a God, He hid Himself.

Every direction I turned, I saw only darkness here.

Chapter Thirty-Two
STOLEN BULLETS

With a stomach empty enough to reasonably enjoy whatever the Army cook came up with, I thought I'd try to find the captain at the mess hall.

The Flying Tigers had been wreaking havoc on the Japanese. The American pilots' bravery in the face of superior Japanese fighter planes and bombers became an inspiration to millions of people back home. So, for the last year, Japanese bombers had been raiding British and American airfields in India. Most of those attacks had been directed at any base of the Flying Tigers. Thus no lights were allowed to show from the ground. Darkness hung everywhere.

Since we were now executing bombing runs around the clock, the Chabua Airfield operated twenty-four hours a day. Even in the black night, a steady stream of British and American servicemen flowed in and out. I followed this informal parade along a winding path, and an American sergeant directed me to the mess hall.

The "hall" was a rough wooden roof, walled by branches and palm leaves. I felt weary, dirty, hungry—and anxious because of the fortuneteller's prophecy.

No one else was eating there, but someone sat alone at the far end of the hall. A group of soldiers sat at another table, playing cards. No officers' or enlisted men's mess here. All soldiers, all equals. Living where you knew that any day you could die served as a strange equalizer. We called it the "democracy of death."

I interrupted the card players. "Excuse me, gentlemen. I'm looking for Captain Fleming."

One of the soldiers nodded in the direction of the solitary figure at the far end. Black mustache, thin as a rail, the man was reading some documents by the light of a kerosene lamp and smoking a well-worn pipe. I figured him to be about thirty years old. He looked up from the papers, over the rim of his glasses, straight at me. "You're new. You just get here? Must be important for you to want to talk to me so soon after arriving, and I'm guessing you haven't had anything to eat. Let's find you some food and a place where we can talk."

Captain Fleming went around to a dark room in the rear and reappeared with a sergeant in an apron.

"He'll bring you a plate of today's dish, some local fowl I hope is chicken, along with some beans. Let's sit over in that corner."

He brought his lantern and papers over, and we sat. It strangely occurred to me that, unlike most other places I'd been at night, I heard no crickets here. It felt like a place of pervasive death.

"Who are you?"

"Corporal Lowell Wood, captain. I was trained as a radio gunner, and then got involved with something more. It's that *something more* I am to talk to you about."

Fleming just stared at me, sizing me up. Would trust me? His grizzled face looked at once cautious and interested.

"Go ahead, soldier. I'm listening." His pipe had gone out; he relit it.

"It seems there are problems in Kunming, Sir. Supplies going missing."

"Corporal, I am well aware of that problem. Is that why they sent you?"

"All Captain Vilani said was to contact you. Did you not know I was coming?"

"If you haven't noticed, there is a war going on here. We aren't at Camp Anza anymore. Not everything gets communicated in a timely manner."

The cook brought a plate of food to our table. Captain Fleming motioned for me to eat. The so-called "fowl" was tough and smelled like old socks. My hunger let me eat every bite of it.

The captain glanced back and forth. "Things are always getting misplaced or stolen. With so much movement of supplies, one could hardly think otherwise. But what's happening in Kunming is different."

He had my attention. I added some salt.

"So much goes missing on a weekly basis that there's got to be an organized effort going on. Just two days ago there was an attack on our forces in Kunming. A squadron of Japanese bombers dropped five-hundred-pound bombs on and around the airbase." He leveled his gaze at me. "In trying to repel them, one of our guns ran out of .50 caliber bullets because two boxes of bullets that were *supposed* to be full were *empty*."

My eyes narrowed, and I began to perspire more than I had before. "Whoever stole those bullets should be shot."

"They will be when we catch them. Tomorrow I fly a C-47 over The Hump to bring supplies to Kunming. Since you're here, I'll take you as my radioman. My regular radioman needs a rest anyway. Jap pilots generally stay away from the northern Himalayas. Too turbulent. But you never know."

"What happens after we get to Kunming?"

"I'll find another radio man to return with me while you stay in Kunming until we uncover the traitors. They might as well be Jap soldiers. That's how much they harm our efforts."

Something moved outside. I stood up to look. Before I could stop him a monkey reached through the window and grabbed the plate, spilling what was left of my food on the floor. I pulled out my pistol, but the captain grabbed my arm.

"Don't! The monkeys are held in high regard in this part of the world. You could shoot a human being and be in less trouble."

This place seemed crazier all the time. Monkeys more important than people. Soldiers stealing ammunition and endangering the lives of their buddies.

I put my gun back. "I'm going to get some sleep. What time do we take off for Kunming?"

"The shipment is being loaded now. We leave in six hours, at 0200. We fly The Lady L, a C-47 named after my wife, Lynn Marie. She has a reputation for never giving up."

"Captain, why so early? I thought I could get some rest tonight."

"Talk to General Hardin. He's ordered us to fly around the clock to keep the supplies moving. Last month he even had the heaters removed from our planes to save weight so we could carry more ammunition. Hope you have something warm to wear. If not, you'll find a pile of warm clothes in the office by the runway. Flying in that plane with no heater will feel like ice fishing in Minnesota in February."

"From the jungles of India to the North Pole in one night!"

"One more thing. Trust no one."

"I understand." Oh, did I understand.

"See you at 0200." The captain left with his papers and lantern.

As I got up, I saw a figure outside the window shooing away the monkey. I wondered if he had been there the whole time and heard our conversation. Before I could get outside, he vanished.

Chapter Thirty-Three
OVER THE HUMP

Two A.M. on a warm night in May 1943. About to fly my first combat mission. Excitement. Terror.

And pouring rain.

I stood beside the plane with the captain, his copilot, and navigator, as Captain Fleming covered one more base. Though he'd consulted the fortuneteller yesterday—the one in her sixties, whom I now found was in her thirties—tonight he'd arranged for the chaplain to pray with us. I had no objection. "Hail Mary, full of grace, the Lord is with thee . . ." He prayed that same Lord would be with us.

And not just because of the weather or the enemy.

Flying the C-47 Commander, anywhere, ranked among the most dangerous flying in the world. The war effort needed the planes badly and so rushed them into action. Testing occurred on flights from the factory to the war zone and during real-time action. One thing the testers discovered: because of an electrical glitch, the first generation of this plane's engines tended to fail at the most inappropriate times. Oh, joy.

"Everybody strapped in?" The captain and copilot completed the last of their checklist. The navigator double- and triple-checked his instruments. We would get no external navigational help once we got into the Himalayas. I made sure the radio functioned, ready to go. The captain, maybe trying to take our minds off what lay ahead, continued his calm conversation.

"Today we are bringing not just ammunition, spare motors, and gasoline, but also two jeeps to our fighting boys. Make sure they are strapped tight, no space for joyrides. Let's get this Dumbo into the air."

Without lights, it took great skill and just as much courage to get us into the black night. Plowing through the water on the runway, the C-47 shuddered and whined its way into the air. The whole crew held its breath, and when we all exhaled, the air pressure in the plane seemed to double.

During the ascent, I felt exhilarated, not because of the ride or the danger, but because finally I would make a real contribution. This was why I had left Jonesville. I knew deep down that it wasn't for adventure or money that I had joined the Army. I wanted to do something valuable.

The flight time from Chabua to Kunming was two hours, a treacherous two hours. I would now experience the famed updrafts, maybe even a storm. Or enemy planes. The presence of Japanese airfields in Burma forced us to fly northeast, over the highest mountains and through the roughest weather, then back southeast to Kunming. We hoped the Japanese would all be sleeping. We hoped they wouldn't feel the urge of bees drawn to a defenseless flower, our transport plane.

As we flew higher and higher, I felt the chill more. When we headed over the Himalayas, I could only hope the mountains had enough snow for the captain to see them in the dark. Without a heater in the C-47, it got so cold that the copilot had to scrape frost from the windshields.

At twenty thousand feet, the plane began to shake and turn side to side, like one of those horses I used to break for Mr. Tillman.

"Hold on everybody," the captain said. "This will only last a few more miles, until we get past the mountain ranges." But to me it seemed like forever. At this point, we had no navigational aids from the ground. If we went down, we would probably never be found.

Finally the shaking stopped. We'd gotten over the Hump.

But now we entered the prime location for Japanese Zeros to find us. I kept my ears pressed to my earphones listening for any chatter sounding like a Japanese fighter pilot. Thankfully, I heard none.

We had almost reached Kunming when the first signs of trouble started.

Both engines of the C-47 began cutting off and then coming back on. This did not inspire the confidence of anyone on board.

"Well, it seems like we may have another bit of information to give to the Army Air Corps about the functioning of this aircraft," said the captain. "Maybe the next edition will be better. Everyone grab a parachute and be prepared to abandon the plane if this gets any worse."

And it did get worse.

Both engines stalled again, and this time they weren't quick to come back on. We were not far from the Kunming airfield. But we were beyond the range in which we could glide to a landing.

The engines completely stopped.

The only sounds were the wind against the plane and the horrible clicking of engines that wouldn't start.

"I am ordering you all to bail out. Now!"

As I secured my parachute, my heart seized up. Something seemed strange. Wrong. The backpack I'd been handed felt wrong.

I opened the pack. No nylon. No parachute. Just a bunch of rags.

The navigator and the copilot left the plane. From the open door I watched the navigator's chute open, but the co-pilot was falling like a missile. No!

The captain was half out of his seat. "I said bail out!"

"Not able to, Sir. The nylon in my chute is missing."

"What? Hang on." He checked his own and gasped. "If you know any prayers, now is the time."

I strapped myself into my seat and prayed, thankful for the prayer I learned at Shirley's church: "Our Father which art in heaven, hallowed be Thy—"

185

Sudden drop.

"Name. Thy—"

Bang! Bang! Didn't know where that came from.

"Kingdom come—" Forgot the rest.

Almost at tree level.

Captain Fleming had slowed the plane as much as he could while still keeping us level. And above the trees. But not for long.

Then the right engine decided to power back on.

I remembered. "Thy will be done on earth . . . um . . . as it is in heaven."

"Trying to pull her back up!" Fleming was incredible. Then the damnable thing stalled again.

This time we went down. The plane clipped a thicket of palm trees, spun, and crashed in a mind-shattering, thunderous cataclysm.

Then stillness.

I sat stunned, facing up. It occurred to me that now might be a good time to exit the aircraft. The plane was tipped up on its port side.

I climbed out of the seat and scrambled to see how the captain was.

"Captain, get up! Captain? We have to get out!"

He didn't move. My heart sank. With the cockpit smashed in, he was probably dead.

Chapter Thirty-Four
PRIVATE HASEMOTO

I pulled myself through the gaping hole that had been the door, careful not to slice my hand wide open on the shredded metal. The top of the fuselage leaned backward against a tall red maple tree. Both wings were partially broken off, the one below me planted in the ground, the one above me reaching up like an arm partly severed. At least nothing caught fire yet.

I climbed out and perched on the fuselage. Then I started to climb down the tree on the side away from the plane. But I found no branch close enough to hold or step on. I finally noticed my body shaking. I sat for a moment, and the shock set in. I was in no shape for tree climbing or descending. I felt helpless, now lying on the fuselage, like bait for vultures. Or easy target practice for enemy soldiers.

By the time I felt ready to shimmy down, the gray light of predawn started to bring the forest around me to life. Birds called—lots of birds, ones I'd never heard before. It reminded me of the morning I woke up under the big tree at the hobo camp after running away from the Bogue Home.

Something else. Footsteps and thwacking. Five or more were making their way through the forest below, coming toward the aircraft.

Fear is a strange thing. Sometimes you want to shout, but the sound gets trapped in your throat. I stayed as still as I could, a duck in a shooting gallery. My ears strained to pick up any hint of who the men below me could be. Japanese? Chinese?

One of the soldiers yelled, "Captain Porter, we've got a survivor." Below the tree stood an American soldier pointing straight at me.

"What are you doing up there, buddy? How about coming down and joining the rest of us?" With that, the man below climbed up the tree.

It shocked me to see that even though he spoke like an American, he looked Japanese. The surprise on my face would have been apparent to him.

"Private Hasemoto at your service!"

He fashioned a lasso out of a rope he carried and lowered me down. I was so happy, I could have cried.

All the airmen had heard of Captain John "Blackie" Porter and his team that rescued flyers, among other expeditions. Now I got to meet them. Porter was unique in his willingness to accept a Japanese-American as a part of his team. Most of the Japanese-Americans fought for the U.S. in Europe. John Hasemoto, an American of Japanese descent, came from Hawaii, and his father's family had lived in Hawaii for many years. His mother was Chinese. Hasemoto proved a valuable recruit to the group because he could speak Chinese and Japanese.

I gave thanks that Americans had found me.

When we were far enough from the leaking gasoline, Porter pulled me aside.

"We heard your plane go down, literally. Not sure we can reclaim all the supplies you brought, but we will try. Those jeeps would sure come in handy. Anyone else with you?"

I pointed at the cockpit. But Hasemoto and two other guys knelt on the fuselage, already tying the captain to a stretcher. There had been no fire, but gasoline leaked out of the lower side of the aircraft. These men cared more about us than whether we all blew up. Hopefully no one would be dumb enough to light up a smoke.

Captain Porter shouted, "What's the status?"

"It's Captain Fleming. He's alive, barely. Bad head wound."

I sighed. "Thank God. I thought he was dead, or I wouldn't have left him."

Still looking up, Porter said, "Where are the other crewmen?"

"When the engines began to fail, Captain Fleming ordered us to put on our parachutes. The copilot and navigator jumped from the plane. But my chute felt funny. It was lumpy. I opened it to check and found a bunch of rags stuffed in the pack. I watched the parachute of the navigator open, but copilot's chute never deployed."

"Damn thieves. They steal the nylon from American parachutes and sell it to be made into shirts. Some of the old Chinese parachutes are even more valuable to them. Those chutes are silk."

I boiled with rage. "Nooo! Those bloody devils! To let men die—for what? A few dollars? It's inhuman. Who would do something like that?"

"They say there's an agreement between American soldiers and a Chinese criminal gang. But no one has been able to catch them."

Whatever I did next in the war would all be to find the people responsible for robbing American soldiers, not just of food or ammunition, but of their lives. For the first time, I gave thanks for having been recruited for undercover work. Up to now it had been a job. Now it became a calling.

"I have to get to Kunming."

"No problem, Corporal. We have a truck about a half-mile from here. Two of my men will get you and the captain to the infirmary. Later we'll bring a crew to salvage everything we can from the plane. Right now we have to find the navigator and the body of the copilot."

A Dodge D-15 truck got us to Kunming over roads with potholes the size of bathtubs. Captain Porter, Hasemoto, and one other set out on foot to find the Lady L's navigator before the Japanese did. Their hunt cleared space in the truck for Captain Fleming and me. I sat next to him in the back of the truck. His head was all bandaged up.

Captain Fleming was starting to wake up. "Wood? What happened? Where are we?"

"We crashed, Captain. Blackie Porter's guys found us. They're taking us to Kunming. You'll be okay once we get there."

"What about the other two? What happened to them?"

"I'll explain when we get to Kunming. Try and stay quiet now."

Fleming motioned me closer. In a tired, low voice he gave me more orders. "Wood, when we get to Kunming, find Major John Lefkowitz . . . He goes back and forth to our airbase in Chengdu . . . If you leave a message for him in the motor pool, he'll find you. He knows you are coming."

I wondered who else knew. It seemed strange to me that two engines of the C-47 would go dead at the same time. Maybe I was just imagining things. Maybe not.

Chapter Thirty-Five
KUNMING

We passed through Kunming and rumbled on to the American base beyond it to the south. This air base in China was ramping up for a major effort to drive the Japanese out of China. We had lost the east of China, but from the looks of the buildup here, I started to believe that the war could actually turn and have us on our way to Tokyo.

Chinese, Indian, British, and American soldiers were everywhere. We had to slowly make our way through the stop-and-go traffic and early morning pedestrian crowds. Oxen pulled wagons, people pushed wheelbarrows, and dog carcasses hanging on street-side butcher stands. This was not Jonesville.

At last the truck driver dropped us off at the base infirmary. Captain Fleming, more alert now, stayed at the hospital. After a brief examination, they released me. I headed straight for the motor pool.

"I'm to report to a Major Lefkowitz."

The lanky private working on the engine of a mud-spattered jeep nodded his head in the direction of an officer with his back to us leaning over a desk.

"Major Lefkowitz, Corporal Wood reporting as commanded."

He stood, a very big man, and turned to me. "Not to be rude, but, what took you so long? And where is Fleming?"

"Plane went down just north of Kunming. Both engines stopped working. The navigator and copilot parachuted from the plane. Only the navigator's parachute opened." I explained about my chute and that Captain Fleming was now in the base hospital. Lefkowitz listened closely.

"Let's go someplace where we can talk, Corporal."

The major led me to a small office in a nearby building and closed the door. Lefkowitz spoke in a slow snarl, his right hand continually working to smooth the hairs on the back of his neck.

"We are facing something dangerous here. A monumental amount of supplies are coming into Kunming and Chengdu, but they are not all the supplies that are being sent from Calcutta. Penicillin and sulfur get diverted somewhere along the way. Bullets too."

"And parachutes."

"Yes, that does happen, but it's small scale."

"So it doesn't matter?"

"No, what I mean is the captain may have been targeted. You too, possibly. But I don't know."

I could easily believe any or all of that.

"You have to be careful, but people here probably won't suspect you. You can go between Kunming and the air base in Chengdu without raising questions. You're an Army Air Corps radio gunner, and everyone knows we need radiomen. So you shouldn't attract attention. I'll get you an assignment in Communications as a radio operator."

"Yes, Sir."

"So nose around. Make friends." He raised a warning finger. "But be careful. If they find out who you are, your life won't be worth much."

He paused and let that sink in.

It sank in.

"There is too much money to be made on the black market for them to let anyone get in their way."

"I will be careful. I'm not stupid." I could only say that because he didn't know my past.

"Wood, I read your record. You started out in the military as an idiot."

I grimaced and kept the mouth shut.

"But you seem to have calmed down."

Hope! "You don't have to worry about me, Major. I can do my job."

"Then do it. But be careful whom you trust."

"Yes. That's what Captain Fleming said."

"Get some rest in the enlisted men's barracks. The sergeant there will tell you where to report next."

The next morning after a hasty breakfast, I wasted no time finding the sergeant who would give me my assignment.

"You're a radioman, Wood? Good thing you're here. We are ramping up operations. Planes and soldiers coming every hour. Busy place. Your orders are to report to the communications building next to the camp entrance. Maybe you saw it when you came in yesterday."

"No, Sergeant. My captain and I were in the back of a truck. Didn't see any buildings until we stopped at the hospital. He's still there."

"I see."

"When do I start?"

"We need you there now, Corporal. It'll take you fifteen minutes to walk there."

So many soldiers. So many jeeps and trucks. This place was crazy. It felt good to walk, though. As I got closer to the gate, I saw the sign for the communications building, but what I saw next almost made me jump out of my boots.

Walking towards me from the building came a figure who looked a lot like Jimmy Riley. That orange hair made him stand out. He had a big grin on his face.

"Woody! We just heard that a Lowell Wood was being assigned here. I can't believe it. My desk is by the window, so when I saw you coming I could have died."

"Impossible. You can't be here. I left you in Calcutta."

"You did, you dirty scoundrel."

"I asked them to send you with me."

"But you're just an enlisted guy."

"And I almost died getting here. That's another story. How did you get here?"

"Instead of taking a train and barge to Assam, I was ordered to fly here with some B-24s that were coming from Calcutta straight to Chengdu to prepare for bombing runs farther east. They needed a radio gunner for protection. When I got here, though, the captain of the B-24 got me reassigned. Let's just say we didn't get along."

I couldn't believe it. My best friend in the military assigned to the same duty station. "So Kunming seems like the nerve center for driving Tojo out of China."

"At least the ears and vocal chords. We help coordinate the shipment of war material all along this battle line. Come on in, and I'll introduce you to the folks inside. Even some females, Woody. Outside of the hospital where the nurses are, this is the best place to meet dames."

"Are you kidding me? What can women do in this place?"

"They send Morse code messages and work the cryptograph machines. This one gal, Genevieve—her father is British, her mother Indian—she's the best soldier we have at breaking codes. The women do as well as any of the men. You'll love this assignment."

Just then, the loud wailing of the air raid sirens broke in. Everyone made their way to the basement. What a welcome party. Reminded me of my welcome when I first arrived in Jonesville.

As committed as we were to expanding our presence, the Japanese were committed to ending it. Their bombers regularly braved the fierce .50 caliber machine guns of our Flying Tigers' P-40 Warhawks and almost always lost. But at least one bomber must have made it through. The bombs started to fall.

"Jimmy, how often does this happen?"

"I'm told the sirens go off every day. Sometimes one of them gets through, but less and less. Lately our P-40s have been able to intercept most of them and drive them away before they get to us."

The sounds of antiaircraft guns and the sirens terrified me. I physically felt fear creep from the back of my neck down my spine, through my legs, to my toenails. The hairs on my arms stood straight up, as if they too prepared to run. This was more frightening than that California earthquake. Far more.

We heard the dull thud of bombs cratering our airfield. Thankfully, none reached the buildings this time.

When the explosions quieted and the all-clear horn blared, Jimmy patted my arm. "It's scary, but the Chinese will be up and repairing the runway as soon as we're are all out of this basement. Let's get to work."

Chapter Thirty-Six
A HARD NIGHT

Jimmy showed me around and introduced me to the small group of radio operators. The soldiers in cryptology worked next door, and we rarely saw them during the work day. *After* work might be a different story. Genevieve was quite the looker. Tall, slender with long, dark hair, she turned heads wherever she went. It only took a week before I became a part of the "communications crowd." We spent our Friday nights at our favorite bar in Kunming: the Dragon Lady.

I thought it wise to get to know Private Genevieve better.

"Hey, Genevieve, some of us are going to meet at the Dragon Lady tonight. Jimmy Riley will be there. Why don't you meet us there?"

"Have to work late," she said. "But some of my friends and I could probably be there around 20:00."

"Great. Leave all your secrets at the office." I smiled at my own humor.

Major Lefkowitz, though, had other plans for my Friday night. Late that afternoon he called me into his office at the motor pool.

"Corporal, you're doing your job too well. They want you to stay in communications; but that's not why you're here. We have word someone may break into our supply depot tonight. We've been chronically short of penicillin and sulfur; these supplies are badly needed by our fighting men. I want you to be part of a detail tonight to catch them or kill them, whichever is easiest. They are worse than thieves. They are traitors."

"What time, Sir? I'm supposed to meet some soldiers around 20:00 at the Dragon Lady."

"This won't happen until midnight or later. That's when it has happened before. Meet your friends so no one gets suspicious. Just be careful. You will be with Corporal Schmidt."

"Al? He's undercover too? I never would have known. I thought he was flying P-40 Warhawks."

"He is. But right now we need him to shoot rats."

"So that you won't be recognized by anyone," he continued, "I'll provide you both with British RAF uniforms. Come by my office at 21:30. You'll be well hidden in a shed at the edge of the south runway, since it's right across from the depot. From there you will have an excellent view. The Indian soldiers will be patrolling by the runway. I'll try to alert them beforehand, but I don't trust everyone there. You may have to be creative if you are caught."

The Dragon Lady did a bang-up business serving Chinese beer and pork barbecue to British, American, Chinese, and Indian military personnel. The Chinese locals everywhere happily took advantage of the opportunity of this polyglot military boomtown. Some went too far, like the illicit gangs of Chinese who befriended my targets, the willing accomplices who shed the military of badly needed supplies.

I had to be careful. "Trust no one," my superiors all said.

If only I'd listened.

I noted the lovely Genevieve as she entered the bar. "Hi," I greeted her. "You got here early. It's only 19:00. And who are these beautiful ladies with you?"

"Jimmy Riley rushed us through. We finished early. Jimmy said he had something to take care of, and he'd meet us later. This is Janie,

Laura, and Millie." She pointed at each of them in turn. "They work in cryptography with me. We love Pilsner, and this is the only bar in town that keeps their beer cold. How about if we buy you one?"

Now this was as close to heaven as I had been in a long time. Four good-looking women and me. And they offered to buy me a beer.

"If you insist." What an evening. My first experience of what a harem might feel like.

As time passed, Genevieve leaned closer. The top two buttons on her shirt were undone, and her right hand worked the sweat away from her neck. The other women became interested in three British airmen on the other side of the bar. This left us alone. Why, oh why, did the operation have to fall on this particular night?

"Jimmy says he thinks you are one of those undercover guys."

"Pffft!" Beer sprayed out of my mouth. I laughed. "Really?"

"You don't have to tell us. It's just you're too good looking for that kind of work."

"We'll just let Jimmy think what he wants. More fun that way."

How on earth did he find out?

She sat and looked at me with inscrutable eyes. Made me nervous. Made me think I'd better go.

"Look, I'm having a wonderful evening but I should call it a night. Can I see you tomorrow night?"

"Really? You have to go? Where? What could be more important than our conversation?"

She was in cryptology, sending and receiving secrets, probably top secrets. Obviously I could trust her. Probably she already knew what we had planned.

"We have word someone's going to break into the supply depot tonight. I have to go. But I would like to continue our conversation again soon."

"Maybe. Go do your patriotic duty." She smiled and fluttered her fingers good-bye, then turned away "Bartender! Another Pilsner."

I moped my way back to the motor pool and to Major Lefkowitz. Because the lights were out to protect against enemy air raids, I felt almost like a blind man trying to find my way along the paths, roads, and buildings. The night had no moon, only the faint light of stars.

I hoped no Japanese bombers would test the growing armada of American fighter planes tonight. Besides the possibility of death, an air attack would light up the skies and probably deter the thieves from robbing the supply depot. It might be a long time until we got intelligence about another of their operations.

I found the door to the motor pool unlocked. A dull light shone under the door to Major Lefkowitz's office; the black shades on the motor pool windows kept what little light remained from escaping. I knocked on the major's door.

Two men sat in the dim room—the major and Al Schmidt. Al had already suited up in the British airman's uniform.

"Where have you been, Wood? Never mind. Get into the British uniform. Have you been drinking?"

"Just one beer, Major. I'm fine. What's the plan?"

"Forget the supply depot. We're changing plans."

"What? Uh, Sir?"

"We believe the gang stealing the penicillin may have gotten word of our original plan. However, a truck's been spotted at a warehouse located near the eastern edge of the north runway. The warehouse holds clothing and boots. Those boots fetch a good price on the black market."

I began drawing a map in my mind.

"Next to the north runway, on the same side as the warehouse, is a shed where we keep the large cement rollers. The rollers are there to repair the runways after they're cratered by Japanese bombs. Earlier today, I placed a .50-caliber machine gun in that shed. It's hidden in a cement bag on the bed of a truck. There is a lock on the shed door, and here's the key."

I took the key and hoped it wouldn't be the key to my death.

"Get to the shed, take the machine gun out, and set it up. Wood, you have training with the .50-caliber gun, so you will stay near the shed and prepare yourself to use it if necessary. Schmidt, make your way without being seen to a spot within twenty yards of the warehouse.

There you will find an old wall that is mostly gone after the last round of Japanese bombing. Wait there."

I tried to imagine how this plan would work.

"Al, if you see someone breaking into the depot, set off a flare. Yell to them to halt and tell them to get down on the ground. If they do not halt or do not get down, shoot them. Wood, you're backup. We want them alive to find out who else is involved, but we don't want to lose any more boots. Questions?"

"What about the Indian soldiers?" I asked. "You said you would contact them."

"I only trust the captain who will be in charge tonight. He knows what we are planning and will have his men nearby."

"Okay, Sir. Al, let's go hunting."

Chapter Thirty-Seven
SHOOT TO KILL

Kunming sits at an altitude of six thousand, two hundred and thirty-four feet, more than a mile above sea level. At that altitude, it's perpetually spring during the day, but gets cold at night. Trudging slowly through the dark and the cold, we found the shed, the cement bag, and the Browning M2 machine gun inside. Together we carried the gun outside and set it up by a clump of tall weeds. The .50-caliber machine gun is capable of firing five hundred bullets a minute.

Nothing that gets into its range escapes.

Schmidt crept over broken concrete, darkened puddles of water, and airplane fuel to the crumbling wall.

Then we waited.

We hadn't brought coats with us, figuring they would get in our way if we had to fight. I'd have given anything for a blanket. I wrapped the empty cement bag around my arms and hands to retain at least a little bit of warmth as I sat, focused on the warehouse, with my finger extended alongside the trigger.

We didn't have to wait long.

All of a sudden the flare shot up and Al yelled, "Halt! Drop your weapon! Down on the ground!"

And the shooting began.

The intruder fired a pistol in Schmidt's direction. I opened up with the M2, firing at the sparks of light from the intruder's handgun.

Right at that moment, spotlights lit up the warehouse. Ten or more Indian soldiers rushed toward the fight. In the light, I saw the intruder holding one arm, as if he'd been hit, but continuing to fire. He hit one of the Indian soldiers, who fell back like a Kewpie doll in a circus shooting gallery.

I opened up again with the machine gun, and this time the pistol went quiet. A truck on the other side of the warehouse roared away.

I ran as fast as I could toward Al.

"Al. Are you okay? Al!"

"Yeah, just a flesh wound. But looks like you bought *him* a one way ticket to hell."

"No, Sir," said the Indian. "Not a 'him.' A woman."

I ran to see for myself. From under the hat, beautiful long black hair splayed out.

Genevieve.

I stood panting. Couldn't believe it.

I've heard people talk about their gut "wrenching." In all the times I'd been disappointed, abandoned, and lied to, I had never felt the way I did in that instant.

When I saw blood everywhere on her body, I doubled over. Not because of any love or concern I had for her, but out of some primeval instinct. Tears gushed from my eyes.

The Indian soldier brought me back to the present. "Both of you guys, come with me. She killed our captain. We're taking you both to jail until we can sort this out."

———

They threw Al and me in with a group of rowdy, intoxicated Brits and Americans. One of the Americans had orangish hair.

"Jimmy, what are you doing here?"

"Woody? Hey! I'll tell you if you tell me. Okay?"

His speech was slurred. Stains and dirt covered his uniform. He looked as if he'd been rolling around the street. Caked blood clung to the skin above his right eye.

There was no way I would tell him what had happened and why I'd been brought to a jail by Indian soldiers. Part of me suspected my incarceration to intentional, an order from the major so that Al and I could gather possible information from talk among the prisoners.

"You look like you met up with some pretty mean fellas, Jimmy."

"I just had a little disagreement."

"With whom?"

"Well, that's my secret, and it will just have to stay that way."

"Okay. Must have been ten of them from the way you look."

"Nah, just three. Oh yeah, a woman too. You know her. Sweet Genevieve."

I couldn't get her dead, bloodied body out of my mind. "What about Genevieve?"

"Okay, Wood. Just don't let anyone else know." He leaned close. "We were going to rescue just a tiny bit of penicillin from the good old U-S-of-A Army. But I told her and them—I didn't know who they were—but I told them it was too dangerous. They had to pay me *mooore*. That's when they whacked me! Not fair. Three against one."

"Where are they now?"

"Why? You want to fight them? Yeah, let's go—you and me. We'll take 'em."

"Can't go if we don't know where they are."

"Probably at Dragon Lady. Two Chinese guys. Tall, skinny guys. Mustaches. One guy with a scar on his cheek. Other guy—Hey! I can't tell you this." He shook his head. "Forget it. Let me sleep."

I didn't want to believe what I heard. Whom could I trust?

Apparently not even myself.

I had been warned.

The next morning, an Indian officer came with orders to free all the British airmen. The American and Chinese prisoners remained behind. Because of our British uniforms, they released Al and me.

I headed straight to the motor pool and Major Lefkowitz. By the end of the day, MPs had the two Chinese guys under surveillance. Jimmy Riley got arrested and went to jail. I never did get to talk to him. I sorta wish that I had. Sure, I had played a role in his going to prison, and he deserved it. But we had been together for a long time—strange how in times of war your emotions get all mixed up. Though a criminal, he was one of us. Besides, I would really like to have asked him if he'd been pilfering as far back as Camp Anza—he always seemed to have money, even then.

And then there was Genevieve.

I know I wasn't to blame, but for years I prayed for forgiveness for Genevieve's death. Why did she have to kill the Indian captain? Why? Oh, the tricks war plays on your mind and the strings it pulls in your heart.

I never found an answer. Only more questions.

The Army moved me to other regions of India and China to continue working as a radioman up front and a detective underneath. The pilfering slowed but never completely stopped.

Altogether, my time in India and China was as close to hell on earth as I ever want to go. The trips over The Hump terrified me every time. Uncovering the seedy world of dishonest, thieving human beings—how they could lie, steal and cheat to prosper themselves and leave their buddies defenseless and sometimes dead—never ceased to disgust me. If not for the courage and sacrifice of so many others, I think I would have gone crazy.

The Army prepared me well for the rest of my crazy life. I only wish there had been an easier way to learn. As I made all that silly trouble in Miami, St. Louis, Georgia, Reno, and Anza, I wish I'd known what waited over here.

Those months in India and China are seared into my memory. I saw the depths and the heights of what human beings can do. During my time in the war, the child in me died.

Yet something in me grew out of that death: I came to want to build, not tear down; love and not be afraid; live, not die.

My last assignment came after the end of the war. I had to return to Camp Anza and help close it down. That assignment I enjoyed most of all.

BUILDING AN
EMPIRE

Chapter Thirty-Eight
HOME AND A NEW HOME

When the military discharged me, I discharged myself straight back home. My family celebrated my return, and I was thrilled to see them. Millie and Gordon were doing much better. They made a fuss over me. Little Robert swore he remembered me and had prayed for me every day.

My, how Dick had grown up. I was equally happy to be back in one living piece. My brother and I spent hours together, although I really couldn't, wouldn't, tell him everything that had happened to me in the war. Dick told me all about his dreams. He wanted to become a cross-country truck driver.

Earl and my mother had gotten their own place, and he was out of the mob, which I liked. I stopped by to say hello, but everything still felt so awkward. Deep down, I still resented my mother. Everyone makes mistakes, but it seemed that what she had done caused me more pain than it caused her. Not fair.

Betty and her child still lived in Jonesville. And she had added a new husband to mix. I felt torn. Should I try to see her? What a mess!

One quiet afternoon, I walked over to the house where she stayed—right across the street from her wacky mother's place. I paused. Would she be home? Would her new husband answer the door? What would I say? Without ever knocking, I turned around and briskly walked away.

After the war, central Michigan slowed down and offered few job opportunities. I didn't want to burden Millie, and she and Gordon now seemed to be doing well enough without my help, especially since with the boys working jobs of their own.

In Jonesville people knew me as "that orphan kid," even if they didn't say it aloud. In the Army, I became a different person. I wanted my life to count. I wanted to be somebody. I couldn't go back—not to the Kiddie Brush and Toy factory, not to break any more horses for Mr. Tillman, and not to emcee at The Scarlet Fever.

This short visit showed me I couldn't stay. I needed a new start.

I purposed to never forget or abandon my Michigan family, to send money back to help my mother or Millie or Dick whenever possible. It mattered to me that the family did well, with or without my presence.

Part of me did not want to go. I feared the unknown future.

Except for Shirley Schuelte.

Was Shirley thinking about me, wondering what had happened to the soldier she had met at the USO club? Her mother had written me several times. I think she just wanted to monitor the state of my physical intactness and make sure I retained all my appendages through the war. I'll never know for sure. I never opened her letters.

Which left me needing to go to St. Louis, if for no other reason than to show Mrs. Schuelte I remained intact.

In 1946, St. Louis Union Station represented a gritty intersection of the nation. Soldiers traveling from all corners of the country transited through this most central of Midwest train stations. The congestion caused delays of hours and days. Families, wives, and girlfriends camped out around the cavernous station waiting for their soldiers to return. No one would be camped out for me.

Two hours from St. Louis, my train got delayed at a small station. During the wait, I stared at a telephone booth and wondered. Then I swallowed hard, gathered what nickels I had, and dialed Shirley's home number.

"Schuelte residence," said Shirley's mother. "Whom may I ask is calling?"

"Mrs. Schuelte, this is the guy you wrote all those letters to and who never wrote you back."

"Who? What are you talking about? Wait. Lowell? Is that you?"

"It's me."

"Oh my. Where are you? How are you?"

"I'm coming on a train that should reach St. Louis about one o'clock, maybe. I am out of the Army now and—"

"Get over here! We're all eager to see you. We want to hear about everything. Look for one of us when you get to the St. Louis station. Lowell, this is an answer to our prayers."

Life never failed to bring occurrences I couldn't believe.

Perhaps I had my future.

The train pulled into Union Station around 2 P.M. on March 26, 1946. The time and date are etched in my memory because it was then that my life began—as if being born all over again.

I had exactly one hundred dollars in my shoe, my mustering-out pay from the Army—all the money I had in the world. Where would I live? With all the servicemen coming home, we already had a housing shortage. Where could I find a job? Those same servicemen would all want work to support their families, but many of the factories that supplied war material to the military had shut down. I knew the challenges.

I also knew I could survive and overcome.

From the back of the milling crowd, I heard, "Lowell, Lowell! Is that really you? I've been waiting for over an hour!"

How May found me among all those people I will never know. And what about Shirley?

"Shirley's out with some friends, should be home about four o'clock. Come on, let's go. There's a trolley leaving in ten minutes." She reached for my small duffel bag, in which lay everything I owned in the world.

"Thanks May. I'll carry it. Very kind of you to come get me." A peace offering deserved a peaceful response.

Spring is the most beautiful season in St. Louis. Summer is hot and humid. Fall is a quick change from hot to cold with no chance for the trees to impress everyone with arrays of color like they do in the Northeast. Winter is icy and cold, a poor substitute for snow. But in spring, the labor of the flower and the human who planted it give rewards of brilliant colors that remind me of the sun's energy pulling life from seeming death. In a similar way, I felt my life also re-beginning.

When we arrived at the Schueltes' apartment on Lisette Street, yellow daffodils bloomed all around the red brick apartment house. Mom Schuelte took me into the apartment and blessed me with a meal she had prepared, a good way to cover the wreckage of the past and begin a new relationship.

Shirley's dad, Gus, waited for us in the fastidiously furnished place. No paintings on the wall, just a lot of photos of Shirley. If May could have "high tea" with her sister every afternoon, I figured Gus should have some title that would match her pretensions. So I called him "the Guv."

Pouring me iced tea, May continued her conciliatory attempts. "Lowell, we thought of you every day. I kept looking for your name in the newspapers. I was certain you had won some significant battle or gotten the Medal of Honor. I always felt there were big things in store for you!"

That wasn't how Shirley's goodbye letter went.

"Yeah, I have a few stories to tell, but not any more than other guys who served. It was a real mess. I feel blessed to be back in the greatest country in the world."

Shirley had no idea I had come. I thought of leaving several times, but where would I go? When May said, "Shirley's coming up the walk," I held my breath.

She came through the door, saw me, put her face in her hands, and started to cry. Then she looked at me. "Forgive me." That's all she had to say.

I took her hand in mine, looked into her eyes and said, "I'm back for good, Shirley. I don't know what's ahead, but I would like it to be with you." I put my arms around her. I thought I saw a tear on the Guv's cheek. Mom Schuelte had a steadier look. The Guv pulled his wife away and into the kitchen. We were alone.

Shirley kept looking at me as if she couldn't believe I was actually there. Then she took my face in her hands and kissed me. "Lowell, I promise I will never leave you again."

Wow. A whole family that wanted me and didn't ask me to support them! I don't think I'd had a happier moment in my entire life.

"Shirley, we start over today. There is a lot I want to tell you, and I'd like to know what you've been doing while I was gone. I know I can find a job. Right now, though, I have no place to stay."

The Guv called from his listening post the kitchen. "There's a rooming house on Forest Park Avenue, near Kings Highway. Rent is reasonable, and it's near the bus and trolley stops. I'll drive you there."

Chapter Thirty-Nine
ON OUR WAY

The rooming house wasn't so bad. The only thing I questioned was the clientele. Women stayed in most of the rooms, single women, or at least they seemed to live alone, some of the time. Most of them slept during the day and worked at night. Usually they left me alone, but not always.

"Hi sweetie, whatcha doin'? Wanna come inside?" I didn't stay in that place long.

I needed to find a job, preferably more than one. If I could make enough money, I'd find a better place to live and save for my wedding. The *Post-Dispatch* newspaper ran several classified ads for tool-and-die makers, and I got hired by the first company to which I applied.

"Shirley, I got a job! I'll be working for the Adler Tool and Die Company. Pay's not bad, and I saw another ad for late-night bakery workers. We're on our way."

"Really, Lowell? Mother won't be too impressed. She has big plans for us. But it's just a first job, you have to start somewhere. Mother is planning a big wedding, Lowell. You'll love it."

I got that second job too, as a "bun popper" at the Freund Bakery, taking the buns from the hot-coal ovens and maneuvering them onto metal trays to cool and be wrapped. I didn't get a lot of time between jobs, so some nights my dinner was spaghetti I ate right out of the can.

I didn't mind the pay, but Shirley was right. Mom Schuelte thought it was beneath her dignity to have a tool-and-die-making bun popper as her prospective son-in-law.

"Lowell, factory work is good for some people, but my daughter deserves more. You were meant to do something else, some executive job." I knew she meant well, but her words made me feel small. She had felt the same way about the Guv, and he managed to live with it. Maybe I could learn from him.

The Guv loved selling, and he was a natural. For a long time, he had sold paper for the Skinner Paper Company. But May insisted he take a "proper" job, and when Skinner offered him an executive position, he told me he stupidly took it though he preferred being in the field. Mrs. Schuelte nagged, yet I know that deep down she wanted the best for her daughter.

What kind of an "executive" job should I look for? I had only been at the tool-and-die shop for a few weeks. I scoured the paper. The Lou Lachau Agency on Seventh Street in St. Louis needed someone to work in advertising.

On Sundays the Schueltes still went to Our Lady of Sorrows Church. The name still amused me but not as much as it once did. The war had shown me the tenuousness of life, and I found comfort in the words of the worship services. It didn't matter to me which mass I went to; they all seemed to offer something mysterious, something I didn't know I needed until I was without it.

One Sunday dinner after church, I said, "I saw an ad for a job at an advertising agency downtown. I'm sort of interested. It even comes with free lunches at the Forum Restaurant."

Shirley said nothing. The rest of the family looked at May.

"I love it, Lowell. There is so much you could learn. And working downtown, you could meet a lot of people and go further. You could get away from that *bun-popper* business." I saw the eyes roll.

But Shirley's father had his head down.

I was curious. "Guv, what do you think?"

"I think you're creative and you'd be successful. I agree you'd learn a lot. I know salespeople, and Lowell, you have the gift." He paused. "I think you'll like the job for a short time, but knowing you, I think you'd eventually get bored."

May was on edge. *Gasp!* The Guv had given a different point of view, sort of. She recovered herself with an offhanded complement: "Lowell, you're too smart to be a salesman. You have to think more of yourself. But go ahead and consider advertising, at least to get started."

The Guv said I had a talent for sales, and I talked my way into a job at the Agency. I did learn a lot, especially how to write effective ads and how to organize an office.

In a short time I fulfilled part of May's fantasy for her future son-in-law to be an executive. I got a promotion to office manager.

I might have gone far at the Lou Lachau Agency, but Lou had two sons in college, and he was grooming those boys to take over the business. My future there looked like a brick wall.

I took my next job with Active Matrix, an old St. Louis advertising company that needed to expand. While there, I honed my advertising and marketing skills. But I wanted to make more money and got a second job filling prescriptions at night with St. Louis Wholesale Drugs. Having no time for family would work out as long as I was single.

I made enough money to support Shirley and me, but the truth is that I didn't feel challenged. Then I read about a new industry. Lee de Forest was beginning a startup in Chicago, building these things called television sets.

"Shirley, I'm bored. I need something more. I saw an advertisement for a new venture I could get interested in, something big, cutting edge, a whole new industry. But we'd have to move."

Maybe she understood, or maybe she saw I was looking to get out from under the matriarchy. Either way, she found a reason to postpone the dream.

"Lowell, we're going to be married soon. Can you just keep doing what you're doing until after the wedding? Then I promise I will support you if you want to change jobs again."

I believed her.

Chapter Forty
DETOUR TO CHICAGO

With Mom Schuelte as the planner, ours would be the wedding of the century. The ceremony took place at Our Lady of Sorrows on August 24, 1946. But even that large church was too small. The place overflowed with flowers. We had sixteen groomsman and sixteen bridesmaids for the largest wedding the church had ever held.

Shirley and I moved into our own apartment, not far from the Schueltes. But the great wedding could not forge a great marriage.

One night, after we had come home from visiting Shirley's parents, I couldn't contain myself. "Shirley, I love you and am very happily married to you, but your mother is driving me crazy. She comes over all the time. She orders you around and tries to do the same to me."

"She loves you, Lowell! She has big plans for you."

"Yeah, I know. But I'm sick of living under the Lisette Street matriarchy. You told me we could move after the wedding. I have to tell you, my skin crawls now whenever I see her coming. "

"Sorry you feel that way. I love St. Louis, and I love my family. Try and be more patient."

"I tried being patient, but I'm twenty-two years old, and I see no future here. I need a challenge."

Shirley gave me an angry stare and went to bed.

Left alone in the now quiet living room, I began to think. *She wants to make her mother happy more than she wants me to fulfill anything in her life.* Hmm. *Why hadn't I seen this coming? There must be a better way.*

Was she betraying me, or was I betraying her?

I didn't know for sure.

Chicago had impressed me. The clanging factories and grinding engines breathed energy into me. The people were willing to try new things. St. Louis felt more attached to the past. People here seemed too satisfied with the way things were. Most people I knew wanted change and talked about change, but they lacked energy and held no deep desire for it.

I went into the bedroom. Shirley lay in bed but not asleep.

"Shirley, I know your family is in St. Louis, but Lee de Forest is starting that factory I told you about in Chicago. They're going to build television sets. This is the future! You know that in the Army I learned to take apart radios and put them back together. I think they'd hire me to help work out some of the processes. I think I could be an executive there."

She pushed herself up from the bed on two elbows, "You'll have to break this to my mother. I'm happy right here."

I wrote to de Forest and told him about my training in electronics in the military. I was half hoping he wouldn't be interested, what with the mess I knew May would create. On the other hand, I saw *opportunity* written all over the move. A week later, I got a letter from De Forest offering me a job as a supervisor in his new factory.

After dinner that night I stepped out on that new limb: "Shirley, I got the job offer in Chicago. More than that, I got information on a rental in Chicago on Drexel Boulevard, three rooms to rent in a house owned by an older woman. We should leave in three days." I actually considered this a reasonable thing to say to Shirley.

"Lowell, we haven't talked enough about this. My mother hasn't even agreed! She has a lot invested in you. She thinks you could go further than my father. We can't move."

"I'm doing exactly what she's pushing me to do."

"Yes, here in St. Louis."

"Too late. I've accepted the job. I'll talk to your mother. Are you coming or not?"

"Why did I marry you anyway? You can't just drag me away like this. I feel safe here. Chicago is too far from my mother and father. Tell Mr. de Forest you've changed your mind."

"I am going to Chicago because I see a better future for us there. You're my wife. We are going to make our own home together. Now, are you coming or not?"

"I don't know."

She started crying.

"Shirley, you swore in front of a priest: for better or worse, till death parts us."

Then came a knock on our apartment door. It was May.

Still crying, Shirley went out and opened the door.

"Mom. Lowell wants us to move. To Chicago." Tears were streaking down her face.

May Schuelte always got her way. But she was also wise. She knew people, had a sense about them. She knew how to put on the pressure, then wait, then twist your words, and in the end get what she wanted.

"Lowell, why? What's in Chicago?"

I explained. I also made it clear I was not going to back down. And that *she* had encouraged me to reach high in my career.

"All right, Lowell. I see you are not interested in hearing what I or my husband have to say. Go try it. See what happens. We can't stop you. Shirley's your wife. She has to go with you. We'll do what we can to help."

Had I misjudged May? Was she actually hearing what I had said? Did she agree with me? More probably she was afraid of a scandal if I left Shirley to go to Chicago so soon after we were married. In her mind, she had probably calculated which would be worse—letting

223

Shirley out of her reach for a while, or being the talk of her south St. Louis friends. Suddenly it didn't matter to me. Shirley and I would go to Chicago, together.

"Thank you, May. That means a lot to me. I'm sure you're skeptical, but I'll prove myself. You'll see."

May forced a brief smile, then turned and left.

Chapter Forty-One
A STOLEN NIGHTIE

With few belongings, we had an easy move to Chicago. Settling in was not easy. At least for Shirley.

In those days, a lot of people were moving to the Windy City, folks trying to get a foothold or work their way up the ladder. Some came from overseas, as well as African-Americans moving from the South to find a better life in the factories around Chicago. These were hardworking, careful-with-their-money people. Others, those who had been in the area a while, struggled. Older folks, who had lived their lives in the neighborhood where we landed, watched it grow, prosper, and then turn seedy. We rented there because we could afford it—and we didn't know the city that well.

Shirley lasted until the second night.

"Lowell, there are some creepy guys in this neighborhood. Why did we have to move here? My old neighborhood was much nicer. I want to go home."

She prattled on and on about how she had a clean apartment in St. Louis, decorated the way she always wanted it.

"I'll never be able to do anything with this place." She moaned. "It's dusty and dirty and dark and drafty. There's no sun!"

With the buildings were too close together, Chicago had grown too big. And the neighborhood scared her.

"Take me back to St. Louis!"

I didn't want to admit it at the time, but Shirley was right about the place. Nowadays we might call the house we lived in a tenement.

As the days passed by, Shirley tried to make friends with some of the neighbors. With the short backyard fence, when she went outside to hang up laundry on the clothesline, she tried to strike up conversations with other women in their backyards doing the same thing. Unfortunately, none of the women ever became more than acquaintances.

I rationalized it all: After all, we had to start out someplace we could afford. Besides, the house was a short walk to the elevated train and not far from the downtown Loop.

To make Shirley happy, I got a home telephone, even though we really couldn't afford one. I called her during the day, just to stay close, but our conversations usually ended with her crying and telling me what a mistake it was for us to leave St. Louis.

I listened, but I wasn't convinced.

I loved the work at de Forest's television factory. I adapted the old radio technology to cutting-edge television monitors. Television mesmerized the public, poised to become more ubiquitous than radio. I saw myself being in the right place at the right time. I would make a fortune in the TV business! I only wish Shirley could have seen that. We had some tense conversations around our small Formica kitchen table at dinnertime.

"Shirley, how many times do I have to tell you this is only temporary? This Lee de Forest is a genius. Besides television, he's trying to develop another machine—I know it sounds crazy—a machine that can cook something in minutes when it used to take hours. He showed it to some of us. It uses what's called microwaves, like in radar."

"Did you bring one home with you?"

"Don't be funny. His ideas are the future!"

"Well I'm concerned. My mother called today. We spoke for an hour on the telephone. Don't worry, she paid for it. I told her about the neighborhood and that I'm scared to go out, even during the daytime. She misses us, Lowell. Both my parents miss us. I'm their only child. We broke their hearts when we moved."

Shirley's tears kept coming. I had nothing to say. But I suspected that May had schemed this scenario from the beginning.

To try and get us into a better neighborhood, I took second job, working in the evenings. An entrepreneur had seen the possibilities in taking parts from old B-24 radios and turning them into ham radios. That work suited me perfectly. But it kept me out until late at night.

When I got home, I'd generally find Shirley in a darkened apartment, and usually her eyes were red from crying. I kept thinking that if I earned enough, we could start looking to buy a place. Maybe Shirley would forget her mother if we had a home of our own. I don't think I ever grasped how desperate my wife became in the days after our move to Chicago. My own dreams and ambitions kept me from seeing clearly what a mistake I'd made—at least for her.

One night I came home later than usual to find Shirley still awake, sitting in the dark. Upset. I turned on a light. Her mouth gaped, her eyes unblinking, and her hands grasped the arms of our secondhand overstuffed chair.

"Shirley, what happened? Why aren't you in bed?"

"Lowell Wood, we are leaving this place. I can't stand it here any longer. Today some perverted criminal stole my nightgown off the clothesline. This never would have happened in St. Louis. I am afraid to live in this place. I am afraid to go to bed without you here. I can't live like this. I won't live like this. I'm going back home. You can come with me or not."

Shirley's mother heard about the stolen nightgown. Just the ammunition she needed. The two women shot me down.

My foray into the world of televisions, microwaves, and ham radios ended with a stolen nightie.

Chapter Forty-Two

WISDOM FROM THE GUV

Back in St. Louis in early spring 1947, I had no car, no place to live, and little to show for my adventure in Chicago. The only two people happy about this were Shirley and May—and maybe Shirley's father. Bitter and frustrated, I wondered what I could do next?

I once came *from* nothing, and now I came back *to* nothing.

Poverty meant worthlessness. It meant shame. The feelings all erupted within me. I had failed in business and failed as a husband.

Worse, I felt powerless, even afraid. I could overcome worthlessness and shame, but powerlessness and fear sabotaged my ability to do anything. These feelings felt like the thieves I had been tasked to root out in the war.

Perhaps I could root out these feelings too.

How could I provide an income for my family?

The Guv helped Shirley and me find a small apartment on Lizette Street. I couldn't afford a telephone. We didn't have a car, so the bus and trolley had to be my transportation. I spent every day depressed.

For the first time since I left the Bogue Home, I had no way to support myself, let alone a family. At night I lay awake, hoping for a way to make my life mean something. The Guv saw I needed help.

One weekend, Shirley wanted to go to the zoo. Of course May and the Guv came with us. When Shirley and May went into the penguin house, the Guv led me to a bench where we could talk.

"Woody, the world hasn't come to an end. You're young, ambitious, and smart. You've got family. What more could you want?"

"A job. No. Not just a job. Work. Work I can be great at. Something that will help me make a lot of money, let me take good care of my family. A job that will get May off my back!"

"May means well. And she's smart, just doesn't know how to keep her nose out of other people's affairs. But this isn't about May, it's about you and Shirley. Don't worry about May or me. Tell me, what is it you really love to do? What is it that would get you to jump out of bed every morning eager to get to work?"

"Well, I think I'm a good judge of people, and I enjoy being around people. I always wanted to get to the office when I was working in advertising, but there wasn't enough money in it. And I didn't like working for someone else. I'd like to start my own business. I think I would be a good salesman. But I don't know."

"Woody, you'd be a great salesman! What would you sell if you could?"

"My mother-in-law."

"Be serious."

"Okay, maybe real estate. I've thought about it before, but I pushed the idea to the back of my mind because of how May feels about salespeople. Guv, it makes sense to me. GIs are coming home from the war and starting families. They need more than just a one-or-two bedroom apartment. I think even the government is beginning to understand this. They've started a program to help GIs buy homes."

"I saw it in the newspaper. One of the best programs to come along in years. Right now you need to put down fifty percent to buy a house, and then you have to pay it all off in only five years. With all of the soldiers coming back, the federal government started a house-buying agency called 'FHA,' Federal Housing Authority."

"And with this government loan you only have to put down ten percent, and they'll give you a thirty-year loan. I started looking into it for Shirley and me. That's something even we might be able to afford, after I find a job."

"You're right on with this, Woody."

"You really think I can do it?"

"You're a born salesman. You could make a lot of families happy finding homes for them."

"And make a lot of money doing it."

"Well, the best salespeople make friends first, then they make money."

"Thanks Guv. That's wisdom. I'll remember that."

And after that conversation, I never looked back. I knew what I wanted to do with my life, and no one would ever stop me again.

I would become a real estate steamroller.

Chapter Forty-Three
HARRY TRUMAN AND
RED SCHOENDIENST

My first interview with the Norman George Company went by quick and to the point.

"Mr. George, I am Lowell Kenneth Wood, my friends call me Woody. I want a job with your company." I hadn't yet learned subtlety.

"Another soldier home from God-knows-where. Okay, how many years have you worked selling real estate?"

"Well, this would be my first real estate job. But I know I can sell. Some people tell me I am a natural-born salesman."

George turned his chair away from me to look at some papers on his desk. "Okay, tell me. What have you sold?"

"You've got me there, Mr. George. I haven't actually made a living selling, but if you give me the chance, you will find no one who will work harder or longer than me."

"Thanks for coming in, Wood," he said as he signed some letters. "Leave your name with my secretary, and if I have anything, I'll give you a call. "

The call never came. But I knew that more and more soldiers would soon be looking to buy their first house, so I kept at it.

A real estate firm on Dago Hill, the Italian section of St. Louis, needed a salesman. Les Freeman was more open to hiring a soldier with no experience. He greeted me, shook my hand, and brought me right into his office.

I got right to the point, which is just how I am. I told Mr. Freeman about my jobs before I went into the Army and what I had done in the service. He listened to every word I said, and his eyes never wandered to the paperwork stacked on his desk. I included the part about working two jobs in Chicago, and he seemed impressed.

"Woody, you're hired."

Mr. Freeman said that I had brains and energy. I just needed someone to give me a chance—and rein me in sometimes.

"I'm willing to give you that chance. Do you have a telephone?

"No."

"Get one!"

It's never easy to get started in business, but real estate is especially difficult. Most people buy their houses from someone they know and trust, or a referral. Starting out cold requires self-confidence and hard work, along with an initial investment to pay for a telephone. For me, the telephone was a lifeline. In those days, every real estate transaction started with a phone call. Fortunately, the Guv helped me out, and we got a phone. With no regular paycheck coming in from real estate yet, I needed another job. The local Wonder Bread factory hired me to deliver bread from 2:30 A.M. to 1 P.M. Not many people looked at houses during those times, and if a few were, I had a little bit of flexibility. I got sleep when I could, but I was young, and that's how we did it in those days.

This became my daily routine for two years straight. Finally, as I suspected, the real estate business began to boom.

———————

One day in 1947, President Harry Truman came to St. Louis for a political fundraiser. Les Freeman had been a prodigious supporter of Truman.

I had suggested to Les that we lobby the president to include real estate training courses in the GI Bill. Truman loved this idea, and after Les told him the idea was mine, the president asked to meet *me*.

Outside the Les Freeman offices on a beautiful spring day, I said, "Mr. President, great to have you here! So, you like the idea of including real estate training in the GI Bill?"

"Good thinking. Practical. Will put people to work. They tell me you fought in the war. Where were you?"

"CBI, Mr. President. I saw the best and worst of humanity there."

"Indeed."

Suddenly some of the president's entourage tried to move him along. One of his Secret Servicemen got a little rough, pushing me away. But Truman saw this.

"Leave him alone, boys. This young man fought the war for us."

The president then turned to me and said, "Let's take a walk." He wore a long coat. He opened it, and I saw a button with a mule on it.

"Young man, are you a Democrat?"

What could I say? I lived in St. Louis and I thought everyone in St. Louis was a Democrat. So of course I answered, "Yes, Sir. I am."

"Young man, you should join the 52/20 Club."

"What is that, Mr. President?"

"Members, like Mr. Freeman, contribute twenty dollars a week, fifty two weeks a year. It will make you friends, son."

I never joined the 52/20 Club, but I did register as a Democrat.

The hard work and long hours I spent selling real estate started to pay off. Around the time I met the president, I received a phone call from Red Schoendienst—yes, the future Hall-of-Fame shortstop for the St. Louis Cardinals' baseball team. He had seen a house for sale on Pernod Avenue, my listing.

I sold Red the house and made $87. In those days, $87 could fund a month's rent for office space and much more. Best of all, Red and I became friends. And Red had big-name friends. I began to get known around St. Louis.

In the 1940s St. Louis, we didn't have a lot of rules, and real estate companies were all small. The government didn't get concerned about who sold houses. Most of us didn't even know we needed to have a license!

Many of the deals were informal. We shook hands on a sale with no signed contract. That was simple enough if you had integrity, but the lack of oversight gave room for dishonest realtors to cheat clients. Customers did not always get the best treatment. I never felt that was the way to earn trust or build a reputation. My mantra—with credit to the Guv—was "Friends selling homes to friends."

Instead of waiting for calls to come into the office, I got leads by randomly opening a telephone book and calling whomever was listed on that page. I called this technique "dialing for dollars." My unsolicited calls irritated a lot of folks, but once in a while, I found someone who wanted to sell their house or who was ready to buy a new one. I knew that if I was going to succeed, I would have to develop a thick skin.

I tried other strategies too. In those days, realtors would go to a funeral of someone who had owned a house. Pretending that I knew the deceased person, I would go and inquire about the family's possible interest in selling. Though not some of my most successful visits, they worked once in a while.

I also went door to door to see if people wanted to buy or sell a house. This was not the most pleasant way to earn a living, but the paychecks from those sales kept me going.

Paychecks helped, because on April 7, 1948, our first daughter, Marlo, was born. Thank God I was on the way up.

Chapter Forty-Four
MY OWN COMPANY

Living in the small apartment on Lizette Street confined us too much. We needed more space.

"Guv, I know May isn't going to like this, but with a kid, Shirley and I need more room. Besides, now I'm making more money and can afford something larger."

"I can understand that, Woody. But before you make a decision, wait a few days. I have an idea I'd like to look into, one that may help the both of us."

The Guv decided he would buy a four-unit apartment building for us. It had larger quarters on the first floor, where he said we could move the family and not pay him rent. How astounding! I did not know that the Guv, May, and Shirley's aunt were planning to move upstairs!

This did not make for a happy marriage downstairs. Shirley and I had more and more disagreements. As a consequence, I spent more and more time selling houses. I thought if I could put aside some money, we could move out of that apartment and find some peace, and happier marriage, in a place of our own.

I got my real estate license in 1948 and entered a partnership with my friend Mel Thomas. At Mel's suggestion, we flipped a coin. Mel would work North St. Louis; I would cover South St. Louis, where I put down deep roots.

On May 10, 1949, the L.K. Wood Realty Company began. Not much of a grand opening: My first office was in my apartment. Any startup looks as though it will not make it halfway through. It's even more frightening in the beginning.

Shirley enjoyed the increased income and having me at home more often. But I worked constantly. She didn't like that. Neither did her mother.

One hot and muggy afternoon, May cornered me in my apartment. I didn't want to listen to another diatribe. "Lowell, why are you wasting your time selling? You have what it takes to be an executive in some big company. You were doing so well in advertising. Why not quit this foolish house selling and get a job where you can be somebody?"

"May, you have to leave me alone." This woman was trying to ruin my life. "I know what I can and can't do. I'm taking care of your daughter and our baby. For once, trust me."

After that, I moved my office out of our apartment. I joined a co-op with seven other brokers. We called ourselves the J. Nash Realty Group, and my first month's rent was $5; overall expenses for the first month were $87, which included my part in paying a secretary for the seven of us.

My life resembled a tornado. I *still* worked for Wonder Bread from 2:30 A.M. to 1 P.M. It was dark and cold when I went to the depot to pick up and load my bread truck. The fumes from the engines in the garage upset my stomach. The lack of sleep made my mind play tricks on me. But all that lifted when I left the Wonder Bread factory at 1 p.m. and did my real estate work. It felt like entering another dimension. I came alive again.

I had identified public phones in strategic locations on my route. While delivering the bread, I would call into the office from public phones to see if I had inquiries from any real estate customers. If so, I would call them back while still making bread deliveries.

Our second daughter, Michaeline, came into the world on November 5, 1949. What a beautiful little girl. When I walked through the door of our apartment and saw my two little ones, I knew why I worked so hard. I didn't want to end up being like my dear father, too poor to provide well for his kids. I never considered that I might sacrifice those very kids in the process.

All during this time, I kept up my cold calling on the telephone. I had to make large numbers. Sure I made people angry. I would be if someone called me at dinnertime or during the baseball game on the radio. But I had to call at the times I knew people would be home.

I stopped and talked to neighbors and even strangers on the street to see if they had thought about selling or buying a home. But it never felt like work. I *enjoyed* the hunt for the sale I knew would eventually come. I also had no problem making sacrifices. My effort to support them was more important. My family didn't see me very much. Many times I disappointed Shirley.

"Woody, my parents want us to come for dinner on Easter Sunday."

"Can't do it."

"But the whole family will be there, my aunts and uncles and cousins. Everyone else will be home with their families."

"Exactly, Shirley. Easter afternoon will be a great time for me to canvass for business. I'm going door to door to find somebody who wants to sell their house, or buy a house."

"You're crazy! People don't want to be bothered by a salesman on Easter. They'll kick you out."

"Probably. Most won't like it. But there is that one out there who has the idea that now would be a good time to buy. And I'll be there when every other realtor is taking it easy."

"All you care about is money! What about your family? What do you love more, us or selling houses?"

I didn't make the distinction. Everything I did at work would be for my family. Someday Shirley would understand. So on Easter Sunday, I went door to door—and many doors slammed in my face.

Then, while dusk fell, I knocked on a door where I found one of the best assets L.K. Wood Realty would ever have.

"Good afternoon. I'm L.K. Wood of L.K. Wood Realty. I wonder if you have been thinking about selling your house."

"Happy Easter, Mr. Wood. You do know it's Easter? Yet you are out here canvassing. Why?"

"I've been starting up my own real estate business, and I need the listings. Are you interested?"

"Probably not in selling our house, but why don't you come in. I'm Sam, Sam Murabito. Meet my wife, Rose."

Sam and Rose were two of the friendliest people you could ever meet. They fed me, and we instantly liked one another.

"Mr. Wood."

"Call me Woody, Sam."

"Woody, I have been putting money aside to buy houses as an investment. Right now I manage a candy company. I want to get out of managing that candy business. I see a future in real estate."

"Is that so? Sam, come work for me. I need someone to manage the office. Free me up to get out and meet people in the community, make friends with leaders in the neighborhoods, get my name known around town. I can't do that sitting in an office all day. What do you say?"

Sam had a great sense of humor, loved his pasta and red wine, and enjoyed a good joke, even one played on him. Rose used to say he would eat every meal as if starving, and that when hungry he would eat anything.

———

From the beginning, my business plan was: "Do good and market well." I meant it, especially the "do good" part. I believed that if I did the honest and right thing, and people saw that, I would succeed. I would be tested on that over the years. My first test came with one of my early hires.

One morning after the Cardinals opening game, one of my realtors came in to see me. He looked a little hung over.

"Mr. Wood, I'm not feeling so good today. I stayed up late last night listening to that ball game on the radio. My wife's a real nag and kept interrupting me, asking me to do things for her, when I was trying to listen to the ball game. She really got on my nerves. To shut her up I belted her. I didn't get much sleep."

I clenched my teeth. "Your wife is in a wheelchair!"

"Yeah, knocked her right out of the chair. She's not going to bother me like that again."

"What? That's the darnedest thing I ever heard. Get out. You're done here."

"Hey, this is none of your business. I can do what I want with my own family."

"No, you can't. At least you can't and work for me. My reputation and the reputation of my business are too important for me to put up with someone who beats his wife and brags about it. Now get out!"

It never pays to ignore a bad situation. Deal with it. Then focus on being the best you can. At least be better than anyone else in your line of work.

I wish I had taken my business wisdom and exercised it at home.

Too often I came home late at night, after the girls were asleep. Shirley did her best to support me, but too many times when I arrived home I was met with silence. Or else she would just ask the same question, "Woody, where have you been?" And then she'd stomp off into another room. What did she think I was doing? She knew I had been meeting with a client or staying late to go over the books.

I couldn't understand it. Because I loved my family, I put my whole self into making life better for the four of us. That's what Shirley wanted, and that's what her matriarchal mother wanted.

My kids wouldn't have to weave cane chairs or collect putrid, worm-infested apples as I did. I saw that they got all the things I missed, but I didn't see what they needed most.

Chapter Forty-Five
AS EVERYONE SHOULD

After coming to St. Louis in 1951 with only a hundred dollars in my shoe, I was now twenty-seven years old and the owner of a booming business. GIs were buying houses like crazy.

I moved out of the J. Nash consortium into a storefront at 3015 Cherokee Street in South St. Louis—a three-story brick building, wide enough for my office on the first floor and narrow flats on the upper two floors. Just one problem: The building only had one bathroom, in the rear of my office. It was a busy place, especially for anyone coming down from the third floor early in the morning. And for the first two weeks, I had no telephone.

The gas station next door, Gramps' Service Station, had a public telephone booth by the road. I finagled as many rolls of nickels as I could get from the bank, and Gramps' public telephone became my office annex. Nothing would stop my dialing for dollars. "Hello, my name is L.K. Wood. Maybe you've heard my ad on the radio, 'L.K. Wood, as everyone should.' I would love to help you sell your house." Doing that every day ensured regular depletion of my stash of nickels.

Shirley took care of our two girls, and she was expecting again. I didn't go home as much as I should. I cared too much about selling houses so we could get rich—the road to happiness.

I didn't realize it at the time, but the way I thought, the way I treated Shirley, the way I overworked and steamrolled my way into the future—all of these rooted deeply in my pain of the past and my fear of the future. I had an irreconcilable need to achieve and create a life of wealth and power that I could control.

With Shirley and me spending so much time and energy away from each other, we weren't as sensitive as we could have-should have-would have been. Our nerves stretched thin. And one day we reached the breaking point.

I was driving one of Shirley's girlfriends to see a house for sale. Shirley's aunt saw us and came to some incorrect conclusions. She went back and told Shirley what she had seen, or thought she had seen. When I got home, my wife met me with a mean stare, a sharp tongue, and false accusations.

All that did was steam me up. I tried to explain; she wouldn't listen. Finally, I gave up. It was another one of those times in my life when I said something stupid, and I didn't know why. "Yeah, sure, okay, you got me, I was fooling around with your girlfriend. So what?" Why couldn't I keep my big mouth shut? But either way, Shirley was ready to believe her aunt and her mother instead of me. That's how things had always been with her. I still fumed.

I finally asked for help from the priest at Our Lady of Sorrows. I explained what had happened. He talked to Shirley. But her response came with an offer I could refuse. "Shirley wants you back, but first you have to give up the real estate business and get a real job."

What planet did she live on? I could see her mother behind that demand. And I couldn't help but think Shirley was becoming her mother. The Guv had told me, "You were created to sell real estate. Stick with it no matter what." And I did.

I thought marriage was for life. So I couldn't believe it when Shirley got an attorney and began divorce proceedings. Shirley and

I were divorced in the spring of 1951. In the fall our third daughter, Meredith, was born.

The Guv never stopped coming by my office. I think he understood things better than anyone else did. Shirley remarried. And sometime later her new husband came as a student to the real estate sales school I established. Go figure.

Divorced from Shirley, I stayed in contact with her and my daughters as much as possible while running the business. I didn't have time to feel lonely or angry. Besides, I blamed myself. I'm not sorry I stayed in real estate, but I should not have run off at the mouth about what I *wasn't* doing with her girlfriend.

I had to stop thinking about that. The office staff became my family. And like a family, we had our differences.

One of my new salespeople, Larry, had a client from out of town. While Larry was out of the office, the client showed up with some questions. After the client had left, Larry returned.

"I heard you talked with my customer. Don't ever do that again."

"Do what?"

"Try to steal my commission!"

"I did no such thing. I just answered his questions."

"You know what you were doing, trying to cash in on the deal I am putting together. Don't lie to me."

That was it. In business, if your word means nothing, you're through. He could not call me a liar and expect me to stand around and do nothing. The others in the office were all watching and waiting to see what I would do. Actually, I didn't think about it at all.

"Get out! You're fired!"

Then I grabbed him and threw him out the door. Only I forgot that I'd closed screen door. It cost me a new screen door, but it was worth it.

When a pre-sunrise dawn of purple fades into a clear blue sky, still dotted with blinking stars, that carries a promise of hope for me. Mornings like that cry out for a new beginning.

After one morning like that in October 1951, I sat in the office when I noticed a good-looking woman opening the store across the street. I asked my secretary, "Who's that across the street?"

"That's Nancy Miner. And that's her store, The Peacock. She owns a string of beauty salons."

An attractive woman who owns and manages a business. That got my attention and held it in the days ahead. As I passed by the front window of my office on Cherokee Street, I found myself more and more fixated on the front door of The Peacock. I found ways to get to my office around the time Nancy might show up for work and would begin a friendly conversation.

In the afternoons, about the time school let out, two young children came to the salon, a boy and a girl. They would wait outside until Nancy showed up, sometimes in the cold and rain. My heart went out to them.

One rainy afternoon in October the children were standing outside waiting. They had raincoats on but jumped up and down to keep their teeth from chattering.

I said to my secretary, "Kathy, those little kids are going to get sick standing out in the cold. Let's go over and invite them to wait for their mom here inside the office."

The children knew us by now and were eager to get out of that bad weather. When their mom showed up, Kathy went out to get her.

"Mr. Wood, thanks for keeping an eye out for my kids. I was caught in traffic, again. Both Larry and Nancy Jane seem to like you."

"Well, if there is anything you need, just ask. We're neighbors, you know."

This became a habit. If they didn't find Nancy at the salon when school let out, Larry and Nancy Jane just came over to Wood Realty. I grew to love both those kids and started buying a lot of candy and ice cream whenever I went to the grocery store.

When Nancy came by to pick them up, we talked and grew close. She had a head for business. She knew her P&L numbers down to the penny. We became friends, and then, more than that.

"Woody, we've known each other long enough. The kids love you. We should get married."

"Hold on a second. I really do like you, but you wouldn't be happy married to me."

"And why is that?"

"I work too much. I'd probably care more about the business than about you. I'd spend more time with my staff than I would with you and the children."

"But this could be good business for the both of us. I'm going to need more property for my salons. And who do you think decides they need more room for their growing families? Women. Women who come to my salons. What other realtor has that kind of edge? Look at is as a commercial venture."

I liked her thinking. Loved it.

Yet I should have been more cautious and remembered Mr. Munzel's advice from years back that "decisions made quickly are never good decisions." But at the time, I couldn't argue with Nancy's reasoning. In 1952 she became the next Mrs. Wood.

Nancy kept her word. My business had been growing, but compared to others, it was small. Nancy had hundreds of customers and, just like me, she was a natural salesman and loved to make money. Now that my real estate sales benefited her, she spread the word and told her customers to call L.K. Wood if they had a house to buy or sell. Just like magic.

Families needed insurance for their homes and for their cars, as well as life insurance. At that time there weren't many ways to insure all of these things with the same company. To address those needs, I started the L.K. Wood Insurance Company as an experiment. It did nothing but grow, and we made more money.

Meeting all the state requirements for selling insurance challenged me and took more work than I could reasonably give. So I hired a smart young man by the name of Dave Kraemer to take over for me.

Honest, Dave showed commitment to the business. After a while, I sold it to him.

My business took off even more.

And I would never again be powerless like my father.

To emphasize that commitment, I decided to print all of our contracts in green, and all of my "L.K. Wood" pens would be green— the color of money.

Chapter Forty-Six
AT THE TOP

Married again, I was euphoric; and in June 1954, my son was born! We named him L.K. Wood II, or "Chip" for short. I now had six children: my beautiful three daughters with Shirley—Marlo, Michaeline, and Meredith—and my three children with Nancy—Larry, Nancy Jane, and Chip. I cherished every single one of them. And I always made sure they had what they needed.

But no matter how I loved them, I loved my business more. And I loved how it just kept expanding. In 1954, I bought the Altmeyer Realty Company and moved the business to its larger quarters at 3352 South Grand. We now had twenty realtors, so many I had to build offices in the basement of the new building.

Taking lessons I learned in my days at the Lou Lachau Agency, I began to advertise more. My slogan, "L.K. Wood, as everyone should," became a standard on radio stations in St. Louis and in the local newspapers. We had visibility.

As we expanded, more and more of my time as the head of my real estate business had to go to meeting other people leading businesses. If someone who knew me wanted to grow their footprint, they would come to me first. If I needed to buy something for the business, or if I needed help with a legal issue, I could get further with a first-rate person I knew. But more than that, I needed my part of the city to do well so I could continue to grow my real estate business.

In 1957, John Dressel, the president of Gravois Bank, a large and reputable bank in St. Louis, asked me to join the board of his bank. He also sponsored my membership in Kiwanis. Before I accepted, I asked him, "What does the word 'Kiwanis' mean, John? A while back someone told me it's an old Indian expression, 'To make noise and have a good time.'"

John said, "Woody, our motto is, 'Serving the children of the world.'"

When I heard that, I joined up. I always had a soft spot in my heart for helping children. And Kiwanis was just one way I met leaders in the city.

One day in 1958 a young insurance salesman, Alphonso Cervantes, pranced into my office and said, "Mr. Wood, I have something for you."

"You have nothing for me! I don't have time for this, whoever you are. Thanks for coming. Unless you want to buy a house, I have some important business I need to attend to. I appreciate the offer, but I can't talk right now."

I had a main rule of, "I don't go shopping." In other words, if a salesman wanted to sell me something, I knew he did it so he would make money off of me. I only bought from people I had already screened, someone whom I invited to come to my office, someone who would give me what I wanted at my price.

Al Cervantes didn't give up. He kept calling my office, but I made myself unavailable until my old friend George Heckmann called me. George was a manager at Cervantes' insurance company.

"Hey, Woody, how have you been? We need to get together for dinner sometime. Don't know if you heard, but I work for the

Cervantes Insurance Company. Would you have time for us to come by?"

I knew George, he was a good guy. So I agreed.

"Woody, thanks for taking George's call. We appreciate the opportunity to earn your business."

"Mr. Cervantes, I am not ready to do business with you. But feel free to tell me what you might do for me, in case I ever do get ready."

I listened to his ideas. Then we switched to politics. Al invited me to join The St. Louis Ambassadors, "a group working for the betterment of the city." Because Al would make the city better, his group worked to get him elected. He had won his seat for alderman in 1953 and 1957. Now he was thinking about running for mayor. I joined the Ambassadors and then got many of my friends to do the same.

Thus began my time in politics.

The business thrived, and I had gained a reputation around the city as someone people could trust to do the right thing, someone who had a heart for the city. Too bad my new marriage began to take a different direction.

Chapter Forty-Seven
BUSINESS WIFE

During our infrequent times together, Nancy and I constantly fought. We were probably too much alike. My working so much to build my business and Nancy's overseeing her salons didn't leave time to work on our marriage. I guess the business arrangement approach to marriage only worked for the business side. Old Mr. Munzel would have thought about that and told me ahead of time. I sure wasn't willing to think about it.

"L.K. Wood, I knew you overworked, but the kids and I never see you. If you aren't at the office, you go out with your buddies. Can't you stay home once in a while?"

"Maybe I would if you and I could talk sensibly to each other. Sometimes I think you married me to be your insurance card. All you see in me is somebody who can make you set for life. I don't know what you're complaining about. I provide a decent living for you and the kids."

"Decent? You call being away from us all day and all night 'decent'? What are you doing staying out late every night? I'm starting to think you're not just with your male friends."

"Don't talk to me about decent. What are you doing with those imbeciles that people say are in the mob? I know they hang around your salons. Those ladies of yours like to take a chance on the numbers racket. Next those mobsters will be making loans to them, or you. They're loan sharks. They charge outrageous interest. You'd better be careful."

"Mind your own business. They aren't hurting anybody."

"As long as you pay them on time. And by the way, it seems to me someone else is paying attention to my business. I found some charges on my real estate accounts that look a lot like things you bought for your salons."

"Go to hell."

We couldn't live this way. If Nancy couldn't face up to reality, I could. We divorced in 1959.

On my own again. Nancy had custody of the three children. I did my best to free myself for time on the weekend to see my children.

As an absentee father, I felt like a failure. So fearful of following in my father's footsteps of poverty, I worked like a madman to make sure neither my family nor I would ever see poverty again. But as that way of life cost me my children for the *second* time, a new fear crept into my thinking—one I'd never had before and did not want to admit. But I couldn't avoid the similarity: In some ways—like breaking up my family and leaving my kids in pursuit of opportunity—I had become like my mother.

This notion disturbed me deeply, too deeply to fully admit or deal with. So I bought a house at 2545 Clifton Avenue, in Dogtown, the Irish area of St. Louis. I built an indoor pool, making it the only house in the city with an indoor pool. My friends loved to come to swim, especially on the first snowfall of the winter. I would send word to all my friends to come to what became known as the "First Snowfall Pool Party." We had wonderful parties that helped me to not think about my life.

Chapter Forty-Eight
MOVERS AND SHAKERS

All through the 1960s, L.K. Wood Realty kept growing. We grew to have twenty-six managers and more than eight hundred realtors.

Sam Murabito took over much of the day-to-day management. Now I spent the mornings looking after business with Sam, and in the afternoon I networked with community and business leaders. Those leaders cared about the community and each other. We came together to make South St. Louis a better place.

Like when Herb Holland, and ad man for the *Post-Dispatch,* came down with muscular dystrophy. He really deteriorated physically at the end, and L.K. Wood Realty bought him an apparatus that helped him steer his car so he could keep driving. I stayed close to Herb and did whatever I could to help him through the last weeks of his life. In those days the people in South St. Louis looked out for each other.

One day my new wife, Mabel, came to my office just before lunch to tell me about a grandfather clock she'd seen while I tried to tie up some loose ends with Herb Richter. He'd come to my office about some real estate we were handling. This Herb owned a flower shop.

After saying hi to Herb, Mabel came around the desk and sat on my lap. "Woody," she said, "I saw the most beautiful grandfather clock at Scruggs downtown this morning. It would really look great in our hallway. Can I buy it?"

"Mabel, I'm busy here, but no. We don't need any more furniture, and besides, I don't want to hear any clock tick-tocking and gonging."

"Woody, you know I've been looking for a clock like this forever. It's on sale. We'll never have another chance like this."

"No, for the last time! Now will you leave us alone? I have business to do."

No excuses. I acted like an unfeeling buffoon. If anyone had ever taught me how to behave, I must not have paid attention.

Mabel got upset and started to cry.

"Mabel, can't we talk about this later?" But she refused to listen and quickly left.

Herb saw the whole thing; I didn't know if it offended or amused him. Anyway, after he left my office, he went back to his flower shop and sent a bouquet of flowers to Mabel with a note, "Dear Mabel, I am sorry for being so rude to you. Please go ahead and buy the clock." And he signed it "L.K. Wood"!

When I got home and saw the clock in the hallway, it made me furious. Thankfully, Mabel wasn't there, but the flowers and the card were—with a note from her telling me it's all right, thanking me for changing my mind! I put two and two together, and I never said a thing to Mabel. But Herb, probably trying to teach me, got an earful from me instead.

―――――――――

Friends asked me to invest in the Valley Park Racetrack, south of St. Louis. I put in $66,000. It was a one-quarter- to one-third-mile track, so we could hold NASCAR races there.

I even bought my own racecar. To house the car, I bought an old nightclub at 9012 Gravois, tore most of it down, and made a garage. I loved racing up and down Gravois, testing that car.

I started out driving it myself, but before I killed myself or someone else, I looked around for someone else to race the car. My former wife Nancy's daughter, Nancy Jane, had a son who was a racecar driver. His name was Bobby. I just loved to watch that "L.K. Wood Car" scream down the racetrack. So did Chip. My son and I could be together doing something that excited him.

We brought the car from state fair to state fair. For the Indiana State Fair, I rented a private jet to fly Mabel and Chip and some of the rest of the family to see us take home a trophy. I knew we would win. The race started out great, and we stayed ahead of the pack until the last lap—and the engine rod blew. That ended it. I quit racing. I had gotten too old, and racing had getting too expensive.

In 1964 we expanded the business by starting Kenneth Investments to speculate on properties. My bank account had grown large. Now we did not just help others buy and sell real estate, we would invest in some properties ourselves.

One of the properties caught my eye: seventy-five acres with a dilapidated farmhouse, an hour southwest of St. Louis. I heard I could raise Black Angus cattle there. I bought the land and decided to restore the house. Only I knew nothing about raising cattle and only a little more about restoring the house.

Euell Colbin, a friend of mine, had been a farmer. I saw him not too long afterward while eating lunch.

"Euell, I've been thinking about you. Mind if I sit down?"

"Heck no, Woody. What have you been up to?"

"Cattle. I bought some acreage in South County, and I believe I can raise cattle there. What do I need to know?"

"Oscar."

"Sorry, Euell, I didn't get that."

"You need to know Oscar. Oscar Euell, my dad. He's been living with me, but he's bored. He had a cattle ranch until mom passed away. All you have to give him is room and board, and he'll raise those cattle. Also gives me some more living space."

I hired Oscar Euell. Chip and I went down on weekends to work on the house. We knocked out the old walls and put up new ones. We painted outside and inside and spruced up a part of the house for Oscar to live in. Chip and I got the closest we'd ever been. I finally felt I was succeeding as a father. And it had nothing to do with money.

Word about my business was spreading. A local television interview led to a series of TV reports in which I gave updates on the real estate market.

By now, the business had become too large to stay where we were. With more agents and the need for offices for my investment company, we needed more space. The Gravois Kiwanis Club met at Al Kirschel's Steak House on Gravois Ave. In 1967, after one of the meetings, Al asked me to stay for a few minutes.

"Woody, I'm ready to retire. I plan to close the restaurant and sell the building. Know anyone who wants to buy some prime real estate on Gravois?"

"I do. If your price isn't out of line, I'll buy it myself. We need more space; our business keeps expanding!" So I bought it with cash and added it to my growing number of offices.

After we'd had the new location for a couple of years, a guy by the name of Metzger opened an office down the street to compete with us. Late one morning, I called him on the telephone to wish him luck. I had Sam with me listening in. I thought I might even invite him to lunch.

"Hi. This is L.K. Wood, Mr. Metzger. Just wanted to welcome you to the neighborhood."

"Well, LK, glad you called. I hope you're ready for some competition. I plan to run you out of business."

My face turned red. Sam saw this and put his finger to his lips, signaling for me to shut up and just listen.

"Is that so? What were you thinking?"

"You'll find out soon enough."

I slammed down the phone. It's a good thing I had Sam there, or I would have punched a hole through the wall. I almost did the next day. The newspaper had a big advertisement for his new business. It said, "While other real estate brokerages charge a commission of 5 percent, the Metzger firm will charge you only 4 percent to sell your house."

I picked up the phone and called his office. When he got on the line, I said, "Saw your ad in the paper today. Yeah, we've been charging a 5 percent commission, but I've decided to change that. Starting today, the L.K. Wood Realty Company is going to charge 6 percent." And we did. I began to get calls from the best real estate sales people in the city, wanting to come to work for me. Metzger did not last long in real estate.

I had become very successful by investing in others, helping them to succeed, helping them to feed their families, send their children to good schools and take their wives on vacation. I didn't need any more accolades, but I knew if the people who worked for me were successful, I would be too.

I developed a classroom in the basement of my new building. We taught our salespeople how to "cold call" on the telephone. Yes, I even told them to call in the evening, during Cardinal games, because that's when the most people would be home. We used a Wollensak tape recorder to tape their calls and then go over them to dissect how to do it better, especially when people cussed at them. Good pay and good support became important for getting and keeping good salespeople.

I helped the people in my business to succeed. Now I had the time, the experience, and the relationships to invest in helping my community become a better place to live.

Chapter Forty-Nine
POLITICIANS

In 1964, the door of political influence opened to me when Al Cervantes ran for mayor. Raymond Tucker had been mayor of St. Louis for twelve years and was considering a fourth four-year term. No mayor of St. Louis had ever served that long. The population of St. Louis had been in decline, and many felt we needed new blood to turn things around. That's when my old insurance buddy, Al Cervantes, came to see me.

"Woody, I can beat Tucker in the primary, but I need help."

Now that I had the time to be more involved, I looked for ways to use my talent and build my influence. "What's your interest, Al, other than that he backed the candidate for alderman who beat you?"

"Tucker is a technocrat. He can get things done, but he can't lead. It's time for new ideas and a new direction. We need someone to give the people hope again, make St. Louis a place where people want to stay and live."

"What can I do to help?"

"I know you're friends with the editor of the *Globe-Democrat*, Dunk Bauman. He's a Republican, but do you think you could put in a good word for me anyway?"

"I can do that. Baumann likes a fight, likes to take sides. He might not be with you in the general election, but he could make a difference in the primary next March."

"Thanks, Woody. And, it'll take a good deal of money to buy publicity. You know that. Tucker has money because he has influence. I need people who will support me because they think I can do a better job."

I got some of my business buddies, mostly the Ambassadors, to step up their support for Al Cervantes. He won the Democratic primary on March 9, 1965, and went on to win the election for mayor.

My support of the Ambassadors got me appointed to a seat on the city planning commission. That was important because the planning commission worked with the mayor to finally finish building the St. Louis Arch.

Cervantes won support for a two-million-dollar bond to complete the Arch. Because of that, the federal government gave the city an eight-million-dollar grant to move ahead and complete construction of this memorial to the pioneers who settled the West, a memorial in the planning since the 1930s.

In 1966, Vice President Hubert Humphrey came to St. Louis to present the check from the government. With the final cost of eleven million, we joked that it cost one million to build the Arch, but ten million to bend it!

The first group of dignitaries who went up in the tram got stuck halfway. They eventually got rescued, but in all the times I visited the Arch with family and friends from out of town, I never went up to the top.

––––––––––––

In 1965 Cervantes formed the Major Case Squad. The mayor appointed me as the only non-police member. The police gave me the unofficial title of "colonel."

The Major Case Squad brought together resources in the region to fight crime. Many of the smaller towns around St. Louis did not have the means to solve some of the worst crimes. The criminals just moved from small town to small town. By bringing investigative help to those municipalities, we would take more criminals off the streets.

I felt we needed to find give more support to the officers patrolling the streets. So I met with Cervantes at his office in the grand old French-style city hall.

"Woody, glad you came. Thanks for the contributions to the campaign. I'd like to help you. What do you need?"

"Help protecting the St. Louis Police, Mr. Mayor. I'd like your support in getting bulletproof vests as well as a mobile crime lab for St. Louis and area townships. What do you think?"

He liked the idea as long as the money did not have to come out of the city budget. I enlisted the help of Captain Jim Hackett of the St. Louis Police Department. Together we managed to involve the television reporter Patsy Drake. Working with her, we got the mobile lab and the vests. That campaign made me more friends among the politicians. One of whom was Francis Slay Sr.

———————

Slay Sr. came to my office on Gravois early in 1969 on a rainy and chilly day in early spring. The city began to come back to life after a cold, wet winter.

"LK, I'm here to get your backing to run for the city's Recorder of Deeds position."

"The hell you are! And why should I help an old geezer like you?"

"Because I can win."

Slay Sr. did not mince words. He was already a fixture in politics in St. Louis, having served for forty-five years as the alderman for the 23rd Ward, after which he won elections in 1966 and 1968 to the state legislature. He had a good track record.

"If you can win, why do you need my help?"

"You have a crazy sense of humor, and I will need some laughs along the way. Besides, you have a lot of money and can help me raise more. The family and I agree we want you to be my campaign manager."

Up to this point, I had only supported campaigns, not gotten involved in strategizing and running a political campaign.

"I'm running against Tom Sargent, the incumbent. This won't be a cakewalk."

I managed his campaign, and we won. Politics had entered my blood.

And when Francis Slay Sr. presided over Wednesday luncheons for the movers and shakers of St. Louis business and politics, he invited me. At the first meeting, it dawned on me that I was now one of them.

Chapter Fifty
SHANGRI-LA DAYS

By the beginning of the 1970s, L.K. Wood Realty Company was one of the top three real estate companies in Missouri. From three-quarters of a million dollars we had brought in fifteen years earlier, we now sold real estate worth thirty-two million dollars a year.

One day in 1972, I had business in south St. Louis County. As I went up the steps into the government offices, I started a conversation with a real estate agent I knew.

"Hi, Stan, what brings you here?" Stan was a southern Missouri guy, sharp, hardworking, and as honest a human being as you will meet.

"Got some acreage in High Ridge I need to sell. It's 181 acres of farm, woods, and streams. But I have to find a buyer right away, or it's going to be foreclosed on. It's a really good price. Know anybody looking for land there?"

"Maybe I'd be interested. What's it good for?"

"Part is in a flood zone, but most of it is good farmland. Someone could do well raising crops like soybeans."

"You know, Stan, I think I'd like to buy it for myself."

We agreed on a price, and I told him he would be hearing from me. We shook hands on it. I called him the next day to put together papers for him to sell me the land, but he told me he had registered the land in my name—did it that same afternoon! That is the way we did business in those days, on a handshake.

I built the massive, seven-thousand-square-foot house I'd always wanted. State of the art. We built it on a slab of natural slate and put in radiant heat flooring. I had a big iron gate erected at the entrance from the road, with a huge "W" on it. In 1974, we sold the house in Dogtown and moved to The Ranch. On part of land we raised soybeans, and on another part we raised cattle and horses. It became my "Shangri-La."

Anybody important in the 1970s came to The Ranch—sports stars, politicians and business leaders. We welcomed them all. They just had to dodge the maddening dogs Mabel collected and the pet monkey she let roam the house. That nasty monkey liked to throw food at you.

One late-winter day, I took some time off at The Ranch when the phone rang. Mabel came running into my office. August Busch was on the line. This was August Busch the Third, grandson of the founder of the great Anheuser Busch Brewing Company.

"Hey, Woody, I need more fields for pairing Clydesdales. Your place is close enough to our plant in South St. Louis. What do you think?"

The world famous A-B Clydesdales—no finer horses existed anywhere.

"What if I say no?"

"You won't. If you do, no one I know will do business with you. Only kidding."

But I suspected he wasn't kidding. He became president of Anheuser-Busch by unseating his own father, Gussie, as president of the company. He lined up the A-B board members to get his father kicked out.

We took the horses. After that, he loved coming out to visit them at The Ranch.

Those huge, beautiful animals, the horses selected to pull the beer wagons in parades, had to have markings that Anheuser Busch considered show quality. According to the official Anheuser Clydesdale book, the ideal horse must be "bay in color, have a blaze of white on its face, a black mane and black tail, and white feathering on all four legs and feet." And The Third enforced this.

The Third had strong opinions besides what his Clydesdales should look like. His father, Gussie, had been a Democrat, but August the Third was a staunch Republican. Once when we attended a dinner honoring city workers, he said to me, "We have the same views; you should be a Republican!" He knew I was a Democrat, but he didn't let labels define someone. He understood people.

And he knew I loved a bargain. One time when he came to watch over his Clydesdales, he told me about some blue goats he was raising.

"Hey, how would you like a couple of blue goats?" he asked.

"What the on God's green earth is that?"

"They're pygmy goats, with blue eyes; they're from Nigeria."

"What am I going to do with blue-eyed Nigerian goats?"

"They make good pets. You can sell their milk, and you've heard of goat cheese, haven't you? Besides, they'd be a great conversation starter. Just imagine Stan the Man coming here and what he'd say about pygmy goats with blue eyes. He might write a song for his harmonica about them."

Well, that sounded reasonable. And he would give them to me for free. How could I refuse?

Stupidest thing I ever did. He sent me one pair. Those goats multiplied in a way that would make rabbits envious. I had goats all over the place, getting their horns stuck in the fences, jumping over the fences, running wild in the road. They escaped in every direction! I got calls from all my neighbors: "Get this damned goat out of my vegetable garden!" I finally got rid of them all. Gave them to the Syrian immigrants in St. Louis who love roasting whole goats. And I don't remember anyone of them saying thank you, either.

When people think you're rich, they think that they deserve to be given things— that I had a duty to give away some of what I earned.

I don't see a lot wrong with that, but it wouldn't hurt if someone had shown some appreciation.

The *Post-Dispatch* did a story on our successes, which got me even more attention from politicians. All of that led to a surprise invitation while on a trip to Washington, D.C., in 1972, when I was forty-eight years old.

I stayed at the Hay-Adams Hotel, across the street from the White House. Beyond the house where the president of the United States lived, the Washington Monument pierced the cloudy sky like an exclamation mark on this great day when I had been seeing all the legislators and clients with whom I had come to speak.

The hotel phone interrupted my first taste of the champagne I'd just opened. The voice on the other end startled me.

"Woody, this is Richard Nixon. What are you doing right now?"

"Who is this?"

"It's Dick Nixon. I wonder if you could come across the street."

"What do you mean, 'Come across the street'?"

"I'd like you to come to the White House. There are some things I need to know about the mood of the people, and they tell me you're someone with a keen sense for where folks are."

"Well, of course I'll come."

I'd heard our president liked a drink (or two) later in the day, so I offered to bring my champagne.

"Of course. And I will have two glasses ready."

"I'll be right there. But where do I go?"

"We'll send someone to bring you and your champagne over. Just wait in your room."

While I waited I thought about how I had come to this place in my life. I turned away from the window and sat on the Italian leather sofa, closed my eyes, and half dreamed of the life from which I had come.

Then I began to cry. I thought of all I had achieved and all it had cost me.

A knock on the door revealed a man who looked like he might have been a brother of Charles Atlas.

"Mr. Wood, I am Agent Decamp. I am here to escort you to the White House for a meeting with President Nixon. May I ask what is in that towel you are holding?"

"Just some champagne, Agent Decamp. Is that allowed?"

"If you don't mind, I will secure it for you. Some minor disturbances around the White House these days. We are being a bit more careful."

With practiced efficiency and flawless security, we left the hotel through an underground maze, got into a black Cadillac, and then drove out of the hotel. Ordinarily this would have been a ten-minute walk or a two-minute drive, but not in the chaos Washington had become.

"Agent Decamp, are these protestors here every day?"

"Yes, Sir. And twice on Sunday."

Hundreds of people walked back and forth on the sidewalk in front of the White House. On this beautiful day in early summer, they looked angry and sad. They protested the war in Vietnam. Their placards and fists moved up and down to the rhythmic chant, "Bring our troops home now, Mr. President." Four bearded ex-servicemen in old military uniforms carried a large banner, "We Won't Fight Another Rich Man's War."

As we rode the officious looking car through the crowds and behind the tall iron gates, I thought how very different this was from the war I fought in.

"Mr. Decamp, I think I can understand why they protest. The threat the country faced in my days in the military came from Germany and Japan. That threat became evident to most Americans. These days, most people wonder what is so important in Vietnam that our young men, through the draft, have to give up so much—years of their lives, and even their bodies. Do you understand it?"

"Above my pay grade, Mr. Wood. But my daughter is out there somewhere with all of those people while my son sits in a jungle in Southeast Asia. All I do is pray."

If he ever allowed himself to think about it, I imagined he would be more conflicted about this war than I ever was about mine.

"Well, here we are."

President Nixon stood in his oval office. Two champagne glasses sat on a mahogany table, but I sensed my champagne was not going to be his first taste of alcohol that afternoon. He put his arm around my shoulder and led me to a very comfortable chair away from his desk. As he did, the smell of alcohol exuded from him, and I had to turn my head.

"Woody, I need your perspec-a-tive." He was slurring his words.

"What can I do for you, Mr. President?"

"Tell the truth. No one tells me the truth. I heard you were like me; you tell it like it is. No bullshit on your shoes."

That was repugnant, not the bullshit part, but they called him "Tricky Dick" for a reason. Congress had him under investigation for ordering the break-in of the Democratic headquarters at the Watergate complex. Was *I* like *him*? I felt a coldness pass over me; inside I shuddered.

"I always tell the truth, Mr. President." But to my shame, that afternoon I did not. I stood at the center of power, talking with the most powerful human being on earth. I clasped my hands behind my back to keep them from shaking.

"What do you think about these Vietnam protestors? Do you think this is going to last much longer?"

Why was he asking me about something I knew nothing about? I'm a businessman. I know real estate, not foreign diplomacy.

"No," I said, lying. "This will pass. Just a bunch of crazies trying to get their names in the paper."

As soon as I said it, I knew it wasn't true. My eyes focused on the blue-and-red carpet. I felt my face turning a deep shade of red. In his state on that afternoon, I don't suppose he noticed.

Why didn't I just level with him? But what would I have said? I sold myself for the sake of what? Trying to make a friend of a man tottering on the brink of reprobation? But worse: maybe I was more like him than I knew.

The President asked me to stay for dinner, but I had come to Washington to host an evening for two hundred real estate leaders. They gathered right now in the reception and dining area on the top floor of the Hay-Adams, probably wondering where their host was.

I am a man with many regrets. I regret I could not honor my father's instruction to care for my little brother; I regret I ran away from my brother at a time he needed me. And even though it wasn't my fault, I regret killing Genevieve.

I regret I did not go back and try harder to work things out with Shirley. Pride is a stubborn mule, harder to break than Mr. Tillman's horses. I deeply regret leaving Shirley and my three little girls to build a business just to make more money.

I could go on and on.

That afternoon with the President surfaced in me a question I had not wanted to ask, and that revealed I was indeed like him: How is it that a man can have everything and still be all alone?

Chapter Fifty-One
THE NEXT GOVERNOR

In 1976, Republican Kit Bond, the popular governor of Missouri, sought a second term. Most Democrats never thought anyone could unseat him. Most, but not all. Joe Teasdale thought Bond vulnerable.

Teasdale, a tough attorney from Kansas City, Missouri, and a hometown boy, had served his country in the 442nd Air Force Reserve Wing while an Assistant U.S. District Attorney. In 1967, he had defeated the incumbent prosecuting attorney in Jackson County and was hungry for more.

Rare for most politicians I knew, Teasdale was not an "angle shooter." He talked straight and had a backbone. And he liked people. Unlike many other Missouri political heavyweights, he didn't think himself above everybody else. He came from outside the regular Democratic Party establishment. Maybe that is why I agreed to talk to him.

"LK, maybe you know no one else has agreed to back me for governor. But I believe I can win, and I want you on board."

"I heard you met with the Slays." They were one of the most prominent political families in St. Louis. "What did they say?"

"They told me they liked me, and at first I thought they would support me. But later they said I didn't have a chance, and they withdrew their support. That's why I'm coming to you."

"Joe, you know my track record backing candidates for governor has not been a good one. No one I backed was successful. What makes you think I can help you?"

"Pardon me, LK, but to be honest, I need your money."

I appreciated his honesty, and I did put my money behind Teasdale. I got my friends to do the same. But Joe didn't make it easy.

One time I had arranged for my candidate to come to The Ranch to meet with potential donors. At the last minute, I got a phone call from him.

"Joe, where are you? I've got sixteen donors sitting around waiting for you."

"LK, I'm sorry, but I won't be coming."

"What the hell? Where are you?"

"I'm in Blue Springs, outside of Kansas City. I'm knocking on doors. Meeting folks and asking for their vote."

"Joe, these are big donors, and we need their money if we're going to win."

"LK, you can handle them. If I'm going to win, I have to do it at the grassroots level. I'm more effective meeting a thousand little guys who will want to go to the polls on Election Day."

I couldn't be angry at someone who respected the common person the way Joe Teasdale did. Sheepishly I went back to my friends and explained what had happened.

"Sorry, folks. Joe's not coming. He's spending his time meeting voters in western Missouri. He loves campaigning more than drinking my good Scotch whiskey. Speaking of which, Mabel, let's get some more of that good stuff to our friends here."

Thankfully, these Democrats understood and appreciated Joe's decision.

The newspapers nicknamed him "Walking Joe" because of how he loved to go door to door, meeting people one on one and listening to their concerns. Then he asked them to vote for him. And they did.

He stunned everyone when he won the election—a great victory, for him—and for me.

One of the first things Teasdale did was give me the job of appointments chief, the one who put together a list of names for the governor to appoint to the 2600 state offices. The Appointments Chief has power, and I would happily use it. Even with friends. I had to put the good of the public before the feelings of the people in power. I had learned that lesson the hard way in Washington as I answered that hard question I'd asked myself ever since: How can a man have everything and still be all alone?

I concluded that it happens when a person values power or money more than he values people.

I had been guilty of doing this my entire adult life. I'd always thought I pursued money to help people, namely my family. But time after time, I neglected them in the process. I made *them* be alone, which made *me* be alone. Nixon, it seemed to me, just did it on a bigger scale than I had.

I resolved not to make the same mistake again.

Not long after, I got tested on this.

One of the police captains in the St. Louis Police Department came to see me. During the Civil War, with St. Louis controlled by Southern sympathizers, the state of Missouri (committed to the Union) took control of the police department. In 1977, the St. Louis Police Department was still under the state's control, so I got to recommend who would become the next St. Louis Chief of Police.

A lot of people wanted jobs. I had the responsibility to find the right people. I sat in my office at The Ranch when Captain Reagan came to see me. He entered my office with a big grin on his face.

"Woody! You look great, for an old fart." He wore in his police captain's uniform. Tall and trim, he obviously he took care of himself.

"What can I do for you, John?"

"To get to the point, I think I should be the new chief of police for St. Louis. You know I have some friends in St. Louis politics. My 'angel' says I'm the best choice. He told me to come and see you." He wouldn't say it, but I suspected this "angel" of his was one of the Slays.

"Yeah, well, in my opinion you aren't ready for that job. I could see you maybe as a major but not chief. Gene Camp is doing a good job as chief for now. He'll be reappointed."

"Okay then, I'll take chief of detectives. We've worked together. You know I'd do a great job."

"No, John. I want to see you get more experience. In time you'll get your chance. Be patient."

Then he did something foolish. His smile vanished. His eyes narrowed. He got angry. "You'll regret this! You'll be finished in politics. I'm going over your head! I've got powerful friends."

"Do that, John. All I'll say is that I'm trying to do the best for the people of Missouri. I want to be fair. You know your way out."

Two days later, I got a call from the governor. "L.K., could you be in my office tomorrow at 9 a.m.? I got a call from one of your St. Louis buddies. He's upset you're not recommending Reagan for police chief."

"You want to know why?"

"No. Just be here tomorrow at nine."

I got to the office at nine, the same time as Reagan. I winced at going into a meeting to defend myself against the complaints of an old friend. The governor sat behind his desk, reading and signing documents. Reagan, dressed in his captain's uniform, avoided looking at me. He didn't wait for the governor to look up.

In a strained voice, he released a torrent of words: "Governor, everyone knows I'd make the best police chief. I have been getting ready for this my whole life. But Mr. Wood here thinks I'm too young. I think he just wants to pay off some old political debts."

Still reading and signing, the governor said, "I'm sure you would do a good job, John. You are kind of young, but I've heard very good things about you. You are the type of professional police leader we need. Your record is excellent. Woody, tell me what your thinking is."

Now he pushed the papers away and looked straight at me.

"Governor, everything you said about the captain here is true. Every time I've worked with him, he has done very good work, and I know he loves the city and the people in it."

"So why not recommend him?"

"Two main reasons. First, there is no good reason to make a change. The current police chief is running a good department. Better than good. If we make a change now, it will cause jealousy and division in the police ranks. Officers who support the current chief will look at it and say we're just playing politics. We'll have a divided and unhappy police force."

Reagan squirmed in his seat. He knew I was right.

"Okay, and what is the other reason?"

"John's time will come, but he isn't mature enough now. Sorry, John, but I think you have to wait until it's clear you have earned the promotion. Work your way up to colonel. You have a lot to contribute, and some more things to learn. I do think you should be given the rank of major, and that is what I am recommending."

The governor agreed with me.

"John, you have a great career ahead of you. I will be eager to see how well you do as a major. Thanks for coming in."

He never did become chief of police, but he did have a long and outstanding career high in the ranks of St. Louis detectives.

Chapter Fifty-Two
CROOKS

To the victor goes the spoils. As appointments chief, I felt no remorse securing for myself an appointment to the Missouri State Real Estate Commission. And as I had learned, I did not do it for power or for money. I wanted to make realtors more professional, institute better testing of people who sold real estate, and encourage continuing education for realtors.

I unfortunately had to address another side of the real estate business—criminals masquerading as honest realtors.

While the vast majority of people licensed to sell real estate are scrupulously honest, I couldn't believe the corruption of some realtors, even some of the most successful ones. What is it about human beings that makes us so selfish?

I don't just mean realtors who made unrealistic promises to potential customers, or the one or two who were caught charging for things that were supposed to be free. I mean the folks who comingled funds in escrow accounts.

An agent would receive a down payment on a house, but instead of properly securing the funds, that agent might use the money to put down a deposit on another property they wanted to buy for themselves. Then when it came time to settle the contract on the first house, the buyer might find that the broker could not bring that down payment to the table. So the buyer could not close the deal. So we created the position of Escrow Examiner to keep the down payments that buyers gave to realtors from being comingled with the unscrupulous realtors' risky investment schemes.

One of the worst offenses was the fraudulent sale of deeds of trust, also known as mortgages. Walter Rumer, president of Cass Federal Savings and Loan, helped me and the Commission uncover these fraudulent deeds. When I became State Real Estate Commissioner, Walter and I found ten or twelve fraudulent mortgages.

One prominent realtor by the name of Murphy had a legitimate business selling deeds of trust. But then he got into selling fraudulent deeds. After hours, he would draw up a fictitious deed, put someone's name on that deed, and go into his secretary's office to get her notary stamp and forge the signatures. He would then sell the deed to someone who might want a safe investment, from which they would collect interest. But he would pay the interest by siphoning the money from other fraudulent deeds he was selling. He got very rich doing this. But this swindle requires always finding new people to cheat—a classic Ponzi scheme. In the end, Murphy's luck ran out, and he went to prison.

I myself almost got burned by someone I'd done business with many times, I'll call him Ralph. When I finally realized his scheme, I called his office and learned he'd gone to his vacation home in Florida. A long-distance call from me was about to ruin his good time.

"Ralph, this is L.K. Wood. I heard you were in Florida on vacation. Sorry to bother you, but I've run into some trouble up here. You have a few minutes?"

"Sure, Woody. What is the temperature in St. Louis?"

"It's twenty-two degrees and overcast. We're expecting an ice storm tonight."

"Aw, that's too bad. It's seventy-six and sunny down here. I put the top down on the Cadillac this morning."

"Ralph, I'm working with a retired couple who are selling their house. When they came into the office, they told me they had paid off their mortgage, but when preparing the paperwork, my assistant found out there is still a mortgage on it. I called the people who own the mortgage, and they said they bought it from you. You have any explanation for that?"

A tense silence came over the telephone. Finally, in a low voice colored by guilt, Ralph explained the scheme to me. It seemed to me that an oppressive gray cloud had come over his sunny day in Florida.

"Woody, only you and I know this. I saw that the property had been paid off, and I drew up a new deed without your clients' knowledge. I advertised the sale of the deed in the *Post-Dispatch* and sold it to an older woman looking for a safe investment. She gets five percent interest every month, which she is very happy with. If you turn me in, she'll lose all that."

"Damn it, Ralph. Why are you doing this?"

"I needed the extra money for the new condominium I bought on Sanibel Island. Hey, I'm not hurting anybody. I'll take care of it. Look, if you keep quiet about this, I can settle the mortgage myself. I'll just tell my investor the owners paid their deed of trust off early. And if you keep this all to yourself, I'll put you on my list."

"What list?"

"You're gonna kill me if you turn me in, so I'll cut you in. I'm already paying two guys at the bank five thousand a month to look the other way. I'll add you to the list."

"What? Who are these two guys?"

I couldn't believe it. The two people he named were people I dealt with at a bank where I kept some of my own money. I knew them both well—a loan officer and his assistant. They made FHA loans for me all the time.

Now I couldn't bear it. Not only did Ralph sell fraudulent deeds, he bribed two people at a reputable bank. And now he had tried to bribe me!

"Ralph, I don't care how many years we've know each other. As far as I am concerned, you're just a crook."

Ralph was able to pay off what he owed; it wiped out all his wealth. And I stood by when he had to appear before the Real Estate Commission and forfeit his broker's license. The two men at the bank who had been in on the scheme lost their jobs.

It seems to me that for some people becoming rich is a destination— they have a figure in mind that once they amass, they can be happy.

But others have an insatiable hunger to keep accumulating. Being rich is not a destination; it's always a journey they are on. This kind of person never has enough. They are never satisfied, not with their bank account, not with those around them, not even with themselves.

As for me, I remained engrossed in my business. Besides running L.K. Wood Realty, I sat as a director on the Board of the Gravois Bank and the insurance firm I started, the L.K. Wood Insurance Company; plus I was a partner in the Murwood Real Estate Company, another business I began, this one to develop new properties. I did all this while Chairman of the State Real Estate Commission.

This all sent me running back and forth between The Ranch, the real estate office in St. Louis, and the state government building. I am thankful for the opportunities I got to make a contribution to the region that had given me so much. But managing any one of those would have been a fulltime job. Deep down, I knew I overstretched myself. And of course my family—whatever that was at this point in my life—suffered.

I had indeed learned my lesson about people being more important than money, and I fulfilled that growth in my character well, and in a big way. I had concern about all the people in the state of Missouri. But I let my own wife and kids get lost in the crowd.

My nerves stood at a breaking point. Most of the time I had no energy. Mabel and I had been married for twenty years, but I wasn't making her happy. More and more, we lived separate lives.

Chapter Fifty-Three
AFTER L.K. WOOD

By the end of the 1970s, the city of St. Louis was enjoying a renaissance. City leadership had led the way for a boom in construction not seen since the early part of the twentieth century. We had new skyscrapers, new shopping malls, and new sites popular with visitors. All this had grown up from a onetime seediness that had held back the Gateway to the West. And L.K. Wood Realty was on the grow.

In 1978, we bought MacFarland Real Estate. We now had eight real estate offices with more than twelve hundred people working for us; eight hundred were full time Realtors. L.K. Wood Realty was closing three hundred deals a month.

This was also the year I had my quintuple (yes, five-way) heart bypass. I hadn't even known there was such a thing. It's hard to explain to someone who hasn't gone through this, but it made me stop and think about the direction my life had taken. There is no greater lesson about the shortness of life on this earth than when you come up against death. I knew I had to find a new direction, some way that would bring me closer to my kids.

Sam Murabito came to see me at Deaconess Hospital.

"Woody, you look awful."

"So would you, ya wop, if you'd had the kind of indigestion I had."

"That was no stomachache, L.K.. Your body is telling you something."

"Don't preach to me, Sam. I'm not ready to leave this earth yet, although that might be a relief. I'm just not sure I can handle everything anymore."

"Mabel is worried about you. She didn't want to upset you and asked me to talk to you."

"I haven't paid a lot of attention to her; she has her own life. She loves those damn animals more than she cares about me. She always has. She just married me because I paid her. She'd be happier without me. A lot of people would be."

I couldn't help thinking about my mother and her gangster husband. Wasn't I just like her? I thought about how when things got bad at home she just picked up and left with the border. Then she hooks up with a lowlife. I thought about her packing her children off to a hospital or orphanage. I thought of her whenever she needed something (I mean money). That's when I'd hear from her. As much as I thought of her, she never thought of me. Believe me, I tried over and over to forge a good family life. Over and over I failed. Maybe they would all be better off without me.

That last part is what stuck me like a knife. I wondered just how many people would be happier without me.

Sam was a true friend regardless of who I was. "Right now you're not thinking straight," he said. "Let's come up with another plan, a plan that gives you some distance from the business. It's a time for change. You know I'll do whatever you need me to."

In 1979 my son Chip was twenty-five years old and had already had his real estate license for seven years. He had learned both the brokerage side of the realty business and the wholesale side. With Sam's and my help we believed he could grow the company. I stepped away, and Chip became the president of L.K. Wood Realty. I was worn out and needed to get away. At least for a while.

Joe Teasdale did not win reelection for governor. He lost in 1980 to the man he had defeated in 1976, the former Republican Kit Bond. Now he could go fishing without standing up any of my Democratic honchos. He told everyone, "For twenty years I was completely consumed by politics. I just want to be a normal person again." I kept that in mind.

Even though it was customary for political appointees to leave when the politician who appointed them left office, I stayed on as chair of the State Real Estate Commission and made Kit Bond fire me.

I was still involved with L.K. Wood Realty as chairman of the board. Chip had a greater vision than I had at this time, and we became involved in buying land and developing more new properties. He knew I wasn't sold on this, and that created tension between us.

By 1982 Chip could buy me out. He did, and I left the board. It was time. I was fifty-eight years old, with a bad heart. I needed a break. Chip now had twelve hundred realtors working out of nine offices around St. Louis.

Then the bottom fell out of the economy.

I went to the office to try and give Chip advice. "You've got to cut back, Chip! With interest rates at 18.5 percent, the business is going to get really rough. Those new houses might have to sit there for a long time."

"Look, Pop, we're doing everything we can to stop the bleeding. We'll get through it, but it isn't going to be easy. Now, excuse me, I've got a phone call I have to make."

I tried to help Chip. Your family is supposed to be the most important thing in the world, more important than your business, more important than your own life. But in pursuit of that, I destroyed as much as I'd built. Even now I wanted to be better about family— without messing up. I had lost both Betty and Shirley; never mind about Nancy. I knew people who'd given their lives for the sake of those they loved and didn't destroy their families in the process as I had. That's why it was painful for me to admit that my marriage to Mabel was not going to last.

One evening it came to a head. "Where have you been, Woody? It's 6:15 p.m., and we're supposed to be at Sunset Country Club at 6:30 for that fundraiser for the high school. You never tell me where you're going or when you're coming back. We're married, you know!"

"Leave me alone. You'll get your dinner. And I did tell you where I was going. You were too preoccupied with those dumb animals of yours to listen. You show them more love than you show me."

"Maybe because they actually care about me. They may be dumb, but they know how to love. I can see their love and the respect in their eyes. All I see in your eyes are dollar signs."

Ouch.

My mother's face hung in the air in front of me. I felt a twinge of fear, or recognition, or maybe both. So many years ago I said the same thing about her. At that instant it seemed to me that the difference between her and me in this regard was simply that I was better at getting the money.

Speechless, I let Mabel walk away in silence.

We'd been married for twenty years, but I'm afraid I did not know who she was any more. Mabel and I knew our marriage was broken. We decided to end the suffering. We divorced in 1982.

Part of the divorce settlement called for me to build a one-million dollar shelter for dogs, with the stipulation that any dog brought to the shelter could never be euthanized. I fought having to build an animal shelter as part of a divorce settlement, but in the end it was just easier to build the thing. If you found a dog that needed a home, all you had to do was pick up the phone and dial 1-800-GODOGEY.

Unfortunately, less than a year after it was built, the shelter caught fire. The whole crazy thing burned down. Contrary to what some people thought, I had nothing to do with it.

Chapter Fifty-Four
RECOVERY

Divorce is no panacea; at best it is an intermission, a break in the storm. A personal fog of regret and guilt persists as life goes on. No matter how bad the marriage might have been, it becomes an empty space you have to live with. And I now had multiple empty spaces. All my life I'd tried to create a real family, and I kept failing. I spent my working life building homes for other families, but could not keep my own family together. I wanted to, oh how I wanted to! But I just kept doing it wrong. Yet something inside me drove me to want to try.

In 1982, single again, I thought I should keep up with all that was happening at L.K. Wood Realty. Chip was now in control, so I had to keep my distance, sort of. My heart was healthy enough for me to get back into the business. Whether he knew it or not, Chip needed the benefit of my experience and knowledge. Unfortunately, he didn't always appreciate my hanging around. I understand wanting to make your own way, but there is something to be said for mentoring too.

One rainy afternoon, I stopped by the office on Gravois. The staff was happy to see me, but I don't think Chip was. His assistant said I should wait in the reception area and Chip would be with me in a while. Twenty minutes later I just went in. He was on the phone, but when he saw me he hung up.

"Pop, why are you here?"

"Chip, you have to focus. You're trying to do too many things. When we started out—"

"I love you, Dad, but you need to call before you come here. I'm trying to run a business."

"My business!"

"It *was* your business. You turned it over to me. Remember?"

What could I say?

My friends in south St. Louis provided companionship, but I needed more than companionship, I needed a purpose, a reason to get up in the morning. I still got a jolt sticking my finger into local politics. One place politicians loved to do business was at country clubs. So I started to get involved at Sunset Country Club.

Sunset is one of the more exclusive St. Louis Country Clubs, the original Adolphus Busch, before Anheuser, built it on land in South St. Louis. It has a beautiful golf course, with rolling hills and hundreds of trees. The clubhouse stands watch on the highest hill and looks out for miles over the Meramec River Valley. Finished in 1910, it was in Anheuser-Busch Beer's earliest Super Bowl ad.

I was afraid my friends at the club would shun me after my divorce. Some did. Henry Jubal did not. Like me, Henry was a self-made millionaire, the founder and president of Spartan Light Metal Products. Henry had built a small manufacturing plant into a worldwide leader in producing automobile engines parts made out of aluminum and magnesium. Henry was unique in another way, one that made him suspect in some parts of the country but which fit in with St. Louis culture. Henry was transparent about his faith.

One afternoon after a late round of golf, I was sitting on the club's veranda. I was alone with a glass of Merlot wine when Henry came and sat down at my table. It was early summer, and the sun was setting behind some tall evergreen trees.

"Woody, how have you been? I'm concerned about you."

"I'm fine, Henry. Just have to get past this rough spot. We all have them."

"You don't have to tell me. Elvira and I have faced tough spots. Starting a company from the ground up is no easy task for a man or his family. And we love our family, but they have caused us to get down on our knees more than once. One thing we found that helped us was our church. Why don't you to come with me on Sunday?"

I liked playing golf with Henry. He wasn't as good as I was, but you knew when he handed in his scorecard, it would be honest. The first thing you saw when you entered his office at Spartan Light was a list of Christian values.

"Thanks, Henry. I'm tied up this Sunday, but I appreciate the concern. I am fifty-eight, and I've done too much in this life to expect God to care what happens to me."

We sat there for a short while. Not saying anything.

Then Henry got up to leave. "Woody, you may not believe that God cares, or even that there is a God. But I want you to believe this: You're my friend, and I will always care about what happens to you."

That was one of those infrequent, serious moments when I had nothing to say. His words penetrated to a place inside me. I think they touched some of my loneliness and lowered a part of the barrier I had built between others and myself.

In early 1983, I was alone at The Ranch. It had been almost two years since the divorce. It was not the happiest time in my life. With my free time, I was making more of an effort to stop by and see my children and grandchildren. If my brothers or sisters needed something they knew I would help them; I even tried to get to Michigan once in a while. Everyone seemed happy to see me, but they had their own busy lives to work out. I was a distraction to them. From time to time I would think about how life might have been, if things had turned out differently. Alone, standing at the window, I looked out over the land

I had hoped would be a family homestead. The phone ringing in the big empty house pulled me back to reality.

"Hey, Woody, it's Bill Rott. Can we tear you away from whatever gin rummy game you're cheating at to play some golf this Saturday? The weather forecast is beautiful."

Bill Rott had been a competitor in the real estate business but in time became a good friend. Before the divorce, Bill and his wife Ruth often travelled with Mabel and me. The only times I saw Bill now was playing cards or on the golf course.

"Always glad to give you a few golf lessons. I need to get outside and brush off some of the cobwebs from winter. Maybe you can fill me in on what's happening in the city. Do you think Shoenmehl will run for mayor again?"

"Probably. I think he's done planting daffodils."

The mayor had thousands of daffodils planted around the city. In the early spring, the whole city buzzed when the flowers broke through the melting snow and dead ground to bloom in dazzling clusters of yellow along highways and around public buildings.

Then Bill shared with me some disturbing news.

"Listen Woody, there is something else I have to say. Other than Ruth I haven't told anybody yet, and please don't say anything to anybody else. I have cancer. The doctors say it doesn't look good. They tell me I only have a short time left on this earth. I need to prepare the family, and that's really why I'm calling you."

"What can I do, Bill? Tell me. Anything you need, just ask."

"It's Ruth. The kids will be fine, but I'm worried about her. She needs someone to stay close to her after I'm gone. I hate to ask you this, but you're the only one I could think of. Woody, would you look after my wife?"

I was shocked.

Bill was my friend. If I could bring him some peace by staying close to Ruth, then that is what I would do. You don't know how much your family means to you until you are close to losing them. I knew all about that. Now Bill knew.

"Certainly. I'll look after Ruth. You'll never have to worry about her, Bill. You've been a good friend for many years. I love you like a brother. I'll be there for your family for as long as I live."

Later that year Bill passed away. It was a loss for the whole St. Louis community, and I felt it very deeply. As promised, I stayed close to Ruth. I took her out to lunch and got to know her and Bill's kids better. In some ways they were like the family I had wished for. Ruth and I saw each other often at country club events. I tried to see or call her almost every day in the beginning, just so she would have someone with her, someone who knew and loved Bill. As the months passed, *she* began to call *me*.

I stopped by her house one afternoon when she was expecting a plumber to fix a leaky pipe. The plumber tried to talk her into a whole new set of copper water pipes, something she didn't need. And I told him so. After he left, she asked me to stay for a while. We talked about Bill and her children.

"Woody, my girls love you. They're happy you've taken the time to keep me company. It is lonely here without Bill. I was wondering, the club is having a dinner dance next Saturday. It's been almost a year since Bill died, and I would like to go. I think I'm ready. Would you go with me?"

I honestly hated those formal dinners, having to get dressed up with a coat and tie. It seemed pretentious. But I wouldn't say no to Ruth. She loved the club for the social scene. I loved it for the golf and eating in the grill. Ruth loved it for the formal dinners and the movers and shakers who went to those things. I went to see old friends; we traded stories about the past and complained about the foolishness of the politicians.

"Okay, Ruth. You know I've never spent a lot of time at those dinners; they make me uncomfortable. But I'll go with you."

That began a closer relationship with Ruth than I had expected. And our mutual children seemed pleased, particularly Chip, who saw this and encouraged us. Maybe he was just happy to get me out of his hair. Ruth added something to my life that I needed more now than I ever felt in the past: companionship. After a while, a warm closeness developed between us. I was beginning to realize that I got along well with women when I was single, but getting married strained me to be the husband they needed. But we both missed being married. I thought maybe this time things would be different. On July 30, 1983, she became the fifth Mrs. L.K. Wood. As I look back, I should have thought about it more.

Chapter Fifty-Five
LOTS OF HOUSES, BUT NO HOME

One thing is for sure, I knew how to sell houses. I put lots of families in lots of homes. Except mine. Oh, they always had shelter, but having a home is another thing altogether. I wasn't very good at that.

In 1985 Ruth and I had been married for two years. Our marriage had started off okay. I tried my best to follow through with my promise to Bill. But I believe I often embarrassed Ruth. I wasn't the slick, cultured businessman Bill was. Ruth was a wonderful woman, but no matter how hard she tried, she wasn't able to shape and mold me into the country club gentleman she wanted. Through my entire childhood and youth, I never had anyone to tell me or show me how to be a gentleman. I only learned on my own how to survive and claw my way forward and upward. And now I was probably too set in my ways. What a sad thing to become. But I saw how hard it was to change one's self-identity after so many years.

As a result, Ruth and I spent more and more time apart. I bought a condominium in Naples, Florida—a place I could retreat, alone. I needed time to think through my life. I felt more and more empty, and I was lonely. I could finally see that simply getting married didn't fix anything.

One morning in St. Louis, I was getting ready to leave for a round of golf. On my way out, Ruth stopped me.

"Woody, what did you decide about going to the dinner to support Kit Bond? My friends are asking me if you would pay for a table. I think they're waiting to see if you can still afford it."

Republican Kit Bond was running for U.S. Senate. Ruth was a staunch Republican; I was still a committed Democrat. She loved the social scene, the dinners and banquets. I hated it. Just let me go down to the Hilltop Bar and be with my old business friends.

"You want me to pay for a dinner to support a Republican? Ruth, this is crazy. And I hate those self-absorbed, narcissistic friends of yours. I hate the way they look down on those of us who made our money by actually working for it. To tell you the truth, I wouldn't trust any of them with my dog."

"So you'd rather hang around with that city crowd. The Democrats just want to take and take from the rest of us. You should know that. If they keep raising taxes the way they've been doing, we'll all be in the poorhouse."

I was not moved.

"Look, Woody, I know you don't like some of my friends, but you'll meet people at the dinner who might be able to help Chip."

Ruth knew how much I cared about Chip—and how to move me. I actually went to this Republican dinner and bought a table her snooty friends could sit at. I only did it in hopes that she was right about helping Chip.

L.K. Wood Realty was now in my only son's hands, and things were not going well. The real estate business is tricky; factors over which we have no control influence the market. Interest rates had risen substantially. All through the 1980s, right into the early 1990s, mortgage rates were above ten percent, making it difficult for people to buy houses. The real estate market continually suffered.

By then Chip had a family to take care of, and I needed to do the best I could for my grandchildren. I felt an obligation to help Chip and my other children take care of those families. When people would ask how my grandchildren were, I'd still say, "I hate kids!" But they all knew it was the opposite. Because I no longer felt I had to work twenty hours a day to make a good life for my family, I was closer to my grandchildren than I had been to my own children. Attending the dinner was just one way to help.

Even though I was not directly involved in L.K. Wood Realty, I tried to support Chip. He listened, but it seemed he preferred I keep my advice to myself. Our relationship became strained. I saw how much it hurt him to see our business declining, but I didn't know what to do.

That's when I asked my friend Jack Bender for advice. Jack was the publisher for the *South St. Louis County News*, and he enjoyed an excellent relationship with his elderly father. Jack went out with his dad at least once a week. I wanted that kind of bond with Chip. One afternoon at The Hilltop I laid it out for him.

"Jack, I love my son, but we just don't seem to get along any more. I've seen how much you love your father. You're always taking him out for a lunch or dinner. I've tried to do that with Chip, but it hasn't worked. What do you and your dad talk about?"

"Woody, it's not so much what we talk about. First, it's about love and respect. I know my father respects me, and I value him. Does Chip know that you respect him?"

"I've done everything I can for him, Jack. I sent him to the best school, brought him into the business, taught him about real estate. He's a great real estate salesman."

"Have you told him that?"

"Evidently I haven't, or haven't told him enough."

My Achilles heel was my family—or maybe *I* was the Achilles heel.

I wanted so desperately for my children to love me. I'd tried to do everything to make their lives secure. I laid a firm financial base for them, but emotionally I failed them.

As I think back, I remember how my father tried to protect our family, and in the end, because of his illness, he wasn't able to and ended up giving me the father's responsibility. I have to say that as much as I'm proud of my success in business, I don't believe I was successful in giving my family emotional security. I honestly didn't give Chip the support he needed.

It is sad how wise we become only later in life. I wish I had learned earlier what I knew now. I would have invested more time and respect in my kids, even if it meant I would have accumulated less money for them.

Benjamin Franklin said, "Life's tragedy is that we get old too soon and wise too late." I would have done so many things differently. If I had only had become wiser. Instead I just got older.

Chapter Fifty-Six
CHANGING TIMES

Sometimes change is forced upon us. Sometimes it is a choice.

I chose to sell The Ranch in 1991 and moved with Ruth to Webster, Missouri. We had been married for eight years, but it felt more and more like a marriage of convenience. She had her social interests in the community and the Sunset club. I preferred the golf at Sunset and checking in from time to time with what was going on at L.K. Wood Realty. At the realty company, change was coming.

We weren't forced to merge with another real estate company, but it made sense. In 1992, the challenges we were facing made it reasonable for L.K. Wood Realty to absorb Emmeneger Real Estate. The new company would grow, and there would be a savings from doing away with duplication in administrative costs. I was not very good at giving Chip the emotional investment he needed from me, but the least I could do was give him the financial help he needed to make this a reality.

Since I was supposed to be retired, I spent more time playing golf at Sunset Country Club. It was at that time that Henry Jubal and I became close friends. I felt I could tell him anything.

Henry was someone I could look up to. He had earned his millions. But more than that, he was honest. I could trust Henry, and his sincerity was one of the things that made him successful in business. When he said something, people believed him. He followed through with every commitment, no matter what it cost. Better to lose a few dollars than your reputation.

He loved his church, and everyone knew that too. But he wasn't one of those holier-than-thou people, like the ones Ruth had stayed close to during our now eleven years of marriage. He didn't care for that hoity-toity group at Sunset Country Club either.

I still saw myself as a committed Roman Catholic. Ask anyone in St. Louis. I donated large sums to Catholic schools and hospitals, and I have the plaques to prove it. Yet my divorces separated me not just from my wives, but also from my church. My church shunned me.

Henry Jubal was a Lutheran, and someone who never missed church. He continually invited me to go with him to his church. I did attend once or twice, and saw one of our salespeople, Patty Ogden, singing in the praise band.

I had several long talks with Henry. Life was short, and mine wasn't extending itself. I was anxious to know more about, well, about God. Growing up, I had an interest in what came after life on this planet. Immersed in war, seeing people torn apart in battle, I had to believe there was more to life. What was the purpose of it all? Why were we alive? Just to be shot dead in a jungle? To be cut in half by a .50 caliber machine gun? Was that it? That did not make sense to me. It seemed to me that every plant, every mountain and valley had a purpose. Didn't hurricanes start with the beat of a butterfly's wing somewhere in Africa? Everything and everyone had to have a purpose.

A few times Henry invited his pastor, Greg Smith, a bear of a man with an impish smile always on his face and dark-rimmed glasses, to play golf at the club. I think at least once in a while it was also to get

Pastor Greg and me together. I'm sure that was true one late May morning in 1994 when he reserved a tee time for just the three of us.

The weather hadn't gotten so warm and humid yet, and Henry rode in a golf cart by himself and let me ride with Pastor Greg. Afterwards Henry invited us to stay for a drink. I thought he meant something more interesting, but he ordered a pitcher of iced tea. He had us in a room away from everyone. The conversation became serious. Henry quietly got up and left the pastor and me alone.

"Pastor Greg, I have seen it all. I don't talk much about the war, but I can tell you I saw things that would make your spine tingle. I don't tell everyone this, but I trust you and Henry. In the war, insane things happen, and, well, I killed my friend."

The pastor didn't flinch.

"It wasn't on purpose. I was assigned to stake out a warehouse from which clothing and boots were being stolen. I was operating a machine gun. We saw a person breaking into an Army warehouse, and we told them to stop. Instead they started firing a pistol. That is when I pulled the trigger. I killed her. There are still times, usually late at night, when I lie in bed and wish it had been I who had died."

Pastor Greg was never at a loss for words, but his time he sat for a while before he spoke.

"There is nothing you can do now, Woody. There is nothing any of us can do. I guarantee everyone alive has done something they would love to undo but can't. What keeps me sane is our belief that God has done something."

"Pastor Greg, I don't think I believe enough in God."

"That's because you're human. No human can believe enough, but it isn't how much we believe that matters. This is the secret: No one can believe enough; no one can love God enough. But it isn't how much *we* love God; it's how much *God* loves us. Moses killed an Egyptian; King David killed the husband of a woman he slept with. God did not stop loving them. Your sin is no greater than theirs."

"What do I have to do?"

"Woody, you see, it's not how much you can do, but how much God has done for you that counts. Out of love God accepts the death of Jesus in the place of our death. We call that 'grace,' God's undeserved love. We have this strong belief that because Jesus came alive, all who love Him will live forever."

The pastor in him was in full swing.

"We Christians also believe God doesn't force anyone to accept His love. Believing is a gift from God. But it is a gift you can refuse. Only when you stop fighting Him and His Spirit comes into your life do you become a changed person. Forgiven. Fully. Forever."

Everything he was saying made sense—and I didn't even know why.

Somewhere the Bible says that when St. Paul the Apostle came to believe, "it was like scales falling from his eyes." I wasn't ready to join a church or anything, but I felt a weight had been lifted, a weight too heavy for me to carry by myself.

"Pastor Greg, I'm going to think about it some more. Just . . . well, thank you."

He put his arm around my shoulder and prayed. As he did, all the regrets I lived with came to mind. I began to cry because now their hold on me seemed broken.

Chapter Fifty-Seven
HURT AND HEALING

It was July 1995, and Pastor Greg Smith had spent a sleepless night. He knew for some time that the church building where his congregation worshipped had outgrown its usefulness. The building was designed for an era when most people walked to church, a time when the congregation was much smaller than it was now.

Over the years the Gothic stone church building gained so many additions that the place felt like a rabbit warren. Getting from one part of the building to another required a map, or better, a GPS. Someone could get lost in there and never be found. Not good for visitors.

Pastor Greg also knew that getting agreement from two thousand people to move from a building that had been Christ Memorial Lutheran Church for more than sixty years would cause heartache for many in the growing church and a pain in the neck for him.

The next morning, awake and nervous, he called Henry Jubal. Pastor Greg trusted Henry for his wisdom and his ability to find a way through difficult situations. Henry would know what to do. Henry told Pastor he would think and pray and asked Greg to stop by his home that afternoon.

Later that day, an anxious Pastor Smith knocked on the Jubal's front door. Elvira greeted him. She knew her own mind and would never be talked into anything by anybody. She loved her church, so Pastor Greg entered the house with trepidation.

"Elvira, I assume Henry told you why I'm here."

"Yes, and all I have to say is, it's about time! We were all wondering when you were going to realize we need a larger campus."

"Elvira, you just made my heart skip a beat. I love you!"

"Henry's out on the porch waiting for you. Would you like a glass of wine?"

Henry was sitting alone at a wrought iron table. He was deep in thought or prayer. Probably both. He was eager to talk.

"Pastor Greg, most of us have known for a while that if our church is to grow, we need more land. I'd like us to meet with L.K. Wood, the realtor."

So they called me. Of course I wanted to help Henry and Pastor Greg. However, that phone call did more than begin a business relationship. I had personal needs I was struggling with. Again.

———————

The Sunday after I received the phone call from Henry Jubal, Ruth was putting pressure on me again. "Woody, you've got to come with me to the Ritz Carlton in Clayton for the next Republican fund raiser." We'd been married for fourteen years and were now at the breaking point.

"You've given a lot of contributions to your friends, those Democrats. It would be nice if you could give the same amount to the Republicans running for office."

"Sorry, Ruth. I don't give money to Democrats or Republicans. I donate to candidates I think can do the most good for the people. After meeting the candidates at the last dinner you dragged me to, I don't like any of them. All they seem to want is power. No, I'm not giving them a dime." I was also becoming *persona non grata* with Ruth's friends at Sunset Country Club.

Ruth didn't get angry. She was trying to keep alive a marriage that we both now knew was ill conceived.

"Woody, you and I live in very different worlds. I keep looking for a bridge, but can't find one. Is there any hope for us?"

I knew it would hurt her, but I believed that it was it was best to face the truth, no matter how coarse it seemed. In business, people benefit the most from honesty. I believe the same is true in our personal lives.

"Ruth, if there's a lesson to be learned about a successful marriage, I have yet to learn it. I think this marriage has been a mistake."

She seemed to want to say something, but didn't.

Then I spoke for the both of us. "We need to divorce."

Maybe she was overcome with emotion, maybe she didn't want to say something she would be sorry for later on, or maybe she knew I was right. She turned around and walked away.

The next day, Monday, Pastor Smith and Henry Jubal came to my office to discuss what would be involved in moving Christ Memorial to a different location. I was glad to help them, but I was emotionally stuck, thinking about my last encounter with Ruth.

"It's good to see you again, Pastor Smith. How can I help?"

Henry explained the need for the church to expand. They weren't sure if they should divide the congregation and buy property for a second location, or if they should move the whole congregation to a larger, new site. We had no way of knowing that our meeting would set in motion a decade-long series of changes that would result in the church selling its building and property and buying a strip mall. Along the way, my life would be redesigned again.

We didn't know all this at the beginning. All we knew was that we'd have many more meetings.

Our meetings took place mostly at night. After one of those I stayed late at the old church, and after the meeting was over, I found Pastor Greg still working in his office. The night provided some anonymity, and I needed to unload a heavy heart.

"Pastor Greg, you don't need to hear all of this, but I need someone to talk to."

"What's up, Woody? Hey, thanks for spelling out the benefits for moving at the last congregation meeting. You and Henry have given excellent leadership."

"It's what I do best, and I'm glad to give it. But there are other areas where I'm not doing so well. My marriage to Ruth is coming apart. She's a wonderful woman, but we are very different. I thought we could make it work. I was doing it for a good friend, Pastor. In my mind, we got married for the wrong reasons. We could have been good friends. Now we just make each other miserable."

"How can I help you?"

"Divorce is a sin, and I've committed that particular one too many times. Our marriage can't end well, and I'm afraid. I'm afraid of hurting Ruth, I'm afraid of disappointing my children and Ruth's children. And I'm afraid of God.

"The last time we talked, I felt better. I felt that my mistakes—you call them sins—I felt I had gotten beyond them. But I didn't. Now I'm back where I started. What's wrong with me?"

"What you are experiencing is what theologians call the human condition. Its proper name is original sin. It's called *original* because it started with the first human. It's trying to take God's place, put ourselves above God, thinking we know better. We all do this, and we keep doing it, over and over. And over and over God offers His grace to all who confess their sin and, as we say, 'hunger and thirst for righteousness.' Divorce is a sin because God's will for marriage is that it would last for our whole life. That is what you swore to, wasn't it?"

"Yes, but . . ."

"And now you want to break that oath."

"No. I don't want to break it, but I know it will be broken. Ruth can't stand me anymore, and I know I'm not going to change. There's something inside of me that is stronger than I am. And I've never been able to change it."

"I think you should hear something St. Paul wrote. Pastor Greg paged through his Bible and read, "'What a wretched man I am! Who will rescue me from this body that is subject to death?'

"He was sick over his sins. Paul sounds a lot like you. But then, listen to the next verse: 'Thanks be to God through Jesus Christ our Lord!'"

"I don't understand."

"Woody, we can never be what God wants us to be. We are broken beings. We mean to do God's will, and maybe for a while we think we are doing what He has commanded. And then, *wham!* Something happens—even to the best of us. We discover again we can't be good enough, for other people, even those we love, or for God. But that's when we remember God's love is greater than our brokenness. Remember? It's called 'grace.' That is what I tried to tell you the last time, but you weren't ready to hear it." His eyes narrowed, and he leaned closer to me. He put his hand on my shoulder, as if to shake me into spiritual awareness. "L.K., God's love is unconditional. You have forgiveness for every sin."

"Even for divorce?"

"If you are looking for a free pass to divorce Ruth, this is not it. It's against God's will for you to divorce. Many people are going to be hurt."

I had way too much experience with that.

"All I can tell you is God will not stop loving you."

"It seems all my life I've been trying to be part of a family that could stay together. Now I've failed again."

"What I have to say to you is what Jesus said to a woman who had been dragged into court for committing adultery. The Bible says she and her lover were 'caught in the act.' The religious leaders wanted to stone her to death. But Jesus said to those self-righteous people, 'Let the one who hasn't committed a sin throw the first stone.' They melted away into the crowd. Then he looked the woman with the steadiest gaze, He who was the only One without sin, the only One who could have thrown that first stone, and told her, 'Neither do I condemn you. Now, go and sin no more.'"

I could tell I needed to learn more about this Jesus.

"Woody, what I have to say to you is, go, hold tightly to God's forgiveness, and sin no more."

"Pastor, I swear to you, if I ever get married again, it will be forever. But I can't do it by myself. I know that. I think I need to spend more time in church."

"With all the work we have to do to with this move, I don't think you're going to have a choice."

Chapter Fifty-Eight
FORGIVENESS

Pastor Greg and Henry Jubal kept the church council informed about the progress for moving the congregation to a new location. More than three hundred people showed up for the congregational meeting in September 1995. Some thought it a great idea to relocate; others were dead set against it.

Pastor Greg knew I could sell. His exact words were, "You could sell a heater to the devil." Henry and I presented the challenge to the congregation, and the majority caught the vision! The motion to relocate passed overwhelmingly. It would take another few years to find the right place and raise the funds needed, but the hard part had been done.

Eventually, the church would buy an entire shuttered strip mall and then rent space to several businesses, among them a pizza parlor and a tire store. The congregation would end up worshipping in a redesigned Target store.

To me, their changing of location was easier than my changing who I was. Pastor Greg knew the challenge he had. I would stop by from time to time to bring him up to date on the search for a new location and also to share with him some of the weight I was carrying. I was passing by Christ Memorial one evening when I saw Pastor Greg's car in the parking lot. I stopped and went inside. He was at his desk preparing a Bible study for a class that night.

"Pastor Greg, do you have a minute?"

"Sure, Woody."

I started to tell him about a location I thought could work, but he interrupted me.

"Woody, you could have told me about this on the phone. Why did you really come to see me?"

"My divorce from Ruth was finalized yesterday."

He sat silently shaking his head.

I felt the weight of whatever he may have been thinking. But I knew he wouldn't condemn me.

"Divorce is not an easy thing," he said. "It's like someone died, but they are still around, and when you see or hear about them, it's a reminder of failure. I hope you are finding strength from God's love and forgiveness."

"I'm trying, Pastor Greg, but I've disappointed too many people. I keep thinking about my children and how I let them down—and all my wives. Ach! I could have stayed with my first wife, Shirley. It was my immaturity, my pride, and a short temper that drove me away. I married Nancy too soon. I didn't know her well enough. Truth is I felt sorry for her kids, Larry and Nancy Jane. The only thing good to come out of that marriage was Chip. Then I put work and politics ahead of Mabel, as I had done with all the ones before. I'm surprised she put up with me for so long.

"But I feel the worst about Ruth. We could have been friends. You know, Pastor, I really don't believe I will ever find someone I could marry and make happy, let alone find happiness for myself. There are people who should never marry. I'm afraid I'm one of them. What a bunch of messes I've made."

"Woody, look, we both know you've put a couple of the commandments on the critical list. But you shouldn't struggle with things you can't change. Accept the fact of who you were, and you are also someone God loves.

"Solomon had more marriages than even you. One of the Roman soldiers at the foot of Christ's cross didn't realize who Jesus was until after he had pounded the nails in His hands and feet and shoved a sword into His chest to make sure He was dead.

"St. Paul was a worse sinner because he probably was present to hear Jesus teach and preach before He was crucified, but then he was part of the mob that killed Stephen, the first Christian martyr. Out of remorse, Paul wrote, 'While we were still sinners Christ died for us.' Woody, that *us* includes you and me." He pulled his chair closer, shifting his weight in my direction, and held out his hands for me to hold. All I remember is how hot they seemed. "Woody, look at me. Do you confess that you have sinned against God and deserved His wrath and punishment?"

"Yes, Pastor. I do."

"Do you desire the forgiveness won for you by Christ's death on the cross?"

"I, I . . . yes. I do."

And then Pastor Smith raised his right hand. At first I thought he was going to slug me, but making the sign of the cross over my broken spirit, he seared these words into my soul: "In the stead and by the command of my Lord Jesus Christ, I forgive you all your sins in the name of the Father and of the Son and of the Holy Spirit."

Wow.

It is said that in New Testament times, sundown was the time at which a new day started. That night in Pastor Greg's office was the beginning of a new day for me.

At first I could hardly think of St. Paul as a sinner, or that he had bouts of guilt or remorse as I did. But I could not doubt that Paul found peace and forgiveness in the same words I had just received. Now I was determined to change my life. I longed to become a better person.

As part of my new life, I thought I could help others by giving the new salespeople extra attention. Every real estate agent knows how hard it is to get started—establishing a name and clientele, the endless legalities, and the fear you'd do something wrong.

I made the time to mentor some of the more talented agents. I wasn't giving them handouts; I was there to give them a hand *up*. That was one of my secrets of success: finding someone with talent and giving them the mentoring and the right tools to succeed.

You can be impressed by someone you've known for a short period of time, but if they continue to impress you over time, then you know you've found someone special.

Patty Ogden impressed us all by her sales savvy and hard work. In the first four years Patty worked for L.K. Wood Real Estate, I knew she had what it took to be more than just a salesperson. She could become a topnotch broker in one of our offices.

She was also deeply spiritual—the one who sang on the church praise team.

One day in the office I stopped her to ask if she was interested in learning more of the administrative end of the business. "Patty, I think you can go beyond just selling real estate—if you are interested. I like to tell people I'm really in the business of 're-aligning the stars for people who were star crossed.' I'd like to mentor you."

"Woody, the years before I came to this job were very difficult for my daughter and me. I love what I'm doing here, and I'd love to go further. I would very much like to be mentored by you. I won't disappoint you."

Tears began to run down her cheeks. I couldn't help it, but my own tears were making it difficult for me to see.

"Patty, to get started, I'd like to buy you dinner."

"Well, Woody, please understand. That may not be a good idea. We should keep this professional. You know what a small city St. Louis is. People talk. There would be rumors."

"Sorry. I just was trying to be helpful. Honestly, I am not ready to get serious with anyone, not yet. But if you are uncomfortable, I understand."

I became Patty's mentor, and she grew in her new profession. In 1997 Chip was going to close the L.K. Wood office in Jefferson County. Instead, I suggested to Patty that she take it over. I bought the office from Chip and put Patty in charge.

All during that time, Patty, Henry, and Pastor Smith were a triumvirate. They kept after me, and in 1998, a year after my divorce from Ruth, I joined Christ Memorial. It was the only place I could find forgiveness and peace. More and more the church felt like my family.

Chapter Fifty-Nine
FAMILY, FINALLY

The members at Christ Memorial welcomed me into their community. Their prayer group continually prayed for me, begging God to bring me to spiritual maturity. I was a seventy-five-year-old spiritual teenager.

I wanted to learn and began spending more time with Patty Ogden, not just to mentor her about real estate, but also to learn from her about spiritual matters. As it turned out, we mentored each other.

During the next two years we grew closer. Her daughter, Bobbi, began to see me as her father. It wasn't something sudden. After all, we had known each other for nine years.

One day at the office in Jefferson County, I pulled Patty aside. "Patty, we've known each other for a long time. I think I've been a help to you and Bobbi, and Bobbi loves me. I want to marry you. We could both start over. My kids all lead their own lives, and they don't need me hanging around. You'd have a good place for Bobbi."

"I don't know, L.K. I'm not sure I'm ready to get married again. It's not just me, but Bobbi suffered the last time I was married. And, if you haven't noticed, there is a big difference in our ages. I think I love you, but marriage—what if it doesn't work out? In God's eyes . . .

"I do love you, L.K. But I'm confused. Let me think about it."

———————

In 1999 my spiritual father in the faith, Henry Jubal, went to heaven. Even though most of the Christ Memorial members accepted me, some remained unsure of my sincerity, and they were protective of Patty. I no longer had Henry to run interference for me.

Then my former wife Ruth passed away. After this, and too late, I increasingly saw how I'd married Ruth for superficial and selfish reasons, unworthy of her and her family. If I could have begged her forgiveness, I would have.

At that time I still was not completely trusted at Christ Memorial. The vicar, their term for intern, and others at the church weren't sure I'd matured enough spiritually to be with Patty--or anyone else; especially wary were those who knew my marital history. Vicar Tony prayed for Patty, asking God to guide her, to keep her from disappointment and sadness. The vicar asked the Lord to give Patty laser insight into what the Lord had in mind for her relationship with me.

My own children had suspicions. They warned me, and they warned Patty, that this could never work. In the minds of some, Patty was a "gold digger." Nothing could be further from the truth. *I* sought companionship from *her*. She was the reluctant one.

Rumors spread at the church and at the country club: "This can't last. She's too young. He's been married too many times before. She's interested in him for his money. He left Ruth for her."

The rumors meant nothing to me, but caused Patty apprehension. In the end, the rumors and innuendos came between us. After church one Sunday, she said what I hoped I would never hear.

"L.K., I can't live with what people are saying. Your family, Ruth's friends, and even some people at church—It's no good. This has to end."

"Patty, please."

"I'm sorry. I don't want to hurt you, but, don't try to change my mind." And that was it. Again. I lost her, a woman I truly loved and with whom I wanted to spend the rest of my life.

I lay on my bed late into the morning, not wanting to move, not wanting to look out a window, not wanting to look in a mirror. I didn't want to see myself alone again. I now knew I would always be alone. I felt like I would never be able to enjoy a complete family.

Then, six months after our breakup, I became seriously ill.

It started with a headache. Then got worse. All of a sudden I became confused. I didn't know where I was or why I was there. Fear engulfed me. I picked up the phone and called the one person I knew would come right away to help: Patty.

"Patty, don't hang up. I need help. I think I'm losing my mind."

"What's happening? You're slurring your words. Are you drunk?"

Very slowly I tried to respond. "Drunk? No. It's 9 A.M. I start a sentence and forget my words. I get dizzy and sometimes forget where I am. I have tingling and numbness in my hands."

"I'll be right over, but you need to go to the hospital."

"I hate hospitals! You remember that Burmese fortune teller told me, 'You spent time in an institution and you will die in an institution.'"

"I'll be right there."

When Patty arrived, she took charge. But the only way I would go to a hospital was if she went with me. Then I insisted she stay with me, or I would leave.

"L.K., the doctors say you've had a series of mini-strokes. You have to stay in the hospital."

"I won't, unless you stay too!"

She stayed. She rarely left my hospital room, even slept there until I recovered. And recover I did! A few days after I entered the hospital, Sam came to see me. "Boss, you look great! No limp, no cane. Your head looks good, and you talk okay. Actually, a few of us hoped you'd lose a little of that ability to talk."

"If I had a cane, I'd whop you with it!"

"Yeah. That's the old boss. He's back."

I give thanks to God for healing me. I am a blessed man. But if there is one human being responsible for getting me through the confusion and pain of a stroke, it's Patty.

"Patty, I think we need to sell the real estate office in Jefferson County. Laura, our best salesperson, could buy it."

"Then what? I need income. I have to support my daughter."

"Marry me. I love the beaches in Naples, Florida. We could move there and make a new life for ourselves."

"Let me think. No, let me pray about it, all right? I don't want to make another mistake."

Several weeks passed, and Patty hadn't said anything about marriage. I knew getting Patty to marry me wouldn't be easy, but I had fallen deeply in love with her. One evening I took her to the Citizen Kane restaurant in Kirkwood, Missouri, an old white clapboard structure and one of the best steakhouses in a city known for fine food. We ate dinner off in a corner of a dimly lit room, under a poster advertising Clark Gable and Vivian Leigh in *Gone with the Wind*. It was arguably the most romantically intelligent thing I had ever done.

"Patty, I love you. I know you love me. I want to marry you. I don't care what others think. You're all I care about." And deep down, within my mind and soul, I meant every word.

"But L.K., your family, what about them? Can they accept me? I don't need them to love me, but I know how much you love them, and I don't want to get between you and them."

"You're right. It won't be easy to win them over. I love them, and I've disappointed them so many times. I've never been good at keeping a family together. I think I have my mother to thank for that!"

My mother. Always my mother. She'd been out of my life for decades and had been quite dead for almost as long. Yet she still defined me. Or at least I let her.

"Yet I don't work and politick like I used to, so I won't neglect you. And I've learned, or at least I'm learning, from my mistakes."

She gently nodded.

"And my kids are old enough to take care of themselves. They're all married and have families of their own. I need someone I can confide in, make plans with, someone to love, and who will love me. Someone to hold my hand, and go out to dinner with. I want that person to be you."

Still not certain of the wisdom in marrying me, she insisted we go to counseling with Pastor Greg. He led us through a premarital compatibility test. This helped us to discuss some very personal things, and brought up for me some very unpleasant memories. One evening as we sat alone, Patty challenged me.

"L.K., after our discussion with the pastor, I have to say this: you still haven't forgiven your mother. I pray every day you will be able to forgive her and find peace."

"I'm not ready," I said. "Maybe someday I could forgive her. Not now. She was the reason Dick and I were sent away to that damned orphanage."

"There's something else. A regret I've been carrying. I know I hurt you too, and I'm sorry for that. I sent you away when I broke up with you. Can you forgive me? I will marry you, and I promise I will never leave you again."

By now everyone who ever knew me was certain that the words *marriage* and *L.K. Wood* were completely incompatible. So the final Mrs. Wood and I didn't even bother asking anyone to come to another wedding. Partly to avoid the whole embarrassment, and partly out of fun, we got married in—of all places—Las Vegas.

Chapter Sixty
WHAT'S MOST IMPORTANT

This marriage surprised everyone. Because it worked.

In 2001, looking to escape the cold and ice of St. Louis, Patty and I started a new life in Naples, Florida. We sold the condo I had bought years before and purchased a new three-story condominium being built on the Gulf of Mexico. Each morning I swam in the pool next to the beach and took long walks in the soft, brilliant-white sand of our Gulf Shore paradise. At night we sat by the pool, watching a blazing orange sun descend slowly through palm trees over the turquoise waters of the Gulf.

Patty's daughter, Bobbi, visited us often. I'd lived seventy-seven years, and all the money in the world could not have made me happier than being with them.

Our family and friends in St. Louis were curious and wanted to see our new home town. I suppose they also wondered about the genuineness of joy in our marriage.

And if it would last.

We traveled less and less to St. Louis. But in 2005, Christ Memorial moved to its new location. Pastor Greg called and asked me to come to the celebration.

"L.K., it's finally going to happen! We have rehabbed the building. You would never know it had been a Target store. All that work, for such a long time. We want you and Patty here to help us celebrate."

We did go and join in the celebration. After the worship service, I talked to Pastor Greg. "Pastor, my dream for this church has come true. Now you have to come and visit us. We have a guest suite where you can stay. And bring your golf clubs."

———————

Patty's and my life together was peaceful, away from work, away from the tensions of political and business deals. We became members of Faith Lutheran in Naples, and Patty sang on their praise team.

I dabbled in real estate and politics. But in all, no one and nothing in Naples preoccupied me or drew me away from Patty.

I buried most of the old regrets. Yet in the mornings when I walked the beach, a particular old bitterness and its accompanying guilt often interrupted my thinking and cause me to walk faster.

It became the steady tormentor in my life. It came late at night and in the pre-dawn dark of the morning. I knew in my mind about forgiveness, but my heart had trouble paying attention to the sermons. Anger and unforgiveness toward my mother filled me until Pastor Greg came to visit us in 2006.

Golf was at the top of his list, but time on the beach and dinner at Shula's Steak House were close behind. Although now in his sixties, Pastor Greg still had a full head of hair, sparkling grey with vestiges of black. Always direct, and he said what he meant.

On the second day of his visit, after breakfast at home, Patty, Pastor Greg, and I sat in the living room watching and listening to the rain. For a while, no one said anything. Even Pastor Greg was unusually quiet.

"Pastor Greg, what's on your mind?"

"L.K., when I first met you, you seemed cynical. There were only a few people you trusted. For a long time, I thought you were depressed. But these days, you seem different. You're calmer and brighter."

"You know, I'm more at peace than I've ever been. I worked hard to build a successful business, not just to make money but to have a positive effect on the lives of people in St. Louis and in Missouri, and I think I was able to do that. When I jumped into politics, it wasn't to make a name for myself. It was to find leaders who had in mind the best interests of the people. But all that came with a cost in my personal life."

The wind slapped sheets of rain against the windows—as if to angrily agree.

"I have had to let go of a lot, all I've done wrong, the people I've hurt. You know the stories. When I joined Christ Memorial, I came to terms with a lot of that."

"You did."

"But can I tell you something? My mother—that's been the hardest. She abandoned the family. I wasn't much more than a toddler. My brother was a baby. She ran away. I could never understand that."

We sat quietly with only the sound of the rain.

Pastor Greg spoke again. "What your mother did was terrible. But do you think you could finally just let it go and forgive her?"

"I don't know. Don't know if I can, and don't know if I want to."

Patty listened, not saying a word.

Pastor Greg spoke slowly and thoughtfully. "No one can be exactly what God wants us to be, whether a son, a daughter, a father, or a mother. For people in the church, forgiveness is not just a command. It is a consequence of having been forgiven. In other words, we've been forgiven, so we can forgive others. Otherwise we become self-righteous, judging others while ignoring our own faults. "

"What mother deserts her babies? How could she deserve forgiveness? Who could ever forgive such a person?"

"God. Forgiveness is not something we deserve; it is a gift. There is no sin that cannot be forgiven. We may run away from God, but God will never abandon us."

"I do remember good things about my mother. I have vague memories before she left us. I also have the heavy-hearted memory of seeing her in Chicago and the first words she spoke to me after not seeing me for more than ten years. She asked me how much money I had."

"L.K., you don't know what her life was like, who she grieved for, what she cried about, what disappointments she felt, including disappointments over her own marriages. And perhaps guilt over leaving you. It is not only you who are broken. You're not the only one to have grown up with pain."

Silence reigned once more. I looked to Patty and found her sitting in stillness, eyes closed. She may have been praying.

In the quiet, I felt something—a new spirit—growing larger in me. This spirit saturated my being like warm water covering a baby. I had to say something.

"I . . . I . . . Maybe I haven't only been cynical and unforgiving. Maybe I'm afraid to say it. Maybe, like you said, I've been self-righteous. In a way, I've wanted to forgive my mother for a long time. I think I might be . . . No, Pastor. I am ready.

The words didn't seem real at first. But they were.

"I. Forgive. Her."

After saying this, I trembled and couldn't stop. Patty put her arms around me and held me.

"Pastor Greg, Patty, I—I tell you, I'm not sure she will be in heaven. I hope she is and that we will have eternity to work things out. It may just take that long."

In July 2010, when I was eighty-six years old, Patty and I celebrated ten years of marriage. I couldn't believe we had been together that long. I couldn't believe I had lived that long.

We walked on Gulf Shore Beach early in the morning, under a blue sky accented by drifting white clouds. Something lay heavy on my heart. "Patty, I want to celebrate our anniversary. And I want our whole family to celebrate with us. I want everyone there. I want to celebrate as a family. I think the only other time everyone would come together would be at my funeral. Let's go all out."

"All right," she said. "What if we reserve the restaurant at the Ritz Carlton in Clayton? We could plan a private party and reserve the whole restaurant in the name of 'The Wood Nation.' What do you think?"

I loved the idea.

The Ritz Carlton in Clayton, Missouri, is a red brick hotel, with three hundred rooms and an indoor swimming pool, which I knew the kids would love. This would be a celebration not so much of Patty and me but of my entire family.

I feared it would not be easy for some of the family to come to this. Some of them had grievances with me; some were upset with others in the family.

Patty felt uneasy, too. "L.K.," she said, "I never wanted to come between you and your children. But I think the resentment they felt when I married you is not as strong as it was then. We had no family with us in Las Vegas when we were married. I think we should do this. Let's invite everyone. It's been at least ten years since most of us were together."

"I hope they all come," I said. "But no matter what happens, I promise, it will be a celebration. I love them all, everyone in the family, even those who don't love me. It took eighty-six years, but I will never let any regret, or any lack of forgiveness on my part or anyone else's part, ever come between me and the people I love. I was forgiven all, and I will forgive all. Like everyone should."

Almost everyone did come: children, grandchildren, and great-grandchildren, along with six couples who were our friends.

Patty says I was a "kid magnet." While the deejay played music, I danced the children onto the dance floor, and soon everyone danced together. We formed a conga line and danced around the room, snaking around tables and chairs, laughing and singing.

The Wood Nation partied late into the night. Patty took the microphone and thanked God for this time to come together as family. She asked God to bless everyone, even the people serving the meal.

She thanked God for the love she and I found in our marriage. She thanked the Lord for our whole family.

By the time we sat down to eat the hummingbird anniversary cake, exhausted abounded for everyone. It was a wonderful exhaustion. Finally—finally!—I felt I had become a unifying force for my family.

This long-awaited culminating success felt more important to me than anything else I had ever achieved.

My son asked to speak. "Congratulations, Pop and Patty for ten years of marriage. We love you both. I also want to say a personal word of thanks to L.K. Wood, my father, someone I am proud to call Pop. He has passed his mantel on not just to me, but to a family. Dad, we will work as hard as you did—but not such long hours—to make L.K. Wood a valued and respected name in our community. Patty, we all want to thank you for taking good care of Pop. He is happier today than he has been for a long time, probably in his whole life."

I had the last word. I felt I owed it to the next generation of Woods, and to my grand- and my great-grandchildren, to say what I did:

"I have lived a long time, but I have only recently learned what is most important and how I should spend whatever years the Almighty allows me to have in this world.

"For too many years I thought to be a good father I only had to provide a substantial income. I measured my success as a husband and a father on how much money I earned. This is hard for me to say, but I was wrong. I want you all to know I don't believe that any more.

"You will have a lot of influences on you, people telling you how to live, where to spend your time and your money. You'll have to figure a lot of that out for yourselves.

My long-ago promise to Dad whispered across my mind.

I looked out at all of them. My family. A real family. Together.

I did it, Dad.

"What I want to tell you today is to treat everyone you meet as a friend. And forgive others. Forgive them more freely than most people will forgive you. Especially your family. Don't just tell them you love them; show them. Don't give up too quickly on someone you have loved. Keeping a friend is more important than maintaining your pride. These are the things that bring real happiness."

With that the band cranked up that conga tune and my grandchildren ran up and pulled me back on the dance floor.

Afterword

On November 6, 2013, L.K. was diagnosed with a stage-four metastatic cancer. On November 16, he attended and regaled a crowd of well-wishers at the celebration of Patty's birthday in Naples at Imperial Golf Club. He went home to be with the Lord on November 22, 2013. The words on his tombstone read: *His branches sheltered many.* His son, L.K. Jr., heads up L.K. Wood Realty Services; L.K. Wood's grandsons, L.K. Wood III and Patrick Wood, manage a fast-growing real estate business called "Wood Brothers Realty."

His record of service to his community continues through his family.

L.K. Wood's Final Word:

Blessed are all who fear the Lord, who walk in obedience to him. You will eat the fruit of your labor; blessings and prosperity will be yours. Your wife will be like a fruitful vine within our house; your children will be like olive shoots around your table. Yes, this will be the blessing for the man who fears the Lord. May the Lord bless you from Zion; may you see the prosperity of Jerusalem all the days of your life. May you live to see your children's children. Peace be upon Israel.

–Psalm 128, New International Version